Conservation and Development in India

T0362146

Despite decades of efforts to integrate conservation and development, India is torn between two very different worldviews of peoples' place in the country's natural environment. This book takes a critical look at nature conservation and poverty alleviation in India. It opens up discussion of the conservation–development nexus in a country that stands at a major crossroads, where forces of neoliberalism, globalisation and urbanisation are driving the future of India's environment.

As the book shows, conservation in India is increasingly concerned with creating 'theme parks' – inviolate, albeit isolated, spaces for wild nature, whereas development is concerned with fast-tracking the construction of built infrastructure while also rolling out nationwide welfare programmes – promising food, clothing and shelter for the poorest of the poor living in rural India. Conservation and development therefore have very different motivations and attempts to find a common ground have been fraught with challenges. This has been particularly so on the fringes of wildlife parks, where the rural poor come in frequent contact with wild animals to the detriment of both people and wildlife.

Chapters are written by leading scholars on India to provide a vision of the future of Indian nature conservation. While focused on India, the book will also be of interest to scholars and researchers of conservation and development more globally. As a 'rising power', the world's eyes are set on India's development trajectory and there is unprecedented interest in the course of development that the world's largest democracy takes in the decades to come.

Shonil Bhagwat is an academic at the Open University, UK. As an interdisciplinary scholar with a background in natural and social sciences, his research interests centre on the links between environment and development. His research addresses the perceived grand environmental challenges within the context of growing discussion on the Anthropocene, the age of humans. He was previously Course Director of the MSc in Biodiversity, Conservation and Management at the University of Oxford. He has DPhil and MSc degrees from the University of Oxford, and MSc and BSc degrees from the University of Pune, India.

Earthscan Conservation and Development series

Series Editor: W.M. Adams, Moran Professor of Conservation and Development, Department of Geography, University of Cambridge, UK

Conservation and Sustainable Development
Linking Practice and Policy in Eastern Africa
Edited by Jon Davies

Conservation and Environmental Management in Madagascar
Edited by Ivan R. Scales

Conservation and Development in Cambodia
Exploring Frontiers of Change in Nature, State and Society
Edited by Sarah Milne and Sanghamitra Mahanty

Just Conservation
Biodiversity, Well-being and Sustainability
By Adrian Martin

Biodiversity Conservation in Southeast Asia
Challenges in a Changing Environment
Edited by Serge Morand, Claire Lajaunie and Rojchai Satrawaha

Conservation and Development in India
Reimagining Wilderness
Edited by Shonil Bhagwat

For further information please visit the series page on the Routledge website:
http://www.routledge.com/books/series/ECCAD/

Conservation and Development in India

Reimagining Wilderness

Edited by Shonil Bhagwat

LONDON AND NEW YORK

First published 2018
by Routledge

2 Park Square, Milton Park, Abingdon, Oxfordshire OX14 4RN
52 Vanderbilt Avenue, New York, NY 10017

Routledge is an imprint of the Taylor & Francis Group, an informa business

First issued in paperback 2020

British Library Cataloguing-in-Publication Data
A catalogue record for this book is available from the British Library

Library of Congress Cataloging-in-Publication Data
Names: Bhagwat, Shonil, editor.
Title: Conservation and development in India: reimagining wilderness /
  edited by Shonil Bhagwat.
Description: Abingdon, Oxon; New York, NY : Routledge, 2018. | Series:
  Earthscan conservation and development | Includes bibliographical
  references and index.
Identifiers: LCCN 2017035716| ISBN 9781138922334 (hardback) |
  ISBN 9781315685908 (ebook)
Subjects: LCSH: Nature conservation—India. | Nature conservation—
  Economic aspects—India. | Economic development—India.
Classification: LCC QH77.I4 C65945 2018 | DDC 333.720954—dc23
LC record available at https://lccn.loc.gov/2017035716

ISBN: 978-1-138-92233-4 (hbk)
ISBN: 978-0-367-59344-5 (pbk)

Typeset in Goudy
by Swales & Willis, Exeter, Devon, UK

Contents

Figures

Tables

Contributors

Arshiya Bose is the founder of Black Baza Coffee, Bengaluru, India – a social enterprise that promotes biodiversity-friendly farming practices in coffee-growing landscapes of South India.

Swati Chaliha is a Program Officer at the Inspire Network for Environment, New Delhi, India.

Ashwini Chhatre is Senior Research Fellow and Visiting Professor at the Indian School of Business, Hyderabad, India. He is also Editor in Chief of *World Development Perspectives*.

Vinita Damodaran is Professor of South Asian History at the University of Sussex, UK. She is also Co-editor of the Palgrave series in World Environmental History.

Krithi K. Karanth is an Associate Conservation Scientist with the Wildlife Conservation Society, New York, USA, and Adjunct Faculty at Duke University and National Centre for Biological Sciences.

Sunpreet Kaur is Program Manager of the Natural Resources Management (NRM) programme at the Inspire Network for Environment, New Delhi, India.

Shikha Lakhanpal is a postdoctoral (faculty track) research scholar in the Climate Change Mitigation and Development (CCMD) programme at the Ashoka Trust for Research in Ecology and the Environment (ATREE).

C. Madegowda is a Programme Associate at the Ashoka Trust for Research in Ecology and the Environment (ATREE) and Research Officer at the Mula Adivasi Study Centre, Karnataka State Tribal Research Institute, Mysuru, India.

Chetna Nahata is an independent researcher based in New Delhi, India.

Nitin D. Rai is Fellow at the Ashoka Trust for Research in Ecology and the Environment (ATREE), Bengaluru, India.

Sushil Saigal is an Institutional Development and Governance Advisor at Forest-PLUS, New Delhi, India, and a member of the Inspire Network for Environment, New Delhi, India.

Ghazala Shahabuddin is Senior Fellow at the Centre for Ecology, Development and Research (CEDAR), Dehradun, India.

Akshay Surendra is an MSc student in the Wildlife Biology and Conservation programme at the National Centre for Biological Sciences, Bengaluru, India.

Rajesh Thadani is Ex-officio Secretary and Executive Director at the Centre for Ecology, Development and Research (CEDAR), Dehradun, India.

Tarsh Thekaekara is a PhD student at the Open University, UK, and founder of the Shola Trust based in Gudalur, India.

Preface

Conservation and development in India

Shonil Bhagwat

Talking about the influence of his work on the United Nations Development Programme's Human Development Reports, Amartya Sen, celebrated Indian laureate of the Nobel Prize in Economics, said in an interview in 2004:

> Human development, as an approach, is concerned with what I take to be the basic development idea: namely, advancing the richness of human life, rather than the richness of the economy in which human beings live, which is only a part of it.
>
> (http://asiasociety.org/amartya-sen-more-human-theory-development, last seen 20 November 2017)

The tension between conservation and development in India arises partly because of the complete disregard for Sen's notion of human development. Conservation in India is largely focused on human-free wilderness areas where the iconic species are protected. Development often comes to loggerheads with this type of conservation because the conservation areas are a significant impediment in building new urban infrastructure to serve the growing middle class in India. The millions of Indian who live below the poverty line also remain below the radar of this type of development.

This book views conservation and development in the grand scheme of things and attempts to reimagine a future where conservation and development both embrace the notion of human development. At the same time, the book is concerned with the Indian wildlife – large and small, charismatic and mundane, unusual and ubiquitous – in all its glory. The conservation of this rich biological diversity – a sort of 'more-than-human development' – needs to happen with people who are nearest to it. This collaboration for conservation must be in a manner that is culturally, ecologically and socially sensitive. A reimagined Indian wilderness hopes to make progress in that direction.

All the authors who have contributed to this volume would like to acknowledge the people and the wildlife of India, encounters with whom have enriched their lives. We dedicate this book to all those 'human' and 'more-than-human' citizens of India who have remained somewhat subjugated by the elite-ness of conservation and development in India.

1 Introduction

Conservation and development in India

Shonil Bhagwat

Background to this book

Kalidasa, a fifth-century Indian poet, imagined Meghaduta, the Cloud Messenger, drifting over the Indian subcontinent. On its journey from the south to the north, Meghaduta reports many beautiful landscapes on its path, where people live in peace with their natural environment. Today one can follow the same journey on Google Earth (Figure 1.1). As one travels from south to north over the subcontinent, the densely populated coastal cities and towns give way to the lush green forests and plantations of the southern Western Ghats. Even the remote forests are dotted with villages and small settlements. There are reservoirs for storing water, clearings in the forest for farming and food production, and the mining operations in the rugged rocky hills of the Eastern Ghats. On the way to the central plains of India, there are rivers criss-crossing the Indian peninsula and without perennial water many riverbeds appear dry until the monsoon rains arrive each year. The central plains are dotted with trees, woodlots and plantations, some of them protected by communities for timber, fuelwood, fodder and shade for their livestock. The sandy desert landscapes of the north-west strike a contrast with the lush green mountains but even there the countryside is dotted with trees, some of them sacred to people. As one approaches the river deltas and the Himalayan foothills, yet again the landscape strikes a distinct note as the forests of the mountain slopes return. Moving further north along the towering Himalaya, and as one moves higher up the mountain range, the rugged landscapes carved out by the mighty glaciers over the geological past strike yet another distinct note and bring us all the way to the 'roof of the world' with some of the world's highest mountain peaks.

Looking at the landscapes of the Indian peninsula from a bird's eye view, the agricultural, ecological and technological transformations that the country has witnessed through its history become evident. This provides a backdrop for the conservation of wilderness in this highly populated country, alongside development of its still largely rural population, which in some cases is entirely dependent on agriculture. The post-colonial history of Indian conservation and development sets the scene for current conservation issues in India. In particular, despite decades

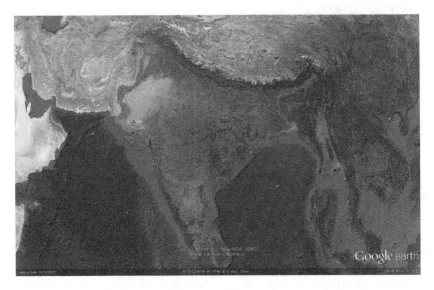

Figure 1.1 A Google Earth snapshot of today's landscapes on the Indian subcontinent
Source: Google Earth, accessed 29 June 2017

of efforts to integrate conservation and development elsewhere in the world, India is still torn between two very different worldviews of peoples' place in the country's natural environment. Conservation in India is increasingly concerned with creating 'wildlife theme parks' – inviolate, albeit isolated, spaces for wild nature that have become a tourist attraction where the urban elite can seek entertainment through wildlife-watching (as the picture on this book's cover photo portrays). On the other hand, development is concerned with fast-tracking mining, construction and other infrastructure development projects that also serve the interests of the urban elite. Simultaneously, nationwide welfare programmes have made promises of food, clothing and shelter for the poorest of the poor living in rural India, but they have rarely delivered on these promises. Conservation and development therefore are both mainly for the elite. Even though they are serving the same constituents, the motivations for the two are very different and attempts to find common ground between them have been fraught with challenges.

Finding this common ground has been particularly challenging on the fringes of wildlife parks, where the rural poor come in frequent contact with wild animals to the detriment of both people and wildlife. Can the 'wildlife theme parks' and the fast-track development model be reconciled with the needs of the poor or will the rift between conservation and development continue to widen as the country embraces modernity? This book takes a critical look at the conservation of nature and the alleviation of poverty in the Indian setting. It aims to open up discussion of the conservation–development nexus in a country that stands at major cross-roads – with forces of neoliberalism, globalisation and urbanisation driving the future of India's environment. The book unfolds through chapters written by leading scholars on Indian conservation and development, and it attempts to paint a picture of the future of nature conservation in India by engaging with key debates. While focused on India, we envisage that this book will be of interest to scholars and researchers well beyond. As a 'rising power', the world's eyes are set on India's development trajectory and there is unprecedented interest in the course of development that the world's largest democracy will take in the decades to come. This book provides a fresh look at the conservation–development nexus, charting the way forward for Indian conservation in the twenty-first century.

Conservation beyond parks

The history of the Indian conservation apparatus is deeply rooted in its colonial past. More than six decades after Independence, the protected area network in India has expanded, but nature conservation is still closely associated with its national parks and wildlife sanctuaries, many of which are former hunting preserves. This brings with it many challenges, not least the conflict between the interests of parks and those of people. This 'parks vs people' or 'tiger vs tribal' issue has informed a lot of the discussion on Indian conservation and development. The challenges of marrying the interests of parks and people both have seemingly compromised the integrity of state-led conservation areas. PADDDTracker. org, for example, monitors the downgrading, downsizing and degazettement of protected areas all over the world. The country profile for India in Figure 1.2 shows the protected areas in India that have been 'PADDDed'. As of July 2017, this database has recorded 510 PADDD events with over 8,500 km² downgraded, downsized or degraded. Common reasons for PADDDing include subsistence needs, infrastructure development or new settlements. This map presents a stark

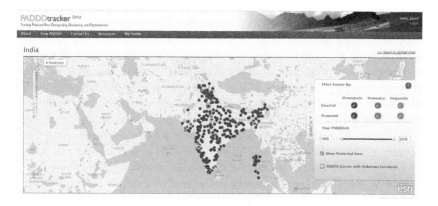

Figure 1.2 Downgrading, downsizing and degazetting of protected areas in India

Source: World Wildlife Fund, PADDtracker. www.padddtracker.org/countries/IND, accessed 29 June 2017

picture of pressures on Indian protected areas as the country tries to balance conservation with development.

Addressing PADDDing requires looking beyond protected areas and finding novel solutions to challenges of doing conservation in a highly human-dominated landscape. But how can charismatic megafauna co-exist with people when the two are coming into increasing conflict with each other? Some instruments of this new conservation approach include creating new incentives for people to tolerate wildlife, e.g. revenues from 'ecotourism'. Other instruments include new categories of protected areas such as 'indigenous and community-conserved areas', based on existing conservation ethos among local communities. But ultimately, the future of Indian conservation depends on whether or not people are able to live with wild animals in their backyards. This requires new ways of thinking about the interactions between humans and wild animals. It also requires the acknowledgement that the need for humans to share space with wild animals is rooted in how conservation and development are conceptualised. Conservation and development in India in turn are themselves situated in the wider discourses on sustainability and a wide range of other environmental issues. The discussion on sustainable development is therefore relevant to the wider context of conservation from perspectives in environmental change, renewable energy, sustainable wellbeing and the Anthropocene. These concepts will inform the future of conservation and development and the future of shared spaces between humans and wild animals.

Conservation with people

With substantial investment from the state in wildlife conservation, parks are arguably still the cornerstones of nature conservation in India, but they have historically disadvantaged certain groups of people, particularly those who live in close proximity to them. In a country that is on a trajectory of rapid economic development, parks are increasingly catering for the elite urban citizens of India, often acting as 'wildlife theme parks' where the elite tourists can regain their lost contact with nature. A large portion of the Indian population, however, does not fall into the elite category, but ekes out a living from natural resource-based occupations, primarily subsistence agriculture, gathering and, in small proportions, hunting. How does Indian conservation play out for their livelihoods? How do the welfare policies for assuring food, clothing and shelter to the poor influence their relationship with natural resource-based occupations? And how do these policies interplay with conservation outside protected areas? This book takes a look at the new policy instruments such as people's right to access forest resources and examines community-based conservation and joint forest management, for which India is known as the leading example, in this context. Attention is also paid to the surge in market-based instruments such as payments for ecosystem services that aim to bring parity between urban elite citizens and subaltern rural communities by aspiring to transfer some economic wealth from the rich to the poor.

Politics of conservation

As a rising power, India has captured the world's imagination for its rapid economic development since the 1990s, when the Indian economy was dramatically transformed by neoliberal economic policies. India's status as a rising power brings with it a sense of national pride that often manifests in the conservation focus on India's charismatic megafauna. The wider Indian political economy also plays a role in determining India's development trajectory through, for example, ambitious national programmes on rural development, employment guarantee or food security. The conservation–development nexus operates within this broad context and is often enabled or compromised by the political setting. So how does the political setting influence conservation? In this context, the politics of a wide range of conservation issues is important: ecosystem service trade-offs, invasive species management, non-timber forest products etc. This also determines the politics of parks, people and their interplay. The book proposes that new ways of thinking about conservation and development are necessary as the Indian economic power continues its upward trajectory. In particular, it critically examines the ways in which parks and people might co-exist in the future. It asks whether such reconciliation is possible and if so in what ways.

Concepts in this book

The book critically engages with a number of key contemporary concerns and opens up new lines of enquiry through empirical case studies. These include the concept of the Anthropocene – the notion that humans have been responsible for a new geological epoch; the range of interactions between humans and non-human species on a human-dominated planet; areas that are protected by people through their own ethical outlook to sharing space with other species; the challenges in governing such areas; and incentives for people to do conservation in places where they live, work and play.

The Anthropocene

The concept of the Anthropocene signals the influence of humans on the Earth's ecosphere and the signature it has left in the Earth's geosphere. Scientists have been preoccupied with finding a precise date for the beginning of the Anthropocene (Zalasiewicz *et al.* 2015) and suggestions vary from as far back as 11,500 years ago when the evidence of first land clearing for agriculture emerges (Ruddiman 2003; Ellis 2015), to as recently as 16 July 1945 when the first nuclear test was carried out (Steffen *et al.* 2015). But it is not just the time of its beginning that varies; what also matters is where on Earth you are. If the Anthropocene started in New Mexico, USA (where the first nuclear test was carried out) in 1945, did it start in India on 18 May 1974 when the first nuclear test was conducted in Rajasthan? Much as the start of the Anthropocene varies in time, it may also vary in space (Damodaran, this volume). If the signature of the Anthropocene is widespread human activity, then this goes back to 10,500 years ago, when Neolithic farm-ers started the cultivation of barley and wheat in north-west India (Gangal *et al.* 2014). On the other hand, despite a long history of human settlement, the Indian subcontinent remains home to some iconic megafauna including Asian elephant, rhino and tiger. This is in contrast with the megafaunal extinctions during the Pleistocene across much of the world, partly driven by the arrival of humans on hitherto uninhabited continents and, since then, substantial human influence on landscapes wiping out many species including through hunting and habitat destruction. Bearing in mind the rich diversity of megafauna that is still extant in India, it can be said that the Anthropocene is yet to arrive. However, the wave of modernisation and neoliberalism in India with capitalist resource extraction may have an adverse effect on the grassroots conservation ethic that has saved species from going extinct up until now.

The Anthropocene has another dimension. It is also about creative engage-ment with novel nature. Human activity transforms the so-called 'pristine' ecosystems to anthropogenic landscapes giving rise to novel ecosystems – novel in their composition, structure and function. Examples of novel nature can be found in India's cities, villages and even protected areas which are never too far from human settlements (DeFries *et al.* 2010). This novel nature comes in the form of 'alien' species that have now been almost naturalised, or plantations of timber species that have been, over time, categorised as forests, or urban parks in cities where nature is distinct in its composition. These novel ecosystems are also a signature of the Anthropocene – nature that humans have created for them-selves, intentionally or unintentionally. To survive the Anthropocene, ways need to be found to live with this novel nature. For example, the spread of one alien species, *Lantana camara*, introduced to India from South America in the 1800s, is so rampant that there is little choice but to learn to live with it (Bhagwat *et al.* 2012). All measures to control the spread of Lantana, let alone eradicate it, have failed and there is renewed interest in looking at ways of using this shrub to make baskets and garden furniture – cutting back Lantana and keeping it under control while also creating livelihoods for people in parts of India (Figure 1.3).

Human–wildlife interactions

With a large number of megafaunal species still extant on the Indian subcon-tinent, a close interaction between humans and wildlife is common in many places. This has been referred to as 'human–wildlife conflict' and is common when animals stray into human settlements or humans venture into protected areas designated for wildlife. In other words, human–wildlife conflict occurs 'when the needs and behaviour of wildlife impact negatively on the goals of humans or when the goals of humans negatively impact the needs of wildlife' (Madden 2004: 248). The well-known negative impacts on humans include loss of crops, livestock or human lives, but the conflict can also lead to diminished psychosocial wellbeing, disruption to livelihoods or food insecurity (Barua *et al.* 2013). The negative impacts on animals manifest through retaliatory killing by

Figure 1.3 Women making baskets from *Lantana camara*, an invasive weed. Living in the Anthropocene will require finding innovative ways to use invasive species

Photo: Shonil Bhagwat

humans who live in places where wildlife is never far away. As protected areas are downgraded, downsized or degazetted and the wildlife habitat shrinks, wild animals come into contact with humans more frequently and such situations can exacerbate conflict. Similarly, when livelihood options for people living in the immediate vicinity of protected areas reduce, people may venture into protected areas more frequently, increasing the incidences of encounter between humans and wildlife. Despite efforts to keep wildlife fenced within protected areas, contact between humans and wildlife is not uncommon in many places. Such contact is often interpreted as conflict and the mainstream approach to dealing with such conflict is to compensate the victims (Karanth and Surendra, this volume).

The issues with human–wildlife interactions are more nuanced, however, and go beyond simply conflict. There is a wide variety of ways in which humans relate to wildlife, and an equally wide variety of ways in which wildlife in turn adapts to living in anthropogenic landscapes. Some human interactions with wildlife occur because of chance encounters. People who have lived near wildlife-rich areas often have their senses tuned to the signs of wildlife presence and are therefore able to avoid direct confrontation with wild animals when chance encounters occur. Other ways of avoiding direct confrontation with wildlife include making noise, lighting fire or burning firecrackers, particularly to dissuade wild animals from coming close to crops or livestock (Barua *et al.* 2013). On other occasions, people actively seek contact with wildlife, often for recreation. This is not just when urban tourists go 'wildlife watching' but also when, for example, youth from the village gather to watch a herd of elephants visiting nearby. Wild animals also often adapt to living in anthropogenic landscapes by changing their home ranges or feeding behaviours. This includes, for example, elephants reducing their home ranges to be near a source of regularly available food such as unguarded crops or garbage dumps. These examples suggest that human–wildlife interactions are more nuanced than those captured by use of the term 'human–wildlife conflict'. In many communities people have wildlife-friendly attitudes and a willingness to living in the vicinity of wild animals (Thekaekara, this volume) (Figure 1.4). The conceptualisation of human–wildlife interactions as conflict and policies to keep humans and wildlife separate are met with mixed results. In the Indian context, human–wildlife inter-actions need to be re-examined and thought of in a more nuanced way.

Community-conserved areas

The community-conserved areas (CCAs) in India have a much longer history than formally protected areas and they are much more numerous than protected

Figure 1.4 Human–wildlife interactions take many different forms. Bonnet macaque (*Macaca radiata*) is seen enjoying juice from Kokum fruit (*Garcinia indica*) on an agroforestry farm in Maharashtra, India. The macaque helps keep the Hanuman langurs (*Semnopithecus hector*) away from fruit trees

Photo: Shonil Bhagwat

areas, with thousands of CCAs spread across the Indian countryside. A well-known form of CCAs is the sacred groves – some estimates suggest that there may be between 100,000 and 150,000 sacred groves in India (Malhotra *et al.* 2007) (Figure 1.5). Some groves are several hectares in size, but most are tiny, measuring a fraction of a hectare (Bhagwat *et al.* 2005a). Despite their small sizes, the network of conservation areas that these groves provide, alongside the quality of habitat between groves, can protect disproportionately large numbers of species (Bhagwat *et al.* 2005b). Other forms of CCAs include wetlands that support wintering populations of migratory water-bird species, thousands of hectares of community forests protected by local communities with support from the government under the aegis of joint forest management schemes, and hundreds of coastal sites that provide habitat to nesting sea turtles (Pathak 2009). This network of CCAs supports the conservation of many habitats and species that are not found within formally protected areas, playing an important role in Indian conservation. The CCAs are upheld by local conservation traditions, value systems and knowledges that recognise the rights of nature and non-human species to exist alongside humans. While some local conservation traditions and institutions are supported by formal government structures, there are more often challenges in the continuing protection of CCAs, including the lack of land tenure security.

The lack of land tenure security is a particular problem for the forest-dwelling communities of India, many of whom are scheduled tribes. These communities, often living in relatively remote locations have remained somewhat distant from the mainstream. To a large extent, they have continued ways of living that depend on forest resources for subsistence. In the process, they have also been instrumental in protecting forest habitats and biodiversity through their own customs of traditions, including resource harvest taboos (Rai and Madegowda, this volume). However, the continuation of colonial forest laws (where forests were seen as the property of the colonial government to be exploited and managed) in post-Independence India disadvantages the practices of the scheduled tribes. To address the problem of land tenure security, to mitigate the legacy of colonial laws on forests and to alleviate the threat posed to their way of living by rapid modernisation in the rest of India, the Indian government introduced the Scheduled Tribes and Other Traditional Forest Dwellers (Recognition of Forest Rights) Act in 2006. While the proponents of the Act are optimistic that it will address the historical injustice done to forest-dwelling communities, some conservationists have issued calls to repeal the Act because they fear it will cause massive destruction of forests. This Act is perhaps illustrative of the wider tensions in India between entrusting communities to look after conservation on their land vs substantial government-led conservation in strictly protected areas. These tensions are unlikely to resolve in a country which still harbours high levels of biological diversity and large numbers of megafaunal species of considerable conservation significance internationally, but the role played by CCAs and their custodians in the conservation of this biological diversity is increasingly being recognised.

Figure 1.5 A sacred grove in Rajasthan, India. Community-conserved areas have
protected thousands of hectares of dry forests and other habitats in India

Photo: Shonil Bhagwat

Governing conservation areas

India hosts a mind-boggling diversity of conservation area categories emerging
partly through the country's colonial legacy, partly through the renewed commitment to environmental conservation since the 1970s and partly through
the strong local conservation ethic among many communities. The categories
include state-led conservation areas such as wildlife sanctuaries, national parks
and tiger reserves; conservation areas that meet India's obligations to international conventions including UNESCO Biosphere Reserves, World Heritage
Sites or Ramsar Sites; and hundreds of thousands of conservation areas governed
locally by communities – sometimes on their own initiative and sometimes in
collaboration with the state. India has robust legislative frameworks that support
environmental conservation and the Indian constitution is forthright about the
duty of every citizen of India to protect and improve the natural environment
(Saigal *et al.*, this volume). There is, however, a mismatch between this seemingly grassroots commitment to conservation – down to the level of every citizen
of India – and the structures that enforce such a commitment in a top-down
fashion. The state-led enforcement of conservation through the huge army of
forest guards and rangers across the length and breadth of India leave little room

for conservation led from the grassroots. Many conservation areas are currently seen by people as the property of the state. To address the lack of trust between the governance structures and the people it is necessary that people are not treated as criminals and culprits, but instead partners and stewards in conservation by supporting the local conservation ethic (Shahabuddin and Thadani, this volume). In the case of CCAs, this is often compounded by the lack of tenure security and the 'ownership' of conservation therefore remains with the state.

Further challenges to governing the conservation areas include conflict between conservation and development, which manifests as, for example, conflict between conservation and renewable energy (Lakhanpal and Chhatre, this volume), or conflict between conservation and livelihoods (Karanth and Surendra, this volume), or conflict between conservation and urbanisation (Saigal *et al.*, this volume). Ameenpur Lake in Hyderabad, India, provides an excellent case of one such conflict (Nanisetti 2017). It is a man-made lake dating back to the sixteenth century, excavated to irrigate a princely garden, but now surrounded by villages, modern apartments and factories. Yet, it is the first water body in India to be declared a Biodiversity Heritage Site because of the populations of migratory water-birds that this lake supports. However, the size of the lake has reduced considerably from over 120 hectares to just under 40 hectares because of encroachment from a brick kiln that supports the urban construction industry. This is compounded by the effluents released from the chemical factories, severely compromising the water quality. Despite this, reports suggest that the declaration of the lake as a Biodiversity Heritage Site has helped improve its ecological quality. The local government have instigated the cleaning of the lake

Figure 1.6 Flamingos at Ameenpur Lake, Hyderabad, India

Photo: Nikhilkobe (Own work [CC BY-SA 4.0 (http://creativecommons.org/licenses/by-sa/4.0)], via Wikimedia Commons: https://commons.wikimedia.org/wiki/File%3AFlamingos_at_Ameenpur_Lake%2C_Hyderabad.jpg)

and the Biodiversity Management Committee has pledged to fence-off the lake to improve its ecological integrity. This case highlights the tensions between conservation and development. Indiscriminate urban development in a rising economy like India is directly pitted here against an ecological habitat that supports migratory water-birds and has received the distinction of being the first water body in the country to be declared a Biodiversity Heritage Site. Governing conservation areas such as this poses significant challenges to those who are in charge of it.

Incentives for conservation

There has been a surge since the 2000s to marry markets with conservation. This form of market-based conservation puts faith in the 'consumer' and aspires to create conditions that prompt consumers to make choices that in turn support conservation. In other words, if a consumer of coffee favours environmentally friendly coffee, then this will prompt the farmer to grow their coffee in environmentally friendly settings such that coffee production also supports conservation of biodiversity. The market-based approach then puts a premium on coffee grown on such estates creating an incentive to the farmer to continue to grow their coffee in environmentally friendly settings. This is seen as a win-win for agricultural production and biodiversity conservation (Ferraro and Kiss 2002). To make this work in practice, the environmentally friendly farms receive 'certification' that endorses their environmental credentials. In order to be certified, the coffee farm needs to demonstrate environmentally friendly production practices, some of which include the provision of 'ecosystem services', the wider benefits from nature accrued by keeping native trees on coffee farms. The premium from environmentally friendly coffee can then help to generate 'payments for ecosystem services'. These payments create incentives for conservation. The incentives therefore operate in complex networks of farmers, consumers, certification bodies and markets (Pagiola et al. 2005). These networks, however, also have to operate within the constraints of local rules, regulations and laws. This is where some of the challenges arise in operationalising the incentives for conservation.

An example of these challenges is the ownership of trees on coffee farms. One would assume that when a farmer owns the land, they would also own the trees on it. However, in some parts of India such as Kodagu, trees are owned by the state. This form of dual ownership is a direct legacy from the British colonial forest management practices, rules, regulations and laws. The colonial forestry departments retained ownership of trees, no matter who owned the land, because they were vital for the British Empire to support activities such as ship-building and the construction of railways (Rangarajan 1996). This mode of ownership continued in post-Independence India, even though the need for ship-building or the construction of railways had long passed. This historical idiosyncrasy has significant implications for conservation in today's India.

In Kodagu, environmentally friendly coffee cultivation demands that native trees are kept on farms, but trees are owned by the state and the state puts restrictions on farmers as to what they can and cannot do with the trees (Figure 1.7). Farmers see trees as property of the state and they are not keen to have someone else's property on their land (Bose, this volume). Even though there are restrictions on cutting native trees, farmers find ways of getting rid of the trees by, for example, girdling them. They instead favour exotic species such as silver oak (*Grevillea robusta*) because farmers have a greater control over management of these trees. This behaviour flies in the face of the objectives of conservation, ecosystem service provision and market-based incentives.

Figure 1.7 Shade-grown coffee plantations in Kodagu, India keep native trees for canopy, but the complex ownership structures of trees create disincentives for farmers to continue to maintain native shade trees

Photo: Shonil Bhagwat

Chapters in this book

This introduction, Chapter 1, sets out the background to conservation and development in India. It also puts the issues specific to India in the context of broader concerns, challenges and opportunities for doing conservation and development simultaneously.

In Chapter 2, 'The impact of the Anthropocene in the locality: Eastern India in the nineteenth and twentieth centuries', Damodaran discusses a complex landscape of conservation – where indigenous people's rights and their pro-environment worldviews come into conflict with exploitative resource industries such as mining controlled by multinational corporations. The manifestations of this conflict include desacralisation of sacred spaces of indigenous people, brutal and forceful removal of people from mineral-rich landscapes and dispossession of indigenous peoples from their ancestral lands, forests and other resources. While Damodaran's discussion is set in eastern India in the nineteenth and twentieth centuries, the tensions she portrays are relevant to the wider Indian landscape. The notion of the Anthropocene elevates human impacts to a geological force of planetary magnitude. The local effects of this planetary force – enmeshed with capitalist resource extraction – are often monumental as Damodaran indicates. She provides valuable perspectives in environmental history, political ecology and political economy through which to examine conservation and development in India.

In Chapter 3, 'For the environment, against conservation: Conflict between renewable energy and biodiversity protection in India', Lakhanpal and Chhatre compare and contrast three case studies of renewable energy projects in India. The case studies include two hydroelectricity projects, one in Karnataka and one in Himachal Pradesh, and one wind energy project in Maharashtra. Many of India's protected areas are located in hilly and mountainous regions, which are also ideal for renewable energy generation. The competing interests between green energy, biodiversity conservation and rural development in these regions provide a complex setting. The renewable energy targets of governments and environmental ideologies of social movements also often come into conflict. Lakhanpal and Chhatre examine in the three case studies how conflicts between diverse stakeholder groups are negotiated and how key individuals often play a disproportionately large role in the outcome of those negotiations. They portray a complex constellation of actors in each of the three case studies and examine how these local constellations determine whether renewable energy concerns are favoured over conservation or whether conservation concerns trump renewable energy.

In Chapter 4, 'Species and sites matter: Understanding human–wildlife interactions from 5,000 surveys in India', Karanth and Surendra report results from one of the largest country-wide questionnaire surveys on human–wildlife conflict. Their study took place in 11 sites around wildlife reserves across four states in India – Rajasthan, Madhya Pradesh, Maharashtra and Karnataka – where they surveyed over 5,000 households between 2011 and 2014. The incidences of conflict reported were assessed in a regression model against a wide range of site-specific variables including distance to nearest forest, water body or reserve; percentage of forest cover vs grassland cover within a certain radius; as well as crop types and the species of wildlife in question. These included a range of species from different animal groups – primates, canids, felids and herbivores – providing a broad spectrum of human–wildlife conflicts. Their analysis identifies correlates between crop and livestock losses and the range of explanatory variables above included in the regression models and informs possible mitigation measures to reduce these conflicts and compensate the affected people for their losses.

In Chapter 5, 'Thinking like an elephant, looking beyond protected areas', Thekaekara portrays the complex interactions between elephants and humans. The elephant is the largest land mammal. Elephants have large home ranges that often span beyond the boundaries of protected areas. This brings people and elephants frequently into contact with each other. All elephants, however, are not alike. They have their own personalities, just like humans. Thekaekara portrays the complex dynamics these personalities generate. While the preservationist model of protection strives to create elephant corridors for seamless movement of these creatures between protected areas, the reality in India is that no corridor can be completely free of humans. The corridors inevitably coincide with lived-in landscapes. How humans and elephants fare in these landscapes is down to their attitudes towards each other. Reviewing snippets of these interactions from his field research in Gudalur at the foothills of the Nilgiris in Tamil Nadu state, Thekaekara puts together a picture that portrays the complexities of what has come to be thought of as 'human–elephant conflict' in the literature. In many of the cases that Thekaekara reviews, this 'conflict' has morphed into coexistence because enforcing boundaries between elephants and people is practically impossible in landscapes where humans as well as elephants live in high densities. The chapter raises a number of practical challenges for conservation management in such landscapes and points to the need for a change in people's attitudes to elephants.

In Chapter 6, 'Biodiversity in community-managed landscapes: A view of the potentials and constraints in the *van panchayats* of the Kumaon Himalayas', Shahabuddin and Thadani examine the social and ecological status of the village commons in two Himalayan villages in the state of Uttarakhand in India. They demonstrate the links between the social set up for the governance and management of the commons and the ecological status of forest vegetation in these landscapes. The focus of their interviews with the village communities was on three main thematic areas: forest utilisation norms, actual usage patterns and functioning of the forest councils (*van panchayats*) as community institutions. They particularly consider in their analysis the process of rule/regulation creation; forest protection and monitoring activities; punishment of the rule offenders and conflict resolution; and management and restoration activities. They also evaluate the ecological outcomes of forest management using indicators that reflect the structure and function of forest ecosystems. Their results suggest that the forest councils as community institutions are ineffective in maintaining the ecological integrity of ecosystems they are supposed to be in charge of. Shahabuddin and Thadani attribute the weakening of these institutions and their ineffectiveness to the top-down interventions from the state, such as the imposition of Joint Forest Management work plans since the 1990s. Such interventionist approach by the state has disenfranchised many community institutions who feel powerless in managing their forest ecosystems.

In Chapter 7, 'Rethinking landscapes: History, culture and local knowledge in the Biligiri Rangaswamy Temple Tiger Reserve, India', Rai and Madegowda challenge the prevalent conservation model of excluding local people to make protected areas 'inviolate'. They trace the history of this exclusion to the British colonial period and point to the historical maps that excluded place names used by indigenous peoples. This omission from the map and the subsequent enforcement of land ownership by the powerful disenfranchised many indigenous and local communities from their ancestral land. Working with Soligas, an indigenous community in an iconic tiger reserve in South India, Rai and Madegowda unravel the intimate local ecological knowledge and place names that reflect this knowledge. They go on to describe the experience of mapping these place names and the resultant sense of elation among the Soliga. They argue that such mapping can not only empower the indigenous community with unique information, but it can also help them assert their land rights under the Indian government's 2006 Recognition of Forest Rights Act. Through the Soliga case study, Rai and Madegowda make a case for a system of knowledge production that is inclusive of local people and incorporates place-based learning.

In Chapter 8, 'Conservation and development: Beyond national parks and sanctuaries', Saigal et al. review the potential of lesser known categories of protected areas in India. While wildlife sanctuaries and national parks are held as the icons of Indian conservation, a number of international and national categories of protected areas also exist. The international categories include Ramsar Sites, Biosphere Reserves and World Heritage Sites. The national categories include Biodiversity Heritage Sites, Conservation Reserves and Community Reserves, Critical Wildlife Habitats, Coastal Regulation Zones and Eco-sensitive Zones. There are international and national legislative frameworks that govern the protection and management of these sites. However, Saigal et al. argue that the implementation of these relatively new categories of protected areas is thin on the ground. They discuss the case of Okhla Bird Sanctuary, one of Birdlife International's Important Bird Areas on the outskirts of the sprawling suburbs of Delhi. The housing development in the area has crept into the buffer zone of this bird sanctuary and is compromising the ecological integrity of the site. Saigal et al. argue that the integrity of these newer categories of protected areas is often trumped by the need to develop suburban housing for the increasing number of middle-class people working in large Indian cities. Saigal et al. suggest that mere legislation to declare newer categories of protected areas is not enough. It needs to be supported by appropriate institutional structures, political will and often influential individuals who can reinforce the protection of these areas.

In Chapter 9, 'Ficus to filter: Understanding complexities of market incentives for conserving biodiversity on private lands', Bose illustrates the complexities of conservation in agroforestry landscapes. Based on the case study of Kodagu, a coffee-growing district of the state of Karnataka in India, this chapter critically examines the increasing tendency to connect markets with conservation. Based on the notion of 'payment for ecosystem services' the market-based initiatives attempt to provide direct payments for private land owners to conserve native trees on their land. In Kodagu, however, right to land does not mean right to trees. This protectionist policy by the government is proving a disincentive to farmers to keep native trees on their land. Kodagu has seen a large-scale transformation of the landscape as the native shade trees on plantations are replaced by exotic trees. Bose argues that this transformation, which is unfavourable to conservation, may be rooted in, among other things, the long history in Kodagu of conflict with the state and the rejection of its power. The certification schemes for shade-grown coffee are also seen in the same light as an imperialist gesture from the West. Many elite farmers therefore refuse to be part of the certification schemes and favour their traditional methods of cultivation, which, according to many farmers, are environmentally far more friendly. Bose concludes by questioning the relevance of market-based mechanisms for conservation in Kodagu, particularly because such an approach is deeply counter to the local politics and therefore fails to achieve its promised outcomes.

In Chapter 10, 'Conclusions: Reimagining wilderness', the book turns to the question of how conservation and development can be reconciled in a country that is on the upward trajectory of development, but still hosts substantial biological diversity.

References

Barua, M., Bhagwat, S.A., and Jadhav, S. (2013). The hidden dimensions of human–wildlife conflict: Health impacts, opportunity and transaction costs. *Biological Conservation* 157: 309–316.

Bhagwat, S., Kushalappa, C., Williams, P., and Brown, N. (2005a). The role of informal protected areas in maintaining biodiversity in the Western Ghats of India. *Ecology and Society* 10(1): 8. www.ecologyandsociety.org/vol10/iss1/art8/.

Bhagwat, S.A., Kushalappa, C.G., Williams, P.H., and Brown, N.D. (2005b). A landscape approach to biodiversity conservation of sacred groves in the Western Ghats of India. *Conservation Biology* 19(6): 1853–1862.

Bhagwat, S.A., Breman, E., Thekaekara, T., Thornton, T.F., and Willis, K.J. (2012). A battle lost? Report on two centuries of invasion and management of Lantana camara L. in Australia, India and South Africa. *PLoS ONE* 7(3): e32407. https://doi.org/10.1371/journal.pone. 0032407.

DeFries, R., Karanth, K.K., and Pareeth, S. (2010). Interactions between protected areas and their surroundings in human-dominated tropical landscapes. *Biological Conservation* 143(12): 2870–2880.

Ellis, E.C. (2015). Ecology in an anthropogenic biosphere. *Ecological Monographs* 85(3): 287–331.

Ferraro, P., and Kiss, A. (2002). Direct payments to conserve biodiversity. *Science* 298: 1718–1719.

Gangal, K., Sarson, G.R., and Shukurov, A. (2014). The Near-Eastern roots of the Neolithic in South Asia. *PLoS ONE* 9(5): e95714. https://doi.org/10.1371/journal. pone. 0095714.

Madden, F. (2004). Creating coexistence between humans and wildlife: Global perspectives on local efforts to address human–wildlife conflict. *Human Dimensions Wildlife* 9: 247–257.

Malhotra, K.C., Gokhale, Y., Chatterjee, S., and Srivastava, S. (2007). *Sacred Groves in India*. Aryan Books International, New Delhi, and Indira Gandhi Rashtriya Manav Sangrahalaya, Bhopal.

Nanisetti, S. (2017). Ameenpur Lake becomes the first Biodiversity Heritage Site in the country: Fish and birds return, but much remains to be done. *The Hindu*, 3 June 2017. www.thehindu.com/scitech/energyandenvironment/fishforeveryone/article18712907. ece, accessed 5 July 2017.

Pagiola, S., Arcenas, A., and Plantais, G. (2005). Can payments for environmental services help reduce poverty? An exploration of the issues and the evidence to date from Latin America. *World Development*, 33: 237–253.

Pathak, N. (ed.) (2009). *Community Conserved Areas in India: A Directory*. Kalpavriksh, Pune/Delhi.

Rangarajan, M. (1996). *Fencing the Forest: Conservation and Ecological Change in India's Central Provinces, 1860–1914*. Oxford University Press, Delhi.

Ruddiman, W.F. (2003). The anthropogenic greenhouse era began thousands of years ago. *Climate Change* 61: 261–293.

Steffen, W., Broadgate, W., Deutsch, L., Gaffney, O., and Ludwig, C. (2015). The trajectory of the Anthropocene: The great acceleration. *The Anthropocene Review* 2(1): 81–98.

Zalasiewicz, J., Waters, C.N., Williams, M., Barnosky, A.D., Cerreata, A., Crutzen, P., Ellis, E., Ellis, M.E., Fairchild, I.J., Grinevald, J., Haff, P.K., Hajdas, I., Leinfelder, R., McNeill, J., Odada, E.O., Poirier, C., Richter, D., Steffen, W., Summerhayes, C., Syvitski, J.P.M., Vidas, D., Wagreich, M., Wing, S.L., Wolfe, A.P., An, Z., and Oreskes, N. (2015). When did the Anthropocene begin? A mid-twentieth century boundary level is stratigraphically optimal. *Quaternary International* 383: 196–203.

2 The impact of the Anthropocene in the locality

Eastern India in the nineteenth and twentieth centuries

Vinita Damodaran

The environmental history of a locality

India today is in the middle of an anthropogenic environmental and climate crisis. As one writer notes, Delhi, the capital city, has one of the worst air pollution results in the world (Kela 2015). The current heatwave has resulted in forest fires stretching across several states in Northern India that have reached the outskirts of Shimla (Times 2016). The heat wave in the preceding year in the Deccan was a sign that extreme weather events such as droughts and floods are set to visit the subcontinent on a regular basis. India's agricultural systems are also in crisis in many states as the soils and the water table are affected in the wake of rampant deforestation and dam building. The damage being done to river ecologies and soils is matched by species loss and habitat loss on an unprecedented scale that should be mapped historically in the context of what currently is being termed the Anthropocene.

For earth system scientists the mapping of anthropogenic change has led them to see humans as a 'geological force' transforming the earth's atmosphere and allowing them to designate the last few centuries the Anthropocene. The period has no precise start date, but based on atmospheric evidence may be considered to start with the Industrial Revolution (late eighteenth century) and the period of Great Acceleration to coincide with the rise of fossil fuel use after the Second World War. A 2015 article in *Nature* using GSSP (Global Stratotype Section and Point) markers notes that agreeing to a start date related to the Industrial Revolution may be used to assign historical responsibility for CO_2 emissions to particular countries or regions. The article also goes on to note a dip in CO_2 emissions in 1610 linked to population decline via diseases carried by Europe and war, enslavement and famine caused by the colonial encounter (Lewis and Maslin 2015). There is agreement using evidence of irreversible climate and environmental change from 1800 and increasing fossil fuel use and since 1950, the period referred to as the 'Great Acceleration' on the future global CO_2 peak and its profound implications for the planet.

For environmental historians the discovery of the Anthropocene (Crutzen and Stoermer 2000) comes as a surprise. After all, the concept of human induced environmental change and human–nature interactions over time has been a core object of research in environmental history. The intellectual origins of environmental history as a self-conscious domain of enquiry can be traced to the encounter of seventeenth and eighteenth-century western Europeans with the startlingly unfamiliar environments of the tropics and the damage inflicted on these environments in the course of European extraction of European empires. The recognition of the role of the environment in modern historical enquiry was heralded when a new phase of global environmental history began with European decolonisation from the 1950s onwards (Grove and Damodaran 2006). The Annales School had since the 1950s elaborated the role of geography and climate in history over long time frames. The relevance of environmental history to earth system scientists was highlighted in 2005, when the Dahlem workshop brought an interdisciplinary group of social scientists and historians (the group included two historians: Richard Grove and John Mcneill), sociologists and scientists including Crutzen on a project to integrate socio-environmental interactions over centennial time scales published as *An Integrated History and Future of People on Earth* (Costanza *et al.* 2006).

Scientists, as Sverker Sörlin has noted, have been described as 'the historians of the future'. By ceding the terrain of history to scientists in this debate on the Anthropocene and foregrounding big narratives on the fate of humanity, one can argue that locality, class, gender and race risk being glossed over (Sörlin 2014). There is therefore urgent need to foreground questions of locality, race and class through a historical lens. This chapter looks at the impact of the Anthropocene in the locality by developing a more pointillist approach to the impact of global climate and environmental change in particular locales and its impact on *adivasi* (indigenous peoples) communities in India and their landscapes. In doing so, it attempts to challenge these planetary debates of earth scientists through a historical and political engagement with capitalism, democracy and resource extraction and to focus on communities in particular periods and specific places in the global South. This has relevance for contemporary debates on conservation. The shifting politics of the climate change debate today from 'historical responsibility' to 'we are all in it together' calls for a radical new political imagination to deal with resource wars, the militarisation of borders and boundaries and problematic ideas of top-down stewardship of landscapes and forest regimes. How do we contribute towards a reframing of Anthropocene debates so that we have 'good Anthropocene' emerging from a 'bad Anthropocene'? Mike Hulme (2011) has noted that the positivist disciplines are ill suited to engaging with and articulating the deeper human search for values, purpose and meaning – yet this search is exactly where humanity's new entanglement with global climate is taking us.

The framing of the debates on the Anthropocene has to be understood in terms of the larger issues of current global political economy and geo-politics as are some of the proposed responses which include top-down, authoritarian ideas of land stewardship, a form of green imperialism with 'Nature to be managed like a garden' including in parts of Africa and also South Asia where the discourse of 'neo-protectionism' is gaining ground (Buscher and Dressler 2007). As Buscher and Dressler have noted when reviewing trends in the conservation–development debate, there has been a neo-protectionist turn among conservation practitioners resulting in a 'commodification of nature' under neo-liberalism. They argue that political science and governance studies need to be integrated with biodiversity conservation and without acute political analysis there can be no effective biodiversity governance (Buscher and Dressler 2007). The current focus on the Anthropocene is increasing the polarisation in the conservation debate with disturbing implications for people and communities. One can argue, that not only do we need participatory conservation as endorsed in the conservation literature but that conservation needs to be situated in the context of wider environmental history, political economy and political ecology. For example, it is only by understanding the use of resources in the past by communities such as those in Eastern India, their ongoing historic struggle to save their traditions and commons against the state and private interests that we can challenge the growing neoliberal enclosures of our landscapes. As Peluso notes 'enclosure is alive and well in the 21st century'. She further asks 'how given the history, politics and social embeddedness of social institutions did state and civil society institutions allow such neo-liberal enclosures representing so few people's interests to proceed?'(Peluso 2007). The movement against mining in Singhbhum in Eastern India today is part of the story of protest against such neoliberal enclosures and its contestations. History, memory and social meanings of the landscape are invoked to contest neoliberal policies in the face of a state that remains constitutive of such regimes and practices.

In their book *Ecology and Equity* Gadgil and Guha (1995) argued for socio-ecological categories relating to resource use for understanding how these are used by different groups. For example, they note that the category 'omnivores', who have been the real beneficiaries of economic development and primarily responsible for the 'abuse' of nature in India, have used their political power to pass on the costs to the ecological refugees and ecosystem people (Gadgil and Guha 1995). While this is true, they did not offer an explanation of how power over natural resources operates globally and nationally and the impact of the exercise of this political and economic power by elites. This poses a problem in conceptualising how their vision of decentralised resource management outlined can be turned into reality especially in the context of the neoliberal enclosure actively endorsed by the Indian state today. The ongoing violent struggle of *adivasi* communities in India today may be the only answer to the neoliberal agendas of the Indian state.

How do we revisit the idea of sustainable development in the Anthropocene? In a 2013 article in *Nature* this idea is redefined as 'development that meets the needs of the present whilst safeguarding Earth's life support system on which the welfare of current and future generations depends' (Griggs *et al.* 2013). It has also been argued that discounting the future and valuing the present is much easier to do in materially poor societies in the global South where survival itself is at stake, but this argument is certainly not true for indigenous societies in Eastern India where attitudes towards the environment are intergenerational and historically conservationist. One needs to challenge the notion that, as many indigenous communities have long engaged in cash economies, they may see little reason to conserve nature in their pursuit of shedding poverty (van Schaik and Rijksen 2002). My research argues that there are communities whose values and ways of co-existing with nature in the past help us learn useful lessons. Research that explores the environmental history and anthropology of particular communities and localities will help uncover alternative ways of living on this earth, detail the impact of the Anthropocene in the locality and allow us to 'reimagine how we live on this earth' (Hulme 2011). Furthermore, a focus on the locality shows the local impacts of global processes and the ways in which the impact of anthropogenic environmental change has a particularly devastating effect in specific locales and on specific communities whose ways of living and being are being transformed. This has a particular relevance in the light of discussions on resilience. The debate on the Anthropocene is wrapped up with ideas of resilience and with security but we need to examine how people have historically understood resilience, the ways in which resilience is mediated and on the ways in which community and place shapes resilience. 'Every day forms of resilience through human agency, collective action and knowledge' is critical to resilience thinking, and in the context of Eastern Indian *adivasis* seeing resistance and resilience as synonyms is important (Brown 2016).

Studies of environmental resistance movements in India have shown how people have historically challenged social processes and built alternatives to capitalist imperatives and the neoliberal perspectives of a corporatist state. For current day developmental specialists working on resilience thinking, I would argue that resilience can be recuperated through resistance. There is a need to bring the politics back to the Anthropocene by focusing on agency and power. Through studying locality and place in a long time frame we can offer examples of 'good' resilience and 'bad' resilience such as in Eastern India where it has been documented that communities less engaged with the market were more resilient to climate vulnerability.

By dealing with scale in terms of time and space in debates on the Anthropocene, by shifting the focus to the locality and to the local effects of human induced climate and environmental change in the periphery, and by looking at the local responses to the effects of global processes both in historical period and more contemporaneously it is possible to reframe debates on the Anthropocene. This will have implications for (a) studies on communities and their landscapes through an understanding of alternative cosmologies vis-à-vis the idea of nature and its uses and what Hulme (2011) calls alternate ways of living on this planet, (b) conservation studies through a reassessment of the debate for governance and management of forest reserves and plantations including ideas of top-down stewardship of the landscape, (c) adaptation and resilience studies.

Here, by looking at the locality as it emerges in the environmental history of Eastern India I hope not just to critique perspectives on the Anthropocene but to enrich our perceptions using the lens of local, regional and national history and local ethnography allowing us to explore issues in complex ways by asking the following questions. How do more-than-human histories and the humanities help reframe questions of boundaries and scale and how do they connect the bodily, local and regional with the global or planetary? Can intimate histories of people and environments bring new perspectives to landscapes with contested values and their conservation? How have particular places and their non-human inhabitants shaped these contestations? Where does environmental history stand in relation to the environmental humanities and ecological and conservation sciences today? This chapter attempts to address some of these questions within the context of South Asian environmental history.

South Asian environmental history

South Asian environmental history has its roots in Jean Filliozat's work on South India, a regional study, was born out his interest in ethnobotany and marked the first steps of the discipline in the 1950s. It was followed by E.K. Janakiammal's contribution to a landmark volume in environmental history and historical geography which has gone unrecognised. As a leading botanist and author of the *Chromosome Atlas of Cultivated Plants* in 1945 she was the only woman and the only non-white contributor to the Chicago symposium held in 1955, which led to the volume of the same name, edited by W.L. Thomas, on *Man's Role in Changing the Face of the Earth* (Grove and Damodaran 2006). An ethnobotanist, her contribution to the volume was on subsistence agriculture in India. A global dimension into these early forays into Indian environmental history was introduced by John F. Richards and Richard Tucker, whose environmental history work emerged from their research in agrarian history leading them to a realisation that a global framework of reference was essential to understand the South Asian environment. This was further developed in Richard Grove's magnum opus on the environmental history of empire, *Green Imperialism*, in 1995. Regional and local histories of South Asia followed first in the edited volume, *Nature and the Orient: The Environmental History of South and South East Asia* in the 1990s and a series of monographs that emerged with Mahesh Rangarajan, Rohan Dsouza, Vasant Saberwal and K. Sivaramakrishnan, whose work described the colonial watershed moment in forest and water history in Central India and Odisha (formerly known as Orissa) and examined colonial constructions of nature and the creation of boundaries of forest and wasteland which partitioned landscapes and defined communities. There were, however, large gaps in the literature of environmental history, particularly at the level of scale both in terms of space and time. Most of the studies concentrated on the colonial period and while there were several small-scale studies of the locality there was little attempt to link the local to the global apart from through the lens of empire. J.F. Richards' project on the land use history of India was an attempt to tabulate the land use and vegetation map of India from colonial records with an eye to understanding carbon stocks, arguing for a decline in carbon stock over the period. Interestingly, they recorded the highest figure of depletion for the 1950–1980 period due to the conversion of forest to other vegetation types and the reduction over time of biomass within vegetation types (Flint and Richards 1991).[1] This was a very significant project whose methodology could be replicated for an earlier period but this is yet to happen. For example, Madhav Gadgil and Ram Guha's book towards an ecological history of India attempted a study of Indian ecological history from the ancient period using qualitative records (Guha and Gadgil 1995). Written by a biologist and an environmental historian, it casts a look at the long-term history of resource use in India with interesting perceptions about caste-based societies and ecological niches in early and medieval India. Its conclusion, that the thousand years prior to British conquest was a period of relatively stable populations, stagnant technologies and only minor changes in the resource use pattern in the Indian subcontinent, is in need of more research. The ecological history of India is still in its nascent stages in terms of soil erosion histories, history of endemics, invasive species and biodiversity histories, histories of disease, history of languages and ethnicities and history of extractive industries. The pre-colonial period is particularly under-researched, though a few edited volumes have emerged.

The collected volume *Nature and the Orient* had highlighted the need not just to focus on the grand theories of environmental history but on very local, small-scale histories of local communities. One cannot over-emphasise the importance of understanding local historical-ecological settings for any study on communities, rights, governance and identity. Neither can one ignore the need to study 'human histories within a multispecies field of histories' (Tsing 2013). Also important is to delineate the local impacts of global processes. This is a sense in which place and locality are being reconfigured in this paper where histories of particular communities and their experience of ecological pressures and change over time can be seen to be part of a broader social agenda aimed at local empowerment and environmental awareness from which emancipatory imaginings can emerge. In anthropology as well, a new multispecies ethnography is emerging as a necessary way to 'write culture' in the Anthropocene, attending to 'the remaking of anthropos as well as its companion and stranger species on planet Earth' (Kirksey and Helmreich 2010). Some research argues that Human ecological relations need to be assessed as a kind of 'knowledge of life' (Canguilhem 2008) related to 'meaningful exchange among human and nonhuman entities' (Whitington 2013). What does this mean for landscapes and people currently in the midst of an ecological crisis? One can argue that environmental history offers invaluable lessons and consequences that, as the writer Kela notes, current conservation practice seeks to understand. He also criticises the question of 'pragmatism' advocated in a volume about working with corporations and private interests to protect landscape and wildlife, noting that an exclusionary approach to conservation will not work in the long run and is unlikely to meet important conservation goals either (Kela 2015). Instead, as noted, conservation debates need to be situated in the context of wider environmental history, political economy and political ecology.

Eastern India in the Anthropocene

Travelling through the mining town of Noamundi, Jharkhand in 2013 and in 2017, I was struck by the presence of red oxide dust everywhere. On my clothes, on houses, on people, on the once brightly painted advertisement for the Tata Company noting that it was a company who valued its Corporate Social Responsibility. There were few amenities and the settlement of Kiriburu further on which overlooked the hills of Saranda hosted no facilities for visitors. As one newspaper report put it,

> Mine areas often have a monochromatic appearance. Coal mining areas are depressingly black, iron ore towns are red, ochre lends a yellow colour and limestone makes everything chalky white. Fine particles of the ore spread as a uniform layer of dust on every available surface in these areas. The pervasiveness of dust is the strongest indication that mining is not a benign activity. Unless carefully planned it can barren the land, pollute water, denude forests, defile the air and degrade the quality of life for people who live and work in the vicinity. Modern technology has enormously magnified our ability to extract minerals. In the process, it has also gravely threatened human lives and the environment.
>
> (Priyadarshi 2008)

Noamundi (Figure 2.1) has a long history as one of the centres of the mining industry, set up by Tata in Eastern India since the early part of the twentieth century. Above the local town with its withered trees and red oxide dust was the officer's colony in Kiriburu with its bungalows and its tennis courts and its magnificent views of the reserved *Sal* forest of Saranda whose proportions set in the colonial period were rapidly eroding under pressure of development following the cleansing of the Maoists in the region. This was a forest which is extremely important in bio-diversity and cultural terms both for local communities and the Indian imaginary. Not only is it part of the cultural world of *adivasi* communities but it fuelled the imagination of Bengali intellectuals such as Bibhutibhushan Bandyopadhyaya who wrote *Aranyak* (a famous Bengali novel written in the late 1930s depicting deforestation and displacement of *adivasis* in Eastern India) around it. Saranda forest was created as a reserved forest by the British in the nineteenth century.

In 1878, the Indian Forest Act was passed, extending policies regarding 'reserved forests' and 'protected forests' to all the provinces of British India. Systematic forestry had commenced after the stabilisation of British rule in the latter half of the nineteenth century. As information gathering in Chotanagpur increased, notably by colonial officials such as Henry Ricketts, John Davidson, S.R. Tickell and Valentine Ball, new regimes of property were beginning to be put into place (Ricketts 1853; Tickell 1840; Ball 1880). On the completion of the demarcation in 1880–1881, the forests of the Singhbhum division

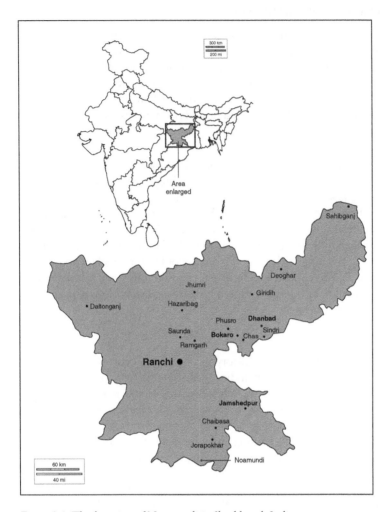

Figure 2.1 The location of Noamundi in Jharkhand, India

comprised Saranda, Kolhan and Porahat. In 1884–1885, Chotanagpur division was constituted, which embraced the whole of Singhbhum, Palamau and
Kodarma. Thus in 1885, 306 square miles of Saranda constituted one 'reserved
forest' range, managed by one forest ranger, three forest guards and six *chaukidars*
(wardens). The history of 'protected forests' dates back to 1903–1905 when 17
blocs were declared protected. There were then various additions and modifications with regard to the area and status of forest. The Kolhan forests were
separated in 1906 to form the Chaibasa division. By 1 April 1924, four forest
divisions had been constituted with their headquarters at Chaibasa for the purposes of control and management of all reserved and protected forests situated
within Singhbhum (Phillips 1924). Every possible safeguard against infringements

(by private rights) surrounded the first-class constitution of 'reserved forests', which were secured by a permanent settlement. The second-class demarcation of 'protected forests', however, offered less sufficient guarantees for stability and protection. There were also private forests leased from political states. By 1898, 33,738 square miles of forest were closed to all animals, and 28,146 square miles were closed to browsers throughout India. The impact of colonial forest reservation on local communities was draconian. While in reserved forests no property rights could accrue, in the protected forests, the colonial state was forced to reconcile customary rights to forest with their agendas for conservation. Protracted resistance followed these demarcations of the landscape all through the late nineteenth century until the Chotanagpur Tenancy Act of 1908, which stabilised the situation in the twentieth century by recognising Mundari land tenure and legislating against further land alienation of the tribes (Basu and Damodaran 2015).

In the post-Independence period, the status of Saranda forest as a reserved forest was carried over. In 2005, the forest, which is part of the core elephant reserve, was in a bid for World Heritage status by the Ministry of Forests. The World Wildlife Fund was also very interested in its status. It later became a Maoist stronghold in the long fight between disaffected intellectuals, local communities and the state over rights to resources and the growing poverty and inequality in the region. Following the purging of Maoists in the region the Saranda development plan sought to hasten the carving up of the reserve into mining leases.[2] The above picture of Saranda is part of the story of Eastern India's rapid transformation in the colonial and post-colonial period and the resistance to this by both local indigenous communities and political groupings such as the Maoists. I had been studying the region for many years as a historian of India's *adivasi* communities. The history of tribal communities was also an environmental history, both 'green' and 'brown', of Eastern India – of a 'sacred' 1830s landscape gradually despoiled since 1800, reserved and protected by British colonial policy, marked by indigenous resistance and state violence, most notably in the 1830s, 1890s and in 2006 resulting in the killing of 12 tribals following their protests against mining by Tata. Mapping this story was an environmental history of globalisation in the region, a history that has resonances with debates on the Anthropocene. This section looks at the complexity of human environment interactions by focusing on India's indigenous communities, *adivasis*, in the Anthropocene and their intimate ecologies.

India and China are becoming the 'Asian Drivers' of the globalising world economy (Kaplinsky 2006; Kaplinsky 2005; Bauman 1998). The consequences for people and environments in both countries are profound as a scramble for resources takes place to feed the demands of industrialisation in both, while environmental governance has failed to keep pace with the speed of change (Bauer 2005). The region of Odisha and Jharkhand possesses among the world's best deposits of the bauxite used in aluminium production, a process which requires the construction of dams to provide electricity. Over 20 mountain ranges in the region are now planned for exploitation by global mining companies. Many of these ranges have complex sacred meanings attached to them by *adivasis* or are priority areas for biodiversity conservation. The inland areas of Jharkhand and Western Odisha can be considered a colony of the coast. Thus the Hirakud dam has its submergence zone in the west but the putative benefits from flood control and irrigation go to the coastal plains. Since 1945 up to 5 million people (mostly *adivasis*, who make up 25 per cent of the region's population)[3] have been forcibly removed and 'resettled' to enable dam building and mining/industrial development, a forced migration rarely equalled globally in the twentieth century. These movements were facilitated by the failure of the Odisha state to redistribute land or rights over the 60 per cent of the region that had originally been incorporated from the princely states in 1947. Such an environmental change has a long history dating back to 1800.

This chapter focuses on the whole of southern Jharkhand with references to Odisha. The poorest districts in these already poor states, such as Singhbhum and Koraput, have the highest percentages of *adivasi* inhabitants; they are also those with the natural resources and minerals currently most targeted by multinational corporations. Research on the history of the ecological distribution conflicts in these areas, as analogues to much broader conflicts, is essential in gaining insight into globalisation forces in rural India as a whole. As the forces of globalisation have accelerated since 1800 vigorous contestations for space and resources have taken place between *adivasis*, peasants, the state and mining and other commercial companies.

Since 1945, and much more since 1990, these contests have involved an increasing level of state and corporate violence against *adivasis* and other peasants, coupled with a rise in violent and non-violent resistance, as well as armed 'Naxalite' insurgency throughout the central interior of India.[4] The Kalinganagar massacre in Jajpur district in neighbouring Odisha, also with a large tribal population, on 1 January 2006 appears a turning point in the breakdown of governance. We question whether central government is motivated at all to effectively control the activities of multinational companies and their agents intent on alienating indigenous land.

Currently over 100 Memoranda of Understanding (MoUs)have been signed in the region between mining multinationals and state governments to promote large-scale open-cast mining of bauxite and iron ore as well as other less important minerals, and to build processing plants and port export facilities. Most of these MoUs ignore Schedule 5 of the Indian constitution prohibiting alienation of tribal lands and a 1996 Act strengthening its provisions; most of them also ignore the legal protection of reserved forests under the Forest Acts. Despite these laws several companies commenced mining operations in both states, including two British mining companies that proposed opencast mines on sacred mountain sites at Niyamgiri (the Hill of Law) and Gandhamardhan mountain. The latter is the most sacred site in Odisha, closely associated with the gods Ram and Hanuman. Thus global mining interests now confront core values in mainstream Hindu as well as tribal religion. Despite the success of the Gond communities in challenging the mining of Niyamgiri, the confidence of multinationals in such plans indicates the seriousness of the plight in which *adivasi* communities and environmental/human rights campaigners find themselves. Under new government plans with the Modi government these pressures on the environment can only grow more severe. In documenting the history of this confrontation in environmental, landscape and human terms, the research fills a critical role (Padel and Das 2006).

A long history of tribal resistance

The history and dynamics of patterns of resistance and violence over the control and allocation of resources by the local communities of the Chotanagpur plateau, now Jharkhand, and the predicament of ethnic identity and culture in the face of unrestrained globalising forces needs to be explored in the *longue durée*. In attempting to understand the nature of resistance one needs to examine the resilience and vitality of tribal culture in the face of exploitation and repression, of crushing inequalities of access to their own resources from the beginnings of colonial rule. The response of communities was not slow in coming and by the mid-nineteenth century there were a series of tribal rebellions.

Beginning with the unrest in Tamar in 1816 and the Munda rebellion in 1832, disaffection continued through the mutiny of 1857, and the last decades of the nineteenth century saw unrest in almost every district of Chotanagpur. W.J. Allen, who made an extensive tour of Singhbhum in 1861, noted 'the love of freedom was the general characteristic of the wild and hilly country of the savage Kols and Santhals'.[5] The Birsa Munda uprising in the 1890s was the culmination of this period of rebellion. Birsa's rebellion originated against the forest laws of the British. British forest reservation laws had long proved irksome to the Mundas and in the context of the degradation of their forest environment, exploitation by Hindu moneylenders and a modernising colonial state, they rose in protest. It can be argued that the despoliation of the forested landscape and the transformation of the people's relationship with their environment in Chotanagpur in the nineteenth century were powerful memories that were revived in periods of cultural resistance. It was also through the mapping of the notion of the *diku* or outsider in these resistance movements that a new sense of community was renegotiated and a radical consciousness began to emerge. As Guha (1999) notes, the Santhals and the Mundas were both determined to be in power in one form or another. The resistance movements of the latter half of the nineteenth century were critical to this growing consciousness. The effects of land alienation following from changes in colonial governance in the 1820s had an immediate and most visible effect in Tamar where the exploitation of Hindu moneylenders, whose activities were bolstered by colonial courts, resulted in widespread protests that continued unabated until the 1830s.[6] In the beginning the communities sought to redress their grievances through colonial courts, wending their way long distances to Shergati in order to resolve land disputes that resulted from the seizure of Munda lands by Pathan moneylenders.[7] When the courts failed to redress their grievances, protest seemed the only answer.

The violent response to transformations in their lifestyle and livelihoods in the Munda rebellions of the 1830s can be explained by the political nature of their actions. Looting along with wrecking and burning occurred on a massive scale during the Kol insurrection. As Guha notes, 'the dominant motive here is political, that of undermining the authority of the gentry by the demolition of its symbols. This inversive function of popular violence is raised to its highest power by insurgency' (Guha 1999: 146). The link between tribe and territory was also well established by the nature of the insurgency; 'they have taken away from us our trees, fishes, lands and jagirs' said the insurgent Singrai. It had been established through the many tribal rebellions over land and the special administrative status accorded to Chotanagpur and it is to this we will now turn (Dalton 1872: 3).

What can be forcibly argued here is that Chotanagpuri understandings of the landscape, their stories of nature, and their lived history were to differ radically from the perceptions of nature and the land of colonial scientists and policy makers and later of a modernising nationalist elite. To say this is not to romanticise indigenous peoples and their relationship to nature. Sahlins has noted that the post-modern attack on the notion of a bounded and coherent culture has occurred at the very moment when groups such as the Maoris, Tibetans, Australian aborigines around the world 'all speak of their culture using that word or some other equivalent, as a value worthy of respect, commitment and defence'. He argues that no good history can be written without regard for 'ideas, actions and ontologies that are not and never were our own' (Sahlins 1995). To the Chotanagpuris therefore the landscape was an important context for their ritual and customary traditions. The destruction of forests that was to occur as a result of colonial intervention in the nineteenth century and later was to change this relationship between the people and their environment. However, the memory of the landscape was to live on and it became a repository of Chotanagpur's nostalgic past, to be revived in complex oppositional contexts (Schama 1995).[8]

That these rebellions forced colonial policy to contend with 'indigenous' ideas of place and being is not in doubt. Native resistance to European land claims forced a recognition of Munda rights and highlighted the limits of colonial power. The process revealed the ambivalence of the colonial state and the 'interaction of indigenous narratives of resistance with narratives of power' (Schama 1995). Some representations of rebellions also make the case for indigenous agency quite strongly. Here, we see a doctrine of human nature where the savages are bestowed with moral judgement, and a sharp sense of injustice that stands in contrast to ideas of the 'noble' or 'ignoble' savage. Through the conscious use of their will to transform their unhappy circumstances into a better social condition the tribes are seen as active agents of their own future. In these accounts, which sees 'tribes' as cultural beings, they are afforded more genuine respect as human beings, resulting in a critique of British imperial policy from within the system that is brutalising fellow human beings and destroying their culture.

Blunt, a member of the governor general's council, who had been located in Chotanagpur, noted in 1832:

I think a serious error was committed in introducing our regulations into Chotanagpur, or in attempting to create a revenue from taxes to be levied from subjects so uncivilised and so poor. It is worthy of remark that the insurrection which occurred in Palamau in 1817–18 was produced by the illegal or fraudulent dispossession of the hereditary proprietors of some of the *jagir* lands in that *Pergunnah*, combined with other local causes. It now appears that in *Pergunnahs* Sonepur, Tamar, Silee, Baranda and Boondooo, in which quarter the insurrection in Chotanagpur commenced, most of the hereditary proprietors the Mundas and *mankis* have been dispossessed of their lands which have been transferred in farm to foreigners whose expulsion and destruction appears to have been a primary object of insurgents. It further appears that the most grievous opposition and exactions have long been practiced by the native officers of government, especially the police *darogas* which alone, amidst a people so poor, might well account for any general feeling of discontent.

(Roy 1912: 121)

The Birsa Munda rebellions of the 1890s further alerted colonial officials to the implications of their policies, especially in the context of the forest reservations of the 1880s. It is clear from the forest reports of the 1930s that old villages that had existed in these reserves had been cleared prior to the setting up of these reserves in the 1880s. In reserved forests this resulted in the dismantling of previous customary rights relating to shifting cultivation, clearing of villages in lands so demarcated and resettling them elsewhere. Control of the forests required that these shifting cultivators be expelled, and in Saranda forest that was what happened (Sivaramakrishnan 1997: 84).[9] The creation of the reserved forests here caused the uprooting of many hundreds of villages. Evidence for this was recorded in Santara, Latua, Loda, Ambia, Ankua, Ghatkori and Karampada, Samta, Tholkabad, Tirilposi and Kodilabad. In Tholkabad, for example, Phillips' working plan for the area recorded that the northern half of the compartment was occupied by what were once the *jhum* cultivated lands of Tholkabad situated on a plateau (Phillips 1924: 98). The impact of forest reservation on local people was therefore dramatic. It is clear that the importance of Saranda as a contiguous forest bloc for the colonial government rendered the issue of indigenous rights in this context illusory.

It is important to note here that not all villages were removed to create forest reserves. Some forest villages were retained to provide labour for the Forest Department. While 27 forest villages were officially recognised, there were other hamlets that existed in order to provide free labour. These villagers were often at the mercy of the forest officials. The provisions of the Chotanagpur Tenancy Act did not apply to them and they had no rights to the lands they cultivated (Phillips 1924: 33). In Saranda forests, while local rights were ignored in favour of the productionist agendas of the Forest Department, this was not the case in Porahat, where increasing local protest highlighted the impact of forest reservation on local communities. Thus the first decades of forest conservancy in Chotanagpur show a variety of competing interests. While some areas like Saranda were dominated by factors such as timber supply and profits from forests, other areas provided less scope for the removal of timber as they were involved with supplying local needs such as the protected forests.

The story of reservation in Porahat is interesting though different from the Saranda story, with important implications for local rights. Here the reserved forest was sometimes recategorised as protected forest, where rights could accrue when recognition was made of errors. The Jesuit writer Matthew Areeparampil notes that the reservation of these 'reserved forests' where no rights could accrue was often done in very haphazard fashion and many survey errors were made. For example, Heremda in Bandgaon was wrongly declared part of the reserved forest. In Dhalbhum, 138 acres of Matigara village was wrongly classified as reserved area. The area was excluded from the reserved forest only in 1938 (Areeparampil 1984: 13–14). Another 160 acres were excluded from the reserved forests of Porahat division after they had been wrongly included in the reserved area. In the case of Chirukubera village in the Porahat *pargana* (administrative district), where the reserved forests were constituted in 1890, revenue from the reserved forest was paid to the local estate holder, Raja Narpat Singh. Chirkubera was a *khuntkhatti* village (meaning that it was the tenure of members of the Munda lineage who reclaimed lands) and included the *tolas* of Saromsoya, Rontuabera, Sasanbera, Jabugadara and Kinduda. All these *tolas* (small villages) were forcibly removed on the orders of the Raja, and the houses of the villagers and their crops were destroyed (Areeparampil 1984: 13–14). Unrest followed in the case of the creation of these forest reserves and their re-categorisation and a long history of resistance dominated the landscape of Eastern India all through the nineteenth and early twentieth centuries where struggles over resources were fought. This was a landscape that was reclaimed and reconstituted through struggle, a struggle with ongoing implications today.

In the post-Independence period the recognition of the 'invented' nature of many traditions and the notion of the constructed nature of culture, race and ethnicity was used by social scientists to approach these questions meaningfully through a historical lens. What emerges then is the links between culture and power and culture and resistance – culture as a form of power and domination, especially when it masks itself as a 'national' culture; culture as a medium in which power is both constituted and resisted as in the case of the Jharkhand movement, which used the notion of a separate ethnic identity to challenge the notion of a homogenous national culture. It was in this context, and given a growing sense of injustice, that the landscape of Chotanagpur became a symbolic terrain for definitions of Chotanagpuri identity. Identities were transformed in the context of this rapid ecological and cultural change (Daniels 1993: 5).[10] It must be noted here that the term landscape is a complex concept. As Cosgrove (1985) argues, the term can be seen as a 'socio-historical construct', a way of seeing projected onto the land which has its own techniques and which articulates a particular way of experiencing a relationship with nature. It can be argued in a similar fashion that the landscape of Chotanagpur has been reclaimed and reconstituted in defining Chotanagpuri identity.[11] Sahlins (1995) has noted, in the context of Hawaii, that the landscape and its legends inscribe a criticism of the existing regime. This criticism manifests itself by reading the landscape as text such that places and names evoke a society that is older, truer and more directly related to the people. In this way were the landscapes of Chotanagpur organised by stories and legends of conquest and through memories of better times. The revisionist point that the forest connection of tribal communities has been overdrawn needs, therefore, to be re-examined.

In the contemporary period, in the context of debates on the Anthropocene, understanding of the vital connections between violence, ethnicity, indigeneity and the environment, the concepts of 'resource curse' and 'environmental justice' need to be examined more carefully. The violent and non-violent responses of *adivasi* people to displacement and state violence is a key concern in contemporary India. Furthermore, the corporations and the Indian state are creating the conditions for a 'landscape of violence'. This manifests in the burgeoning autonomy or ethnicity movements and even full-scale armed insurgency or 'terrorism'. Equally, the extent of breakdown of governance with respect to law, human rights and the environment in India exacerbates these concerns.

Post 1991

It can be noted that there are no sacred frontiers today as far as mining is concerned. Across the country, mining is taking place inside and outside reserved forests, protected forests, national parks and wildlife sanctuaries (Centre for Science and Environment 2008: 75). Saranda forest, protected by the British by alienating tribal land, is now part of the new frontier. The story of foreign direct investment (FDI) in India is alarming. Until the 1990s, FDI was not encouraged in the mining sector. Mineral concessions were restricted to companies with less than 40 per cent foreign holding. The national mineral policy, 1993 changed this by allowing FDI up to 50 per cent. In 2006 this was raised to 100 per cent. Since 1994, the government has approved 73 proposals of FDI in the mining sector, envisaging an investment of Rs 4,044 crore, including from mining giants De Beers, Rio Tinto Minerals Development Ltd and BHP. De Beers has acquired prospecting rights to several large tracts of land in Odisha (over 8,500 km^2), Andhra Pradesh (679 km^2), Chhattisgarh (9,000 km^2). Rio Tinto has diamond and gold prospecting rights in Madhya Pradesh (7,650 km^2) and diamond prospecting rights in Chhattisgarh (6,000 km^2). Broken Hill Proprietary Company (BHP) of Australia has acquired nickel, gold and cobalt prospecting rights in Madhya Pradesh (2,293 km^2) (Centre for Science and Environment 2008: 27).

For Odisha, as Felix Padel, notes the plans are how to expand bauxite mining and aluminium manufacture, iron mining and steel plants, as well as build new mega dams for supplying both industries (Padel and Das 2006). A British registered company, Vedanta Resources, has an important profile in the industry.[12] The company's annual report since 2005 notes that it engages in 'sustainable mining'. The reality is that mining is a highly destructive industry. As Roger Moody notes 'natural resource extraction cannot be reconciled with long term sustainability. For industry spokespeople to claim (as they often do) that there is such a thing as "sustainable mining" is a transparent oxymoron' (Moody 2007: 7). The company aimed to mine Niyamgiri Hill in Kalahandi district, which is a wildlife sanctuary and an elephant reserve. As a Centre for Science and Environment report notes, 75 per cent of the area is covered with thick forests, with more than 300 species of vegetation including 50 species of medicinal plants. It has a number of perennial hill streams, which serve the irrigation and drinking water needs of tribals living in the foothills. The hill is also considered sacred by the Dongria Kondh tribals who call it Niyam Penu. Unfortunately the area also has rich deposits of almost 195 MT of bauxite (Centre for Science and Environment 2008: 260). Another Indian company, Tata, also attempted to construct a new steel plant in the region. When the tribals protested, several of them were killed in police firings in Kalinganagar. This event highlighted, as Padel and Das (2006) note, the numerous iron ore and steel projects in the state and a highly controversial deal with the Korean company Posco to mine Odisha's iron and build a steel plant near Paradeep. These projects had support from the Chief Minister of Odisha, and the Odisha government was adamant not to let anything come in the way of Odisha's progress. However Deogi Tina did stand in the way. She was a 35-year-old Ho woman who came from a village in Champa Koila and her religion was the Ho religion in which the hills and the mountains were the residing place of the deities in which she believed and which fed the streams and hills that were also sacred to her and her kinsfolk. She was shot from about five feet away. Subsequently the bodies of 12 others killed in the protest were mutilated. This incidence has many parallels with the deaths of activists in Nigeria, Ecuador, Columbia, Peru and the Amazon who stand in the way of the extraction of minerals from their homelands by multinationals who depend on the state as their middleman to legitimate or force the handout of lands they need to extract minerals.[13]

In Jharkhand, in Hazaribagh, the requirement for Environment Impact Assessment, which had been mandatory ever since the 1970s, was undermined by a 2001 draft notification where carte blanche was given to mining projects with a lease up to 25 hectares, widening of highways and modernisation of irrigation without the displaced people's prior informed consent or a public hearing. The Naxalites have controlled this area for 20 years, but in the last few years Indian paramilitaries have been launched against them. The forced relocation of 600 tribal villages has been spurred by trying to cut the Maoists support base and to open up the land to corporate ventures. As Padel puts it, 'the civil war is an example of resource curse where a region's mineral wealth leases were below 25 hectares excluding them from Environmental Impact Assessment. It has been estimated that 50,000 *adivasis* will be displaced in Jharkhand alone. In neighbouring Bastar, the opening up of the region to unrestricted mining becomes a cause for breakdown of social norms' (Padel and Das 2006, citing Dias 2006). In Odisha, the entry of government-sponsored mining companies and other huge industries as well the construction of multi-purpose power projects have meant the uprooting of thousands of people. It has been pointed out that in the four districts of Odisha, namely Dhenkanal, Ganjam, Koraput and Phulbani, over half the land was lost to non-*adivasis* over a 25–30-year period. In Koraput district alone over 100,000 *adivasis* were dispossessed of their land, including 1.6 lakh hectares of forest on which they depended for their survival. The local communities have responded by setting up *Bhumi suraksha sangathans* (organisations for the protection of lands). In Saranda, local action against the Saranda Development Plan and the crisscrossing of this magnificent forest by mining leases has been brilliantly documented by the indigenous rights activist Gladson DungDung, who has included in his documentation the many human rights violations by the state here engaged in suppressing protest (DungDung 2015). As India hurtles towards an uncertain environmental future in the Anthropocene, plagued by extreme events such as the 2016 droughts affecting 300 million people, the protection of such a rich natural heritage should be paramount for the nation and more globally.

In conclusion, then, while long present, economic globalisation in Eastern India has vastly accelerated since the advent of 'economic reform' after 1991, especially with the rapid expansion of foreign direct investment in large-scale open-cast mining of bauxite, iron ore and coal but also of asbestos, uranium and chromite. There has also been acceleration in the rate of construction of large dams built to service mining and smelting processes. These changes have been characterised by an increasing level of state violence accompanying attempts to vacate tribal land for mining and dams. These have frequently involved, since 1998, mass shootings and related incidents arguably genocidal in effect and intention, along with unregulated or illicit environmental impacts involving deforestation, pollution and species decline. This undermining of the law by state mechanisms poses grave threats both to human rights and to the implementation of environmental protection. In Odisha, in particular, a major transition was marked, as we have noted, by the notorious massacre of tribal people at Kalinganagar in January 2006 as a multinational company cleared land for an iron mine and works. Many multinational companies are alleged to have been associated with the killings of environmental activists by state police. This increasingly violent trajectory and the connections between the economic agents of landscape degradation and the human agents behind incidents involving the killing and mutilation of *adivasi* peoples are compelling.

The historical causes and environmental consequences of these developments have been very little researched to date but need to be understood if local cultures and heritages are to be sustained alongside biodiversity protection. Piers Vitebsky (1993), David Hardiman (1987), Amita Baviskar (1995) and Nandini Sundar (1997) have made a start at understanding tribal cosmologies in the region and assessing the historical impact of globalisation on *adivasi* society and its environment. A much fuller understanding is now needed, especially as the role of state and popular violence has now become rapidly more widespread and threatening to *adivasi* livelihoods. Comparable approaches to this dynamic have been attempted by Michael Watts, in the case of oil drilling in the Niger Delta, while the effects of 'resource curse' are a part of the global impact of resource demands on 'indigenous peoples'. *Adivasi* identities and beliefs are based on ancient linguistic, religious and literary conceptualisations and on cultural origin myths in which important deities are believed present in the distinctive mountain and deltaic landscapes and especially in the sacred woodlands (*sarnas* or *deswalis*) of the region. Environmentalist claims build on this landscape–identity nexus and encourage activist resistance to forces threatening the moral economy of the landscape. Increasingly *adivasi* organisations assert 'minority' identities by promoting landscape and historical sites of significance in resistance history as places of secular historical importance for state protection. Because the resource frontier impinges on *adivasis*, an understanding of economic choices induced in globalising resources is enmeshed in the issue of the *adivasis'* future. As is well known, the concept of indigenous peoples is now upheld in international law and this new indigenousness is internationalist and highly sympathetic to environmentalist agendas. The new indigenism claims group control over resources in regions as far afield as Bolivia, Ecuador and Nigeria. For the mineral globalisers it becomes essential to crush new notions of internationalised indigenousness. This is now happening. Conversely the new indigenousness may be potentially a major bulwark against globalised environmental destruction especially in South America and South Asia.

This chapter will be thus be of utility to those activists and scholars developing an alternative model of development and conservation appropriate to the poor majority of Eastern India, in place of the failed science and extractive industry-based model, which has brought only intense changes and severe ecological degradation in Eastern India in the age of the Anthropocene. This resistance history of Eastern India's *adivasis* needs to be understood as part of a much more politicised resilience thinking in the context of the Anthropocene. As Lewis and Maslin (2015) note 'the power that humans wield is like any other force of nature and can be used, withdrawn or modified . . . the recognition that human actions are driving far reaching changes to the life-supporting infrastructure of the earth . . . has philosophical, social, political and economic implications'. But it may already be too late to do very much about it.

Notes

1 The John F. Richard's project built a time series (1880, 1920, 1950, 1980) of estimates of land use and carbon content of vegetation for a contiguous area in northern India, Bangladesh, and Burma and by incorporating official agricultural and forest statistics with ecological, botanical, historical, geographical and demographic data for 149 administrative units, aggregated into 39 ecological zones. The project estimated the area and carbon content for different land-use categories: net cultivated area, settled–built-up area, forest–woodland, interrupted woods, grass–shrub complexes, barren–sparsely vegetated areas, wetlands, and surface water.

2 There is a Public Interest Litigation suit in the Jharkhand High Court filed by Saryu Roy, convenor of the Save Saranda Campaign. He has also convened a seminar

in Calcutta to highlight these issues with the media. There are several excellent reports on this by Prerna Bindra, for example, 'Mining: Death knell for Saranda: The world's finest Sal forest' (http://prernabindra.com/2013/02/16/mining-death-knell-for-saranda); see also 'More mines fewer schools in former Maoist stronghold' (www.thehindu.com/news/national/other-states/more-mines-fewer-schools-in-former-maoist-stronghold/article4820577.ece). Both stories show clear agendas at work and the mining–politician nexus in today's Jharkhand.

3 *Adivasi* population today in Jharkhand is 7 million out of 26 million, 26 per cent of the total population; 90 per cent of them reside in villages.

4 Based on a 2005 Lok Sabha Report: Lok Sabha Committee on Scheduled Tribes, *Atrocities on Scheduled Castes and Scheduled Tribes and Pattern of Social Crimes towards Them* (Parliament of India, Delhi, 2005).

5 Home public 150–152 dt. 26th Sept. 1861, quoted in Kumar (1991: 87).

6 See file on Tamar disturbances, *Hazaribagh District Collectorate Records*, 1819.

7 Report of the Munda rebellions in the 1830s in Dalton's, *Descriptive Ethnology of Bengal* (1872).

8 Simon Schama (1995) has noted that 'Landscapes are culture before they are nature; constructs of the imagination projected onto wood, water and rock . . . once a certain idea of the landscape, a myth, a vision establishes itself in an actual place, it has a peculiar way of muddling categories, of making metaphors more real than their referents; of becoming in fact part of the scenery'.

9 Sivaramakrishnan (1997) notes that the debate on shifting cultivation in Chotanagpur did recognise that shifting cultivators rarely extended cultivation by denuding forests.

10 As Steve Daniels (1993) notes (and this is certainly true both of ethnic and national identities), 'Identities are often defined by legends and landscapes, by stories of golden ages, enduring traditions, heroic deeds and dramatic destinies located in ancient or promised homelands with hallowed sites and scenery. The symbolic activation of time and space often drawing on religious sentiment gives shape to the imagined community of the nation'.

11 For more recent writings on history, landscape and identity see Lowenthal (1991).

12 Vedanta Resources plc, *Annual Report, 2005*. Balco, India's third largest aluminium company, was disinvested in 2001 to Sterilite industries, now Vedanta Resources, which also owns Zambian Copper Mines (KCM). A London listed company, it is 54 per cent owned by Indian mine financier Anil Agarwal. See Moody (2007: 25–26).

13 Personal communication with Richard Grove, Kalinganagar, Odisha, March 2006.

References

Areeparampil, Matthew (1984) Forest reservation and denial of tribal rights in Singhbhum. Tribal Research and Training Centre, Chaibasa, May 1984.

Ball, Valentine (1985 [1880]) *Tribal and Peasant Life in Nineteenth Century India*. Usha Publications, New Delhi [first published in 1880 as *Jungle Life in India, or the Journeys and Journals of an Indian Geologist*].

Basu, Paul, and Damodaran, Vinita (2015) Colonial histories of heritage: Legislative migrations and the politics of preservation. *Past and Present* 226(Suppl. 10): 240–271.

Bauer, J. (ed.) (2005) *Forging Environmental Values: Contested Environments in China, Japan, India and the United States*. M.E. Sharpe, New York.

Bauman, Zygmunt (1998) *Globalisation: The Human Consequences*. Polity Press, Cambridge, UK.

Baviskar, Amita (1995) *In the Belly of the River: Tribal Conflicts over Development in the Narmada Valley*. Oxford University Press, Oxford.

Brown, Katerina (2016) *Resilience, Development and Global Change*. Routledge, Abingdon, Oxon.

Buscher, Bram, and Dressler, Wolfram (2007) Linking neo-protectionism and environmental governance: On the rapidly increasing tensions between actors in the environment–development nexus. *Conservation and Society* 5(4): 586–611.

Canguilhem, G. (2008) *Knowledge of Life*. Fordham University Press, New York.

Centre for Science and Environment (2008) *Rich Lands, Poor People: Is Sustainable Mining Possible?* Sixth Citizen Report, Centre for Science and Environment, Delhi.

Cosgrove, D (1985) Prospect, perspective and the evolution of the landscape idea. *Transactions of the Institute of British Geographers* 10(1): 45–62.

Costanza, Robert, Graumlich, Lisa J., and Steffen, Will (2006) *Sustainability or Collapse? An Integrated History and Future of People on Earth*. MIT Press, Boston, MA.

Crutzen, P., and Stoermer, E. (2000) Living in the Anthropocene. *IGBP Newsletter* 41: 17.

Dalton, E. (1872) *Descriptive Ethnology of Bengal*. Office of the Superintendent of Government Printing, Calcutta.

Daniels, Stephen (1993) *Fields of Vision: Landscape Imagery and Identity in England and the United States*. Cambridge University Press, Cambridge, UK.

Dias, Xavier (2006) Kalinganagar, before and after. *Mines Area Coordination Committee*, 16 January.

DungDung, Gladson (2015) *Mission Saranda: The War for Natural Resources in India*. Bir Buru Omapay Media & Entertainment, Ranchi.

Flint, E., and Richards, John F. (1991) Historical analysis of changes in land use and carbon stock of vegetation in south and south-east Asia. *Canadian Journal of Forest Research* 21(1): 91–110.

Gadgil, M., and Guha, R. (1995) *Ecology and Equity: The Use and Abuse of Nature in Contemporary India*. Penguin, New Delhi.

Griggs, D., Stafford-Smith, M., Gaffney, O., Rockström, J., Öhman, M.C., Shyamsundar, P., Steffen, W., Glaser, G., Kanie, N., and Noble, I. (2013) Sustainable development goals for people and planet. *Nature* 495: 305–307.

Grove, Richard, and Damodaran, Vinita (2006) Imperialism, intellectual networks and environmental change: Origins and evolution of global environmental history, 1676–2000, part 1. *Economic and Political Weekly* 41(42): 4497–4505.

Guha, R. (1999) *Elementary Aspects of Peasant Insurgency in Colonial India*. Oxford University Press, Oxford.

Hardiman, David (1987) *The Coming of the Devi: Adivasi Assertion in Western India*. Oxford University Press, Oxford.

Hulme, Mike (2011) Meet the humanities. *Nature Climate Change* 1: 177–179.

Kaplinsky, R. (2005) *Globalisation, Poverty and Inequality: Between a Rock and a Hard Place*. Polity Press, Cambridge, UK.

Kaplinsky, R. (2006) *Asian Drivers: Opportunities and Threats*. Institute of Development Studies, Brighton.

Kela, S. (2015) Who cares about the environment? Some notes on the ecological crisis in India. *Kafila*, 12 July. https://kafila.online/2015/07/12/who-cares-about-the-environment-some-notes-on-the-ecological-crisis-in-india-shashank-kela/ (last seen 14 July 2017).

Kirksey, S.E., and Helmreich, S. (2010) The emergence of multi-species ethnography. *Cultural Anthropology* 25(4): 545–576.

Kumar, P. (1991) *Mutinies and Rebellions in Chotanagpur*. Janaki Prakashan, Patna.

Lewis, S.L., and Maslin, M.A. (2015) Defining the Anthropocene. *Nature* 519: 171–180.

Lowenthal, David (1991) British national identity and the English landscape. *Rural History* 2(2): 205–230.

Moody, Roger (2007) *Rocks and Hard Places: The Globalization of Mining.* Zed Books, London.

Padel, Felix, and Das, Samarendra (2006) Anthropology of a genocide: Tribal movements in central India against over-industrialisation. South Asia Analysis Group (SAAG), New Delhi.

Peluso, Nancy Lee (2007) Enclosure and privatisation of neo-liberal environments. In Nik Heynen, James McCarthy, Scott Prudham, and Paul Robbins (eds.), *Neoliberal Environments* (89–93). Routledge, Abingdon, Oxon.

Phillips, P.J. (1924) *Revised Working Plan for the Reserved Forests of Saranda and Kolhan Divisions in Singhbhum.* Superintendent of Government Printing, Patna.

Priyadarshi, Nitish (2008) Impact of mining and industries in Jharkhand. *American Chronicle*, 28 October. www.sacw.net/article302.html (last seen 14 July 2017).

Ricketts, H. (1853) *Report on the District of Singhbhum.* Bengal Military, Orphan Press, Calcutta.

Roy, S.C. (1912) *The Mundas and Their Country.* Kuntaline Press, Calcutta.

Sahlins, Marshall (1995) *How 'Natives' Think: About Captain Cook, For Example.* Chicago University Press, Chicago, IL.

Schama, Simon (1995) *Landscape and Memory.* Routledge, London.

Sivramakrishnan, K. (1997) *Modern Forests: Statemaking and Environmental Change in Colonial Eastern India.* Stanford University Press, Stanford, CA.

Sörlin, Sverker (2014) Historians of the future: Emerging historiographies of the Anthropocene. Paper presented at the World Congress of Environmental History, University of Minho, Braga, Portugal.

Sundar, Nandini (1997) *Subalterns and Sovereigns: An Anthropological History of Bastar, 1854–1996.* Oxford University Press, Oxford.

Tickell, S.R. (1840) Memoir on the Hodesum. *Journal of the Asiatic Society of Bengal* 9(2): 694–710.

Times (2016) Forest fires threaten former Raj capital. *The Times*, 4 May, 30.

Tsing, Anna (2013) More-than-human sociality: A call for critical description. In Kirsten Hastrup (ed.), *Anthropology and Nature* (27–42). Routledge, Abingdon, Oxon.

Van Schaik, C., and Rijksen, H.D. (2002). Integrated conservation and development projects: Problems and potential. In J. Terborgh, C. van Schaik, L. Davenport, and M. Rao (eds.), *Making Parks Work: Strategies for Preserving Tropical Nature* (15–29). Island Press, Covelo, CA.

Vitebsky, Piers (1995) *Dialogues with the Dead: The Discussion of Mortality among the Sora of Eastern India.* Cambridge University Press, Cambridge.

Whitington, J. (2013) Fingerprint, bell weather, model event: Climate change as speculative anthropology. *American Anthropologist* 107(1): 44–54.

3 For the environment, against conservation

Conflict between renewable energy and biodiversity protection in India

Shikha Lakhanpal and Ashwini Chhatre

Introduction

Global concerns for climate change mitigation and the need for sustainable development are manifested locally in various forms. Practices of conservation and expansion of renewable energy are two such manifestations of this global sustainability discourse (Adger *et al.* 2001; Zimmerer 2006; Bridge *et al.* 2013; Zimmerer 2011). But there are instances when the two forms of this discourse come into conflict with each other. This chapter draws on a comparative analysis of social movements against renewable projects located next to conservation spaces across India. In doing so, we show how the local opposition to renewable projects is dynamic and influenced by the broader politics of environment and development, which has itself evolved over time. Until now, the arguments for and against development projects near conservation spaces have been straightforward and presented a clear case of environment against development. However, the conservation–development debate has expanded to include development projects that can themselves be justified on environmental grounds (like renewable energy). We chronicle this shift and contend that the same conflict is manifested either as an environment versus environment contestation or as an environment versus development conflict, contingent upon the scale of analysis.

The undermining of conservation in protected areas due to large-scale development projects has received much attention (Chhatre and Saberwal 2006; Zimmerer 2006). Renewable energy projects provide an alternative to large-scale development projects and have intended benefits that simultaneously allow for mitigating climate change and economic development (GEF 2010; IPCC 2012). However, these intended benefits are sharply contested when such projects are located within reserved forests, protected areas and wildlife migration corridors. This conflict is particularly interesting because the stakeholders can justify their positions either for or against the renewable project, by channelling aspects of the same discourse on sustainability. The novelty of this chapter lies in explaining the use of the conservation of biodiversity against development projects that are justified as environment friendly.

Two seemingly contradictory arguments, the need for economic development and the urgency to protect the environment, are used in conjunction to justify a renewable energy project. As countries transition to low-carbon forms of energy and expand renewable installation, resource conflicts accelerate (Zimmerer 2011). This merits a closer examination, especially in the global South, where access to natural resources is a highly contentious issue and deepens social disparities (Guha and Martinez-Alier 1997). In the Indian context, the conflicts over access to land, rivers and forests that arise as a consequence of renewable expansion have not been given much attention. Our study, spread across three Indian states – Karnataka, Maharashtra and Himachal Pradesh – fills this current gap in scholarship to advance theory on social and political concerns that emerge as a result of renewable expansion especially in areas important for biodiversity protection.

The rise of the sustainable development discourse has led to the creation of new actors debating the environment–development sphere (Sivaramakrishnan 2000). Affected people who live at the site of the contestation lend great complexity to the opposition to renewable projects in close proximity to conservation landscapes. A diverse set of actors connected with the conflict in different capacities act in accordance with their own contexts, ideologies and interests. Conservationists that oppose renewable energy projects galvanise support for the biodiversity aspect and proponents of renewable energy, both channel the sustainability discourse to justify such projects. The outcome hinges upon which aspect of sustainability is channelled by various actors and the mobilisation of local opposition around it.

We start by focusing on the local scale and establish the cases, including how and why are local people protesting and the context in which the conflict plays out. Subsequently, we explain the mobilisation of actors around two aspects of the same global discourse: conservation of biodiversity and renewable energy as sustainable development. We first explore the arguments in favour of renewable energy. Later we detail the mobilisation of actors around the conservation of biodiversity discourse. By showing the mobilisation of actors around two aspects of the same global discourse – conservation of biodiversity and renewable energy as sustainable development – we aim to illustrate the peculiar dynamic nature of this conflict. What appears to be an environment vs environment conflict at the outset morphs into an environment vs development conflict as we move from higher scales to the local scale.

The three cases: Karnataka, Maharashtra and Himachal Pradesh

The three cases detail the opposition to a wind power project, next to Bhimashankar Wildlife Sanctuary in Maharashtra; a small hydro power project near Puttur in the Western Ghats of Karnataka and a series of mini-hydel projects in Tirthan, next to the Great Himalayan National Park in Himachal Pradesh

(Figure 3.1). All three cases exhibit a differential outcome. In Maharashtra the local opposition was unsuccessful and the high court ruled in favour of the project officials. In Karnataka, the project is stalled as three village councils (*panchayats*) oppose the project even as one is in favour of it. In Himachal, the local activists won a long, drawn-out legal case against the mini-hydel project developers and as a result the Tirthan watershed has now been declared a 'No project zone'. Thus, in Karnataka and Himachal Pradesh the opposition to the renewable projects has been successful in either ousting the project or in stalling it. In Maharashtra, the opposition was unsuccessful and the project developers won the court case. The local actors in Karnataka and Himachal Pradesh successfully channelled the conservation aspect of the sustainability discourse as opposed to Maharashtra.

Across the three cases, the affected people at the local scale are protesting because the project does not provide adequate development outcomes at the local level and/or threatens to disrupt their traditional livelihoods and interrupt their cultural norms. The protection of biodiversity is not an explicit motivation for the local people to protest against the project, even though the project threatens to disrupt the biodiversity of the area. However, there are various actors at higher scales for whom the underlying motivation for opposing the renewable energy project is conservation of biodiversity. For local actors in favour of the project, sustainability of the project is not a consideration. Simultaneously the

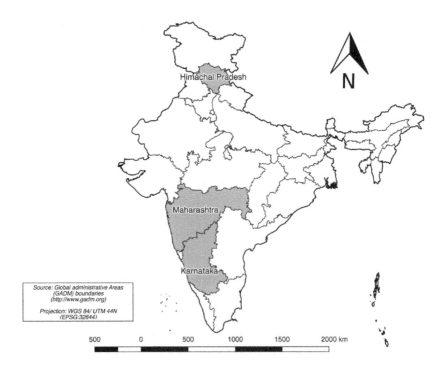

Figure 3.1 The locations of the three field sites

justification for the project predicated on the sustainability of renewable energy comes from actors at higher scales. We employ the local opposition as a starting point to unravel this complexity of the conflict. The following three sub-sections detail the cases across Karnataka, Maharashtra and Himachal.

Karnataka case study

The Kukke small hydel power project is proposed by Greenko International Limited, 90 km off the coast of Mangalore in the rich biodiversity hotspot of the Western Ghats. It is located at the confluence of the Kumaradhara and Gundia, both tributaries of the Netravathi, a major river in south India and a rich fresh-water biodiverse region. Even as the project has been approved and sanctioned by the government, it has not yet been able to start construction. This is because the local people are protesting against the proposed 24 megawatt (MW) small hydropower project, as they believe that it is going to cause submergence of the lands that the activists own and cultivate and disrupt their livelihoods.

All development projects need the prior approval of the village-level local elected bodies, *panchayats*, in the form of a no-objection certificate (NOC) (Government of India 1992). The Kukke small hydel project in Karnataka requires the no-objection certificate from four *gram panchayats* (village-level local elected bodies). Three *gram panchayats* are opposing the project and have refused to give the NOC to the project developers. Only one *gram panchayat* has issued the NOC to the company officials and is explicitly in favour of the project.

The rice fields in the valley, where the project is to be constructed, are irrigated with perennial streams from the forested hill slopes. The rivers and land support cultivation of coffee, tea, rubber, pineapple, cocoa and cashew. The Kumaradhara river winds its way through steeply descending slopes and joins another river, the Gundia, at Kunthur Perabe. It is here, at the confluence of the two rivers, that the proposed small hydropower project is to be situated.

The project is at an altitude of 74 m in the Puttur Taluka of Dakshin Kannada and about 64 km downstream from the origin of Kumaradhara in Kodagu district. It aims to build a dam across the Kumaradhara, a powerhouse with sub-station, control room, a tailrace pool and tunnel. The local activists and those opposing the project claim that in doing so, it will submerge 123 hectares of rubber plantation, 522 hectares of areca nut gardens and 35 hectares of cocoa plantations (Ramachandra *et al.* 2013). A reserve forest wedged between the Kumaradhara river on the south and the Gundia in the north is also threatened by the project. Interestingly, the project is also a threat to an existing mini-hydel system of 4.8 MW and its associated generator house. Thus, according to the opposition, patches of riparian forests, agricultural land and horticulture areas are likely to be submerged because of the project.

The leader of the agitation, Pradip Kumar, lives in Kadaba, 12 km away from the project site. The imposing threat of land submergence and the resulting loss of livelihoods for him and many others, including *panchayat* members, is the major reason for their protest. Local people opposed the projects on livelihood, environmental, religious and cultural grounds. Through strategic alliance with conservationists, the local activists have been successful in highlighting the rich biodiversity of the area and encasing their arguments in the sustainability discourse. As a result, the project developers have not been able to gather the mandatory no-objection certificate and the nodal provincial agency (KREDL) has asked the company to discontinue construction.

Himachal Pradesh case study

The Tirthan river originates in the upper mountain glacial region of the Great Himalayan National Park, which lies in the globally significant 'Western Himalayan Temperate Forests' eco-region in the northern Indian state of Himachal Pradesh. The Great Himalayan National Park is characterised by riverine forests, meadows and alpine peaks and is part of the Himalaya biodiversity hotspot (UNESCO 2014a). It includes a rich assemblage of species including the globally endangered western tragopan (*Tragopan melanocephalus*) and musk deer (*Moschus leucogaster*). The park demonstrates outstanding significance for biodiversity conservation and is the source of several glacial rivers, including the Tirthan, which support human settlements downstream (UNESCO 2014a)

In 2002, the local people living downstream of the Tirthan in the eco-zone bordering the Great Himalayan National Park had protested against a series of nine mini-hydel projects proposed on the Tirthan. The dams were proposed by private investors, notably Swastik Companies Private Limited, which has its headquarters in Calcutta. The project had the active support of HIMURJA, the regional-level renewable energy authority. The loss of local livelihoods was the prime reason for opposition to the mini-hydel dams. The nine power projects would have obstructed the water flow of the Tirthan and disrupted the *kuhls*, the local irrigation network, and rendered the *gharats*, water flourmills, inoperable and useless.

In 2006, the local activists won a long, drawn-out legal battle against the private companies that were building the mini hydropower (less than 5 MW) projects. The high court banned the construction of any hydel power project on the river and as a result, the Tirthan river that flows within the eco-zone has been designated a 'no-project zone' – the only such watershed of its kind in India (GoHP 2006). However, the legal outcome was because of the proximity of the construction site to the Great Himalayan National Park, now proclaimed as a UNESCO World Heritage Site. Even as the opposition to the small hydropower projects was primarily because it threatens people's livelihoods, it is the protection of the Himalayan ecology that convinced the court. The Himachal case is a great example of the effective mobilisation of local people around the discourse on conservation and preservation of biodiversity.

Maharashtra case study

The Andhra Lake 132 MW wind power project, developed by Enercon India, is situated next to Bhimashankar Wildlife Sanctuary (BWS) in the prime conservation area of the Western Ghats in Maharashtra (Byatnal 2011). The Western Ghats are prized for their outstanding ecological significance and the area has been designated as UNESCO World Heritage Site for its biodiversity (UNESCO 2014b). The Bhimashankar Wildlife Sanctuary, located in the Pune district, exhibits a mosaic of different vegetation patterns and harbours 529 species of animals. Large tracts of contiguous forests in and around the BWS form an upper catchment of River Krishna. These forests are the northernmost stretch of semi-evergreen and seasonal cloud forests and home to endangered fauna and flora such as the Indian giant squirrel (*Ratufa indica*), the leopard (*Panthera pardus*), some rare medicinal plants and the bio-luminous fungus (*Armillaria mellea*), among others.

The project is set up in an extension of these forests that form the southern buffer of the wildlife sanctuary. A total of 192 acres of forest land was allotted to Enercon India for the 132 MW wind power project (Byatnal 2011). The construction of the project required felling trees, cementing an access road from the lower *ghats* to the project site, widening the access road to allow for wind turbines and construction of a power sub-station and linear transmission lines for power evacuation. The project violates the Supreme Court order that stipulates that every state should declare a 10 km radius buffer zone as an ecological sensitive zone (ESZ) around protected areas that should be free from developmental activities (MoEF 2011). The state of Maharashtra has not declared the buffer zone of the sanctuary an ESZ, even after strong protests and lobbying by conservationists (Aggarwal 2014).

The primary motivation of the local people to agitate against the project was the lack of development outcomes as a result of the project and not the conservation of biodiversity. However, the local activists contested the case in the Bombay High Court on environmental grounds and claimed that the project threatened the rich biodiversity of the Western Ghats. The Bombay High Court, however, was not convinced by the argument and ordered the project to proceed as long as the developers carried out compensatory afforestation (Byatnal 2011). The project developers channelled development outcomes to selective villages and weakened the opposition to the project. The mobilisation of local actors by conservationists was unsuccessful in this case.

We now present details of the mobilisation of local activists by actors that uphold aspects of the global discourse on sustainability. First we present arguments in favour of the renewable energy project at the three sites, using the sustainable development discourse. Subsequently we present the uptake of the conservation of biodiversity discourse by local actors.

Mobilisation of actors around renewable energy as sustainable development

India's renewable energy context

India is one of the top five leading countries worldwide in terms of renewable installation (UNEP 2015). Various central government legislations and policy mechanisms have played a pivotal role in enabling this transition. The federal National Electricity Act of 2003 was the most important legislation in this direction. This act devolved renewable policy making to provincial level authorities and mandated a policy framework to develop a market for renewable power. Through incentives and capital subsidies, these provincial level nodal agencies aggressively attract private sector investment in the renewable sector. In addition, they also actively facilitate land acquisition, evacuation of power and building of access roads to enable renewable projects. Project developers can also avail themselves of federal incentives, like accelerated depreciation, tax benefits and capital subsidies, along with the provincial level incentives. The combination of both federal and regional incentives makes renewable energy a highly lucrative sector for private power producers, developers and investors.

Across renewable technologies, the wind energy sector has seen the highest growth in capacity, especially in the post-2003 scenario. The state of Maharashtra, with an installed capacity of 4,500 MW, is the second leading state for wind power capacity after the south-eastern state of Tamil Nadu (MNRE 2013). The wind power sector has grown immensely through private sector participation and has been subject to allegations of forcible and illegal land acquisition, especially in the poor and tribal belt of Maharashtra (Jamwal and Lakhanpal 2008). Even as such claims are reported in the national media, the wind sector has remained relatively free of controversy as compared to the hydropower sector.

Large hydropower projects in India have a long history of being opposed on accounts of predatory land acquisition, submergence and the resultant loss of livelihoods (McCully 2001; Singh 2002). As a result the discourse has now shifted in favour of small hydropower projects. Small, run-of-the-river hydropower projects are considered the environmentally benign, sustainable counterpart to large hydropower projects, primarily because they don't involve storage of water and instead divert the river flow through turbines that spin generators. Consequently, the Indian state considers small hydropower as renewable and large hydropower projects as non-renewable. The small hydropower sector in India comprises projects that are equivalent to or less than 25 MW and comes under the federal Ministry of New and Renewable Energy. On the other hand, dams above 25 MW are considered large and come under the purview of the federal Ministry of Power. Furthermore, small hydropower dams that require less than 5 hectares of land are exempt from an Environmental Impact Assessment (EIA), which is carried out to assess any damage to the environment because of the project (MoEF 2006). In addition such projects don't require the mandatory clearance from the federal Ministry of Environment, rather are mandated to furnish a clearance certificate from the regional Forest Department (MoEF 2006).

The National Mission on Small Hydropower states that, 'Small hydro projects are run-of-river and are environmentally sustainable. These projects do not encounter the issues associated with large-scale hydro projects. There is no deforestation, resettlement or rehabilitation' (MNRE 2015). Such projects, however, hide the threat to livelihoods, cultural norms, land and biodiversity that the run-of-the-river projects can cause. As a result there is now a growing concern from environmental activists and many non-profit organisations are encouraging protests contesting the sustainable nature of these dams (Das and Chopra 2012).

Karnataka has the highest installation of small hydropower across Indian states (950 MW), followed by Himachal Pradesh at 550 MW (MNRE 2013). The state offers high tariffs to small hydropower producers and has utilised the majority of its hydropower potential through dams that range from 8 to 24 MW capacity. Deviating from the federal categories of hydropower sector, Himachal Pradesh considers dams that are less than or equal to 5 MW as small and renewable (GoHP 2006). The state explicitly promotes mini-hydel dams (less than 5 MW) because they are easier to construct in the Himalayan terrain (GoHP 2006). The hydropower sector has been a major source of revenue for the state government and there are a total of 655 mini-hydel power projects across the state (HIMURJA 2014).

It is against this backdrop that the three cases involving opposition to small hydropower and wind energy power unfold across Karnataka, Maharashtra and Himachal Pradesh. We now present the mobilisation of local actors around the sustainable development discourse by considering arguments used in favour of renewable energy projects.

Karnataka

The Kukke small hydropower project is opposed by three village *panchayats* and favoured by one *panchayat*, which has given the no-objection certificate to the project developers. Nagamma, the president of the Perabe *panchayat*, argued in favour of the project and used the logic of local benefits like employment, education and electricity to provide justification for the renewable project. 'Perabe village is closest to the project site and hence is likely to get more local development outcomes', she reasoned. Interestingly, none of the actors at the local level, including Nagamma, draw upon the *sustainability discourse* to favour the project. At the village level, the project is construed as any other economic development project and therefore the justification for the project is centred only on development outcomes.

The opposing *panchayats* counter the development claims because the project developers destroyed the existing development benefits in the village. The company officials blocked access to a public road by constructing a gate and banned the local people from accessing the road (Figure 3.2). When the locals protested, the clashes turned violent. This incident was instrumental in cementing the belief of the local activists that the project officials are never going to invest in development outcomes for the villagers. The opposition to the project thus rejected all claims of development benefits that the project officials promised. Kadaba village, where most of the agitation committee resides, comprises 700 households, and 94 per cent of the workforce is engaged in main agricultural work (Government of India 2011). The relative prosperity of Kadaba and surrounding villages is relevant because it tells us that the protestors are not in dire need of local development outcomes like schools, electricity and jobs. Even if the project

Figure 3.2 Access to public land has been blocked by the developers of the Kukke
hydropower project. This image shows the signboards restricting villagers' entry

does lead to local development outcomes, it is not a priority for the actors at the
local scale in Karnataka because it will destroy their livelihood. The local activists are well entrenched in the urban setting of Bangalore and even when faced
with a choice to re-locate to Bangalore, choose instead to stay in the village and
cultivate their lands.

Other actors that support the project but are not located at the local scale, justify
the project on the basis of national development, local economic benefits and the
environmentally friendly sustainability discourse. The justification for the project is
contingent upon the audience and the motivation of the actors to espouse aspects
of the sustainability discourse. For instance, the district RSS (a Hindu nationalist
political outfit) leader, in an attempt to dissuade the protestors, justified the project on the basis of national development during a speech. At an agitation march
where the locals were protesting, he intervened to say, 'We must allow the project
because it will lead to India's development. And if a few individuals lose their land
for India's growth then one must not protest'. The rhetoric of national development, however, did not appeal to the agitating villagers. In conversations with me,
however, the RSS leader had reasoned in favour of the project explicitly using the
sustainability discourse, saying, 'At least it is a renewable project and not a coal
power plant'.[1] His diagnosis of the agitation was that through employing violence,
the project developers had hardened the stance against the project. It would have
been easier for them to implement the project if they had formed strategic linkages
at the local level and provided some development outcomes to the protestors.

The actors that draw clearly upon the sustainable development discourse are at higher scales. The chairperson of the provincial nodal agency responsible for implementing renewable projects (KREDL) is based at Bangalore and supports the project by drawing upon the sustainability discourse. For him, it is a battle of coal power projects versus renewable energy projects and he firmly asserts that India needs to mitigate climate change and hence renewable projects are necessary. However, he also contends that the only answer to address local opposition to the renewable projects is to offer broad development outcomes at the local level. The logic being that the likelihood of projects encountering local opposition decreases if it offers local economic development outcomes. Hence, the dire need to encase and package the project so that it caters to the demands and aspiration of the local people. In Karnataka the mobilisation of locals around the sustainable development discourse was unsuccessful.

Maharashtra

At the site of the Andhra Lake wind power project in Maharashtra, the mobilisation of the local people by actors who draw from the biodiversity discourse was unsuccessful. The actors favouring the project offered differentiated development outcomes for the local people. These outcomes, however, were contingent upon their political orientation and the existing level of development in the village. Development benefits were channelled to villages that were relatively well-developed and to individual supporters of the political party of the ruling member of the legislative assembly.

An elected member of the state legislative assembly strongly supported the project. He mediated the conflict by offering electricity and employment to the local people spread across three villages (Pallavi 2011). The local political economy and the geography of development in the villages played a crucial role in the mobilisation of the development discourse in the region. Kharpud, the village closest to the project site and also the wildlife sanctuary, is an *adivasi* village and is the least developed of all the villages in the area. Shivegaon, is located farthest away from the sanctuary at a distance of approximately 10 km. Shivegaon is the most developed village in the vicinity of the project site. Kude, a village at a distance of three km from the project site, is more developed than Kharpud but less so than Shivegaon.

Kharpud received the fewest development outcomes from the project in terms of local employment. Interestingly, the incessant movement of heavy vehicles carrying the huge turbines to the project site destroyed the access road between Kharpud and Pune city. This affected the locals in Kharpud adversely as it cut off their access to schools and the industrial layout that are located *en route* to the city. This incident was crucial in exacerbating the animosity between the villagers and the project officials. In Kude, however, where the pre-existing development context is relatively better than in Kharpud, the agitation against the wind power project was systematically weakened. Supporters of the ruling political party were given jobs as security guards contingent upon their withdrawal from the protest against the wind power project.

In Shivegaon, the local people withdrew their protest when development outcomes were channelled to the village. The project developers constructed a community hall in the village and also gave a substantial number of jobs to the local people. The project re-made the categories of development, by destroying the access road between Kharpud village and Pune city, and by offering local development outcomes in certain villages. As a result of the selective channelling of economic benefits, the mobilisation of local actors around the development discourse was effective in Maharashtra and the opposition was weakened.

Himachal Pradesh

The actors in favour of the mini-hydel power projects justified them using the rhetoric of national and local development but they were unsuccessful in mobilising local actors. In Tirthan valley, which lies in the eco-development zone of the Great Himalayan National Park (GHNP), the local activists are well aware of the empty rhetoric of development outcomes employed to dam the Himalayan rivers. A few kilometres downstream of the Tirthan is the Sainj, another river that flows through the GHNP (Figure 3.3). Sainj river valley has been the site of ruthless hydropower dams and this has declined water availability, denuded the hills and altered the social and cultural fabric of the valley (Rai and Srivastava 2014). Closer to the GHNP, people have witnessed their loss of land and livelihoods for the greater common good of national development in the form of a behemoth, the 1,100 MW Parbati hydroelectric project (Chhatre and Saberwal 2006).

The local activists have well-entrenched networks with Delhi-based nonprofit organisations like SANDRP that strongly oppose all hydropower projects and question their claims of sustainability using the argument to protect ecology. Through these and other interactions the local opposition has deftly incorporated the biodiversity angle to negate the development claims of the hydropower project developers. The additional power secretary for the state of Himachal Pradesh at the time had sanctioned and approved the mini-hydel power projects. Yet he was instrumental in guiding the local activists to use the biodiversity angle to oppose the projects. 'Location matters', he had insisted when one of the authors (Lakhanpal) asked him his reasons for protecting the Tirthan, even as hydropower development continues elsewhere in the state. He underscored the importance of hydropower development as long as it was not built in proximity to conservation landscapes. The CEO of Himurja, the regional body that promotes mini-hydel projects in the state, reiterated that post-Tirthan they are now very careful not to allot any hydropower projects near sites that are ecologically significant.

Local livelihoods are intimately connected with river use. Water flourmills, traditional channels that irrigate the fields and the brown trout (*Salmo trutta*) are useful for subsistence farming and tourism, which form the bulk of the livelihoods of the people in the eco-zone. The creation of the GHNP formally restricted the use of grazing lands and prevented the locals from collecting herbs and other medicinal plants from the forests that now form the national park. The

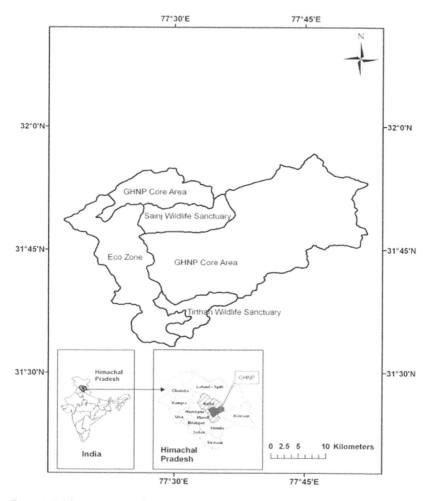

Figure 3.3 The Great Himalayan National Park along with the eco-development zone. The GHNP is located in the Kullu district of the northern hill state of Himachal Pradesh, India

Source: Kumar *et al.* 2016

mini-hydel power projects would have destroyed the livelihoods of an already vulnerable population and as a result the local people were not amenable to the promised development outcomes from the village.

The existing development context in which the local activists operate is of utmost significance. Unlike the Maharashtra case, the local activists in Himachal are relatively well off. The director of the local NGO, SAHARA owns and operates a guest house in addition to cultivating farmland. The villages are electrified and the influx of tourists has ensured that economic benefits are available to the local people. Development is undoubtedly a concern for the local people but not at the cost of their land, tourism opportunities and traditional livelihoods. The mobilisation of local actors around the development discourse in favour of the renewable project was unsuccessful in Himachal. The local political economy of development and the experiences of the local activists with hydropower projects were crucial components in rendering this mobilisation unsuccessful.

Mobilisation of actors around the conservation of biodiversity

Conservation context in India

India has followed the exclusionary model of conservation by setting aside large spaces devoid of human pressures for biodiversity protection (Lewis 2003; Agrawal and Redford 2009). The exclusionary practice of conservation is predicated on the need to preserve biodiversity threatened by human practices, especially predatory development projects. The Indian Wildlife Act, 1972 was instrumental in encouraging Indian states to constitute wildlife sanctuaries and national parks devoid of human presence. Protected areas have constituted the terrain for conflict by impinging upon the rights of traditional forest dwellers and threatening their livelihoods. Since the 1980s, agrarian expansion, extraction of industrial raw material and other development projects have been increasingly prioritised by the developmental state (Gadgil and Guha 1995). The modern Indian state has repeatedly accorded priority to securing the resources for selective commercial elites as against the forest dependent communities. As the global focus tilted in favour of integrated conservation and development programmes, Indian policy makers have also focused on participatory programmes like community-based conservation and joint forest management. The experience from such projects has shown, however, that by and large participatory rhetoric has failed to translate into reality (Sarkar 2009). Fast tracking of mining, construction and other development projects has resulted in diluting the conservation efforts in India while simultaneously dispossessing and alienating forest-dependent communities. It is against this backdrop that sustainable development projects are being implemented across conservation landscapes in India.

In the following sections we present the mobilisation around the conservation discourse across the three case studies. We show the linkages between the local activists and other actors at higher scales that are rooted in the conservation discourse. We build upon these linkages to trace the effectiveness of mobilisation on the basis of biodiversity across the three case sites.

Karnataka

In Karnataka, a constellation of actors were crucial in mobilising the affected people for the conservation discourse. The chief conservator of forests in Mangalore is strongly against any development projects in the forest areas. He identified himself as an environmentalist first, a forest officer later. He was instrumental in inviting Ananth Hegde, renowned conservationist and ex-chairperson of the Western Ghats Task Force, to visit the site of the contested project and to high-light the rich biodiversity of the contested site. Ananth Hegde raised the issue in the state legislative assembly, assured the locals that they will not lose the land and highlighted the case in the national media. He also invited eminent profes-sors from the Indian Institute of Science (IISC) in Bangalore to report on the biodiversity of the project site. The report published by IISC highlighted the rich flora and fauna in the area, chiefly the tree *Madhuca insignis* that is endangered as per the International Union for Conservation of Nature (IUCN) and was re-discovered after 125 years at the project site. The team also reported the threat to 56 fish species that are found especially at the confluence of the Kumaradhara and Gundia rivers. Eight of those fish species are listed as threatened as per the IUCN and 11 are classified as vulnerable (Ramachandra *et al.* 2013). This report formed the basis for challenging the project using the biodiversity argument in national and regional media as well as international fora like the United Nations Framework on Climate Change Mitigation.

Activists from the Delhi-based NGO SANDRP and other conservation-ists urged the local activists to challenge the CDM status sought by the Kukke project developers. CDM or the Clean Development Mechanism is an interna-tional instrument that allows developed countries to pay for reduction in carbon emissions through channelling funds to eligible projects in developing countries (UNFCCC 2002). The comments submitted by the local activists to UNFCCC, the international body that governs the CDM, effectively stressed the rich biodiversity of the project site and highlighted the impending destruction of ecology as a consequence of the dam. The comments reiterated that in doing so the small hydropower project is highly unsustainable and not worthy of CDM finance (Dandekar 2013). This strategy proved to be extremely effective and the UNFCCC has not yet validated the CDM status for the project. A crucial factor that made the local people amenable to the use of the conservation dis-course is the overall development context in the village. The locals protesting against Kukke are not the marginalised, poor victims of exclusionary conserva-tion, rather they are plantation owners with highly successful rubber, cocoa and areca nut plantations. Interestingly, even before conservationists like Ananth Hegde and Parineeta Dandekar, approached the local people, the protestors had garnered a stop work notice from the Karnataka Renewable Development Authority Limited (Letter no. KRED/06/SH205/Kukke MHS/2012/634). The members of the agitation committee had written to the managing director of KREDL, complaining that the project impinges upon the livelihoods of the local people. They did not employ the biodiversity angle when writing to KREDL, the provincial agency for implementing renewable energy across Karnataka state. In the words of Pradip Kumar, 'KREDL supported us when we told them about our livelihoods. But for the big international organisations like UNFCCC, we had to approach through the biodiversity angle'.[2] This underscores the importance of rooting one's arguments in the global discourse on sustainability, especially when contesting the project at the global scale. In other words, as one moves from the local to the global scale, it is imperative that the argument is framed as a threat to biodiversity and not merely livelihoods. Thus, in the Karnataka case, the mobilisation of local activists employing the biodiversity discourse was very effective.

Maharashtra

The Andhra Lake wind power project, developed by Enercon India, is one of the relatively rare cases of a wind power project next to a protected area. The project was sanctioned by the federal Ministry of Environment and Forests and was aided by a letter from the Principal Chief Conservator of Forests (PCCF) at the regional forest office. The PCCF had stated that the buffer zone of the sanctuary does not contain any wildlife and the project will not cause disruption to the ecology of the Western Ghats (CCF (T) Pune's Letter D-1/Land/FCA-164/1092/2009-10, dated 19 November 2009). The subordinate to the PCCF, the range officer, however, negated this claim. In his investigation report, the range officer claimed that 'the area is known to be the habitat of endangered mammals, reptiles and birds, particularly, including the Giant Squirrel and leopards, among many other flora and fauna species' (Letter No. Wind Mill/952 of 2008-09, Chakan, dated 28 December 2008 to the Deputy Conservator Forest, Junnar Division). However, the project was allowed to begin construction and is currently functioning barely a few kilometres from the Bhimashankar Wildlife Sanctuary.

In the wake of the indiscriminate creation of resorts, tourist guest houses that have been constructed in the buffer zone, the conservationists had been arguing for the buffer zone to be declared an ecological sensitive zone. The construction of the wind power project sanctioned by the federal Ministry of Environment and Forests, in the buffer zone of the sanctuary exacerbated the situation. The project was embroiled in the national-level controversy between two federal committees set up to decide the course of conservation and development projects in the Western Ghats; the Western Ghats Ecology Experts Panel (WGEEP) and the High Level Working Group (HLWG) on Western Ghats.

The Western Ghats Ecology Experts Panel (WGEEP), chaired by Madhav Gadgil was asked to review the conflict related to the Andhra Lake wind power project, on the recommendation of Jairam Ramesh, the acting federal Minister for Environment and Forests at the time (Aggarwal 2014). The opposition to the renewable project was also able to garner the support of Madhav Gadgil and Renee Borges, influential and renowned environmental activists. Renee Borges, a professor at the Indian Institute of Science (IISC), filed a complaint with the central-level Ministry of Environment and Forests (MoEF), explaining the ecological destruction caused by the project (Kulkarni 2011). Madhav Gadgil, visited the project site with his team and published a detailed case study on the wind power project near BWS in the WGEEP report (Gadgil 2011). The Western Ghats ecology experts panel recommended that the wind power project be subject to Environmental Impact Assessment and the eco-sensitive zone should be declared and hence should be free of any development activity that threatens the ecology of the landscape (Gadgil 2011).

The WGEEP report, however, was entangled in a controversy at the federal level because it posed a threat to the indiscriminate mining and other development activities in the Western Ghats (Gadgil 2014). The report had recommended zoning 75 per cent of the total area under the Western Ghats into levels of ecologically sensitive areas by discontinuing power projects, mining and tourism operations that threatened the biodiversity of the Western Ghats. Concerns about accelerated growth, the need for national development and expressions of concerns about local livelihoods in the Western Ghats were cited as reasons for creating another committee – the high-level working group (HLWG) – to review the WGEEP proposal and suggest alternatives to the conservation–development debacle (Nandakumar 2013).

The HLWG, also known as the Kasturirangan committee, diluted the recommendations of the WGEEP to favour 'growth' (Gadgil 2014) and partitioned the Western Ghats into cultural (63 per cent) and natural landscapes (37 per cent). The natural landscapes are mostly forested landscapes that are to be preserved using the conservation-by-exclusion format (Kasturirangan *et al.* 2013). This area, the report had recommended, should be out of bounds for a range of industrial, mining, quarrying and related activities. The cultural landscapes are areas that also include all freshwater habitats (that are biologically diverse and highly ecologically significant) and are critical for local livelihoods and are laid open to developmental activities though subject to Environmental Impact Assessment. Renewable energy projects, however, by virtue of being sustainable, are deemed as category B2 and allowed in both natural and cultural landscapes (Kasturirangan *et al.* 2013). The report recommends that Environmental Impact Assessments be carried out for all renewable projects including wind energy. Once the federal Ministry of Environment and Forests issues the clearance, renewable projects can start construction in ecologically sensitive areas (Kasturirangan *et al.* 2013).

The recommendations of the Kasturirangan report were accepted 'in principle' by the federal Environment Ministry in 2013, then under Jayanthi Natarajan (Bhave 2013). The rhetoric of development and accelerated growth were the key factors in accepting the Kasturirangan committee report. The casting aside of the WGEEP report spelt doom for the opposition to the Enercon wind power project next to BWS. This is so because, in comparison with the Gadgil report, the Kasturirangan committee report diluted the area designated under ecologically sensitive zones and explicitly favoured and legitimised renewable energy development in prime conservation areas on the basis that it is sustainable.

In Maharashtra, the mobilisation of different constituencies around the conservation of biodiversity discourse was not effective. Lack of support from the Forest Department, influential and politically powerful actors in favour of the project, the differentiated development context of the neighbouring villages and selectively targeted development outcomes were some of the factors responsible for the lack of effective mobilisation around the conservation discourse in Maharashtra.

Himachal Pradesh

In Himachal, the local activists used the conservation discourse to successfully oppose the mini-hydel projects in the Tirthan valley. The Forest Department officials, notably Sanjeeva Pandey, ex-director of the Great Himalayan National Park, was instrumental in steering the protest in order to incorporate the conservation agenda. Sanjeeva Pandey, a committed conservationist, regards the GHNP as his temple and was the key actor in its creation. The timing of the protest was key, he emphasised, as the proposal for GHNP to be considered as a UNESCO World Heritage Site was being prepared by the Forest Department. From the state's point of view, it was imperative that the GHNP be declared a UNESCO World Heritage Site for tourism development in the Kullu district.

In addition to the Forest Department, an ex-member of the legislative assembly from the area, Dilaram Shabab, had approached the additional power secretary, J.P. Negi. Shabab urged him to visit the area and suggest ways to counter the mini-hydel power projects. Negi's visit to the Tirthan was crucial because he emphasised that the local activists should use the biodiversity angle to their advantage. Later, as one of the authors (Lakhanpal) interviewed him, J.P. Negi pointed out that the Himalayan ecology angle would have worked better to stave off the hydropower projects in the region and hence he had emphasised that the activists should stress the biodiversity angle.

The global discourse on sustainability has permeated the local livelihoods discourse. Because of the creation of the National Park, the tourism sector has emerged as a substantial employment sector. The Great Himalayan National Park was designated a UNESCO World Heritage Site in June 2014 (UNESCO 2014a). Since its creation, the Forest Department and the state administrative department have peddled the GHNP as a vehicle for development and an opportunity for the local people to develop alternative livelihoods like tourist guest houses. The cool, clear, pristine waters are important for drawing tourists and the folding of these alternative local livelihoods into the sustainability discourse allows the local people to claim access to natural resources. Petitions made by the village *panchayat* leaders to the minister for power, district commissioner and the Environment Ministry, underscored the dependence of the local people on the tourism industry and the need to keep the valley free from hydropower development.

The involvement of the state-level Department of Fisheries strengthened the biodiversity angle in Himachal. Kullu district has the largest number of private trout farms in the state (GoHP 2011). The department has a fish stocking programme and also attracts anglers from around the globe. The angling activities are supported through the Himachal Angling Association and an annual angling competition is held in the Tirthan valley (Baker 2014). There are both private and government hatcheries in the district and especially downstream of the hydropower project locations. The Tirthan is home to brown trout (*Salmo trutta*) that requires clean, cold, highly oxygenated water to breed and hatch. The trout hatcheries raised the stakes and strengthened the case against small hydropower projects. The projects would have led to the accumulation of silt in the river water thus destroying the habitat for aquatic species.

The Himachal Angling Association, an active organisation that promotes sport fishing, and the state Department of Fisheries supported the resistance against the mini-hydel power projects in the Tirthan valley. The Angling Association held its 2012 Trout Anglers Meet at Sai Ropa on the Tirthan river. The keynote address at the angling competition, given by the Association's secretary-general, advanced strategies for strengthening 'Angling Tourism' and denounced the negative impacts of small hydropower development on fisheries and the livelihoods they support (Baker 2014). As a result the Tirthan valley has now been declared an angling reserve by the Himachal government to further strengthen the biodiversity of the region (GoHP 2013).

The eventual backing of the protest against small hydropower projects by the Fisheries Department, Himachal Angling Association, Forest Department and the proximity of the proposed sites to the UNESCO nominated Great Himalayan National Park aligned to strengthen the biodiversity agenda in Himachal Pradesh. The instrumental decision to join forces with the conservationists helped them couch their argument in the sustainability discourse and hence successfully oppose the renewable energy projects.

Conclusion

A social movement is powerful precisely because its meanings are ambiguous and shifting (Baviskar 2005). The motivations for different actors to oppose a renewable energy project near a conservation site can be manifold and depend upon the scale at which they are located. At the local scale the conflict is clearly a struggle between environment and development. But as we move from local to higher scales, the justification for the renewable energy project is increasingly located in the sustainability discourse. This allows the conflict to morph into an environment versus environment contest. Urban, metropolitan actors and audience give more credence to the sustainable aspect of development projects. Following from this, the constellation of actors that support local struggles is key to understanding whether conservation will trump renewable energy or vice versa. Local activists in Karnataka and Himachal, as opposed to those in Maharashtra, had a wider support base in the metropolitan audience as they deftly incorporated aspects of biodiversity conservation.

Locally grounded social movements are nested within and influenced by the broader politics of environment versus development. The current global focus on sustainable development and resulting pressure on policy makers to incorporate environment-friendly projects has led to new ways of staking claims over nature. This shift in the environment–development debate has opened up new avenues for grassroots mobilisations to strategise, network and instrumentally align themselves with broader ideologies that cater to a metropolitan audience and have great currency. In sum, this has given rise to ideologically hybrid social movements that increasingly harness aspects of global discourses to negotiate contradictions between diverse groups.

Notes

1 Personal communication with T.V. Bhat, Kukke, March 2013.
2 Personal communication with Pradip Kumar, Kadaba, March 2013.

References

Adger, W.N., Benjaminsen, T.A., Brown, K., and Svarstad, H. (2001). Advancing a political ecology of global environmental discourses. *Development and Change*, 32: 681–715.

Aggarwal, M. (2014, 30 September). MoEF leaves the ball in Maharashtra governments' court to decide eco-sensitive zones. *DNA*. Retrieved from www.dnaindia.com/india/report-moef-leaves-the-ball-in-maharashtra-governments-s-court-to-decide-eco-sensitive-zones-2022495.

Agrawal, A., and Redford, K.H. (2009). Conservation and displacement: An overview. *Conservation and Society*, 7: 1–10.

Baker, J.M. (2014). Small hydropower development in Himachal Pradesh. *Economic & Political Weekly*, 49(21): 77–86.

Baviskar, A. (2005). Red in tooth and claw: Looking for class in struggles over nature. In R. Ray and M. Katzenstein (eds.), *Social Movements in India: Poverty, Power and Politics* (161–179). Oxford: Rowman and Littlefield.

Bhave, R. (2013, 18 October). MoEF approves Kasturirangan panel report on Western Ghats. *First Post*. New Delhi. Retrieved from www.firstpost.com/india/moef-approves-kasturirangan-panel-report-on-western-ghats-1180911.html.

Bridge, G., Bouzarovski, S., Bradshaw, M., and Eyre, N. (2013). Geographies of energy transition: Space, place and the low-carbon economy. *Energy Policy*, 53: 331–340. doi:10.1016/j.enpol.2012.10.066.

Byatnal, A. (2011, 10 April). Green energy project poses threat to wildlife in Maharashtra. *The Hindu*, 1. Mumbai. Retrieved from www.thehindu.com/todays-paper/tp-national/green-energy-project-poses-threat-to-wildlife-in-maharashtra/article1684118.ece.

Chhatre, A., and Saberwal, V. (2006). *Democratizing Nature: Politics, Conservation and Development in India*. New Delhi: Oxford University Press.

Dandekar, P. (2013, 22 August). Neither small, nor green. *The Hindu*. New Delhi.

Das, S., and Chopra, K. (2012). Towards 'green growth': Measuring the trade-off between conservation of protected areas and hydel power generation. *Economic & Political Weekly*, 47(51), 59–68.

Gadgil, M. (2011). *Report of the Western Ghats Ecology Experts Panel*. New Delhi.

Gadgil, M. (2014). Western Ghats Ecology Expert Panel: A play in five acts. *Economic & Political Weekly*, 49(18): 38–50.

Gadgil, M., and Guha, R. (1995). *Ecology and Equity: The Use and Abuse of Nature in Contemporary India*. New Delhi: Penguin India.

GEF. (2010). *Focal Area: Climate Change*. Washington DC.

Government of Himachal Pradesh (GoHP). (2006). *Himachal Pradesh Small Hydro Power Policy*. Shimla.

Government of Himachal Pradesh (GoHP). (2011). *Trout and Carp Fish Farms in Himachal Pradesh: An Assessment Report*. Shimla.

Government of Himachal Pradesh (GoHP). (2013). Angling reserves in Himachal. Retrieved 15 October 2015 from http://himachal.nic.in/index1.php?lang=1&dpt_id=4&level=1&lid=168&sublinkid=146.

Government of India. (1992). *Constitutional Amendment to the Panchayati Raj Act*. Retrieved from http://eci.nic.in/archive/instruction/compendium/state_elec_comm/comm133a.htm.

Government of India. (2011). Houselisting and Housing Census Data Tables (District Level) – Karnataka, Office of the Registrar General and Census Commissioner, India, Ministry of Home Affairs, Government of India. *Retrieved form* www.censusindia.gov.in/2011census/hlo/District_Tables/HLO_Distt_Table_karnataka.html?q=kadaba (last seen 20 September 2017).

Guha, R., and Martinez-Alier, J. (1997). *Varieties of Environmentalism: Essays North and South*. London: Routledge.

HIMURJA. (2014). Small Hydro Projects MoU signed. Retrieved 23 October 2015, from http://himurja.nic.in/mousigned.html.

IPCC. (2012). *Renewable Energy Sources and Climate Change Mitigation*. Potsdam.

Jamwal, N., and Lakhanpal, S. (2008, 15 August). Fanning an Alternative. *Down to Earth*. Retrieved from www.downtoearth.org.in/coverage/fanning-an-alternative-4855#0.

Kasturirngan, K. *et al*. (2013). *Report of the High Level Working Group on Western Ghats*. Delhi.

Kulkarni, S. (2011, 9 November). Windmills near Maharashtra mascots home, green brigade rings alarm bells. *Indian Express*. New Delhi. Retrieved from www.wind-watch.org/news/2011/11/09/windmills-near-maharashtra-mascots-home-green-brigade-rings-alarm-bells/.

Kumar, A., Chauhan, V.K., Kumar, S., and Singh, R.D. (2016). Relevance of satellite derived net primary productivity data in monitoring of protected areas in Indian western Himalaya. *Asian Journal of Geoinformatics*, 15(4): 19–24.

Lewis, M. (2003). Cattle and conservation at Bharatpur: A case study in science and advocacy. *Conservation and Society*, 1: 1–21.

McCully, P. (2001). *Silenced Rivers: The Ecology and Politics of Large Dams*. New York: Blackwell Publishing.

MNRE. (2013). *Ministry of New and Renewable Energy: Annual Report*. New Delhi.

MNRE. (2015). *Draft National Mission on Small Hydropower in India*. New Delhi. Retrieved from www.indiaenvironmentportal.org.in/files/file/Draft-national-mission-on-SHP.pdf.

MoEF. (2006). *EIA Notification*. New Delhi. Retrieved from http://envfor.nic.in/legis/eia/so1533.pdf.

MoEF. (2011). *Guidelines for Declaration of Eco-sensitive Zones around National Parks and Wildlife*. New Delhi.

Nandakumar, T. (2013, 16 December). Protest against Ghats report disastrous: Kumaraswamy. *The Hindu*. New Delhi.

Pallavi, A. (2011, February). Wind farm threat to forests. *Down to Earth*. Retrieved from www.downtoearth.org.in/news/wind-farm-threat-to-forests-32970.

Rai, S.C., and Srivastava, A. (2014). Small hydro power projects and community participation. In R.B. Singh and R. Hietala (eds.), *Livelihood Security in Northwestern Himalayas: Advances in Geographical and Environmental Sciences* (239–248). Tokyo: Springer.

Ramachandra, T.V., Subash, M.D.S., Shenoy, H.S.P., Rao, G.R., Vinay, S., Mukri, V., and Naik, S. (2013). *Kumaradhara River Basin, Karnataka Western Ghats: Need for Conservation and Sustainable Use*. ENVIS Technical Report 54. Bangalore: Centre for Ecological Sciences, Indian Institute of Science.

Sarker, D. (2009). Joint forest management: Critical issues. *Economic & Political Weekly*, 44(4): 15–17.

Singh, S. (2002). *Taming the Waters: The Political Economy of Large Dams in India.* New Delhi: Oxford University Press.

Sivaramakrishnan, K. (2000). Crafting the public sphere in the forests of West Bengal: Democracy, development and political action. *American Ethnologist,* 27(2): 431–461.

UNEP Collaborating Center. (2015). *Global Status Report 2015.* Paris. Retrieved from www.ren21.net/status-of-renewables/global-status-report/.

UNESCO. (2014a). Great Himalayan National Park conservation area. Retrieved 15 October 2015, from http://whc.unesco.org/en/list/1406.

UNESCO. (2014b). Western Ghats. Retrieved 16 October 2015, from http://whc.unesco.org/en/list/1342.

UNFCCC. (2002). Clean development mechanism. Retrieved 15 August 2015, from https://cdm.unfccc.int/.

Zimmerer, K. (2006). *Globalization and the New Geographies of Environmental Conservation.* Chicago, IL: University of Chicago Press.

Zimmerer, K. (2011). New geographies of energy: Introduction to the Special Issue. *Annals of the Association of American Geographers,* 101(4): 705–711.

4 Species and sites matter

Understanding human–wildlife interactions from 5,000 surveys in India

Krithi K. Karanth and Akshay Surendra

Introduction

Understanding and managing human–wildlife interactions remains a global conservation priority. Most often, the interactions that emerge from the literature focus on negative interactions such as crop damage, livestock loss, property damage, human injury and death (Treves and Karanth 2003; Graham *et al.* 2005; Madden 2004; Lagendijk and Gusset 2008; Dickman 2010; Kansky and Knight 2014). Little effort is exerted towards documenting neutral or positive interactions between people and wildlife (Peterson *et al.* 2010). Despite a vast body of literature devoted to understanding human–wildlife interactions – particularly conflict – many fundamental questions remain unanswered. At the core of these interactions is examining how different species influence people's perceptions, attitudes, reporting of conflict and retaliation against species and whether these differences can enable improvements in policy, compensation and mitigation efforts (Bagchi and Mishra 2006; Barlow *et al.* 2010; Dickman 2010; Karanth and Kudalkar 2017).

In our multi-site, multi-species evaluation and comparison of conflict across India, we adopt an approach that focuses on understanding conflict from a species perspective. Specifically, we examine crop and livestock loss reported by households to understand differences at the species and site level. We might expect some herbivore species to exhibit different preferences for specific crops and carnivore species to exhibit different preferences for livestock (such as elephants versus pigs or deer, felids versus canids). We also expect differences in loss experienced to be a function of environmental and landscape-level factors at local site level that influence species differently (Michalski *et al.* 2006; Karanth *et al.* 2013b). Lastly, we are interested in examining if mitigation measures used by people have an effect on conflict. Although conflict is often localised, we are interested in discerning commonalities among groups of species (for example canids or felids) that might help target mitigation efforts (White and Ward 2010). Our large database (over 5,000 surveys) combined with incidents attributed to 12 species (across 11 study sites) in India allows to explore these questions in a systematic and robust manner. Our efforts will help disentangle the multiple dimensions of human–wildlife interactions, especially with respect to developing targeted species programmes. This is much needed in a country where 81,000 conflict incidents were reported and compensated for in one year, and there exist wide variations in how species are covered by states (Karanth and Kudalkar 2017).

Methods

Study sites

We selected 11 sites around wildlife reserves across four states in India – Rajasthan, Madhya Pradesh, Maharashtra and Karnataka. Four sites are situated in the Aravalis of northwest India, two of them in central Indian forests and five sites lie in the Western Ghats of southwest India (Figure 4.1). The four sites in the Aravalis were Jaisamand, Kumbalgarh, Phulwari-ki-nal and Sitamata. In central India, the sites were Tadoba and Kanha. The five sites in the Western Ghats were Anshi-Dandeli, Bhadra, Biligiri Rangaswamy Temple (BRT), Bandipur and Nagarahole. The total surveyed area covered 16,488 km², ranging from 622 km² around Jaisamand to 3,084 km² around Kumbhalgarh (Table 4.1).

The sites cover a range of vegetation types including thorny scrub, dry deciduous, moist deciduous, semi-evergreen and evergreen. These reserves support significant mammalian diversity, including threatened species such as tiger, leopard, wolf, hyena, dhole, sloth bear, elephant, gaur, sambar, chital, chinkara and nilgai. Annual rainfall ranges from 425 mm in Kumbhalgarh to 4,000 mm in Anshi-Dandeli and elevation varies from 3 m in Dandeli-Anshi to 1,587 m in Bhadra (30 m DEM; Table 4.1). Human population density varies from 94 people/km² around Tadoba-Andhari to 443 people/km² around Nagarahole and

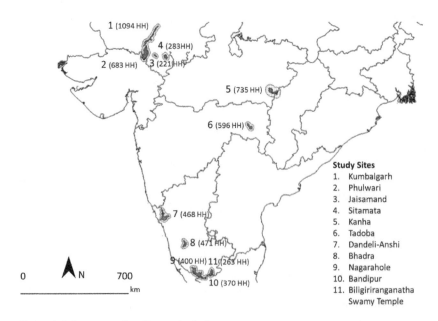

Study Sites
1. Kumbalgarh
2. Phulwari
3. Jaisamand
4. Sitamata
5. Kanha
6. Tadoba
7. Dandeli-Anshi
8. Bhadra
9. Nagarahole
10. Bandipur
11. Biligiriranganatha
    Swamy Temple

Figure 4.1 Location of study sites in India

Bandipur (Census of India 2011; Table 4.1). Livestock population densities range between 69 heads/km² around Tadoba-Andhari to 445 heads/km² around Dandeli-Anshi (Livestock Census of India 2007; Table 4.1). Other site characteristics are in Table 4.1.

Survey design and field data collection

We surveyed 5,154 households across 11 sites between 2011 and 2014 (Table 4.1). Human research ethics protocols approved by Columbia University, USA, Duke University, USA and the Centre for Wildlife Studies, India were followed in all questionnaire surveys. Across all sites a total of 3,074 villages were selected within a 10 km buffer of each reserve. A total of 1,286 grids of size 13 km² were surveyed, and about 60 per cent of the villages within each cell were randomly selected (Karanth *et al.* 2012, 2013b, Table 4.1). In each grid cell, between one to ten households were opportunistically surveyed. In villages where we conducted more than one survey, we ensured that households surveyed were located as far away from each other as possible. Teams of trained volunteers and research assistants conducted the surveys in Hindi, Kannada and Marathi, and all surveys were later transcribed into English.

In each household we interviewed both adult female and male respondents, and in our sample about 60 per cent of surveyed individuals were men. Common to all sites were questions on demographic and socio-economic characteristics, nature and type of conflict, species involved, agricultural and livestock characteristics, and mitigation measures employed by households. Additionally, spatial variables such as distance to protected area, distance to water body, distance to forest cover, percentage forest cover within a 3 km buffer and percentage of grassland/scrub within a 3 km buffer were extracted for each surveyed household (Karanth *et al.* 2012, 2013a, 2013b).

Variable and model selection

Each interviewed household reported experiencing crop loss and/or livestock loss in the most recent year, and we recorded all species reported by people. If a species was reported by at least 30 households of a particular site, that site was selected as a subset for that particular species (to ensure minimum sample sizes were met). Reports of incidents with bonnet macaque, rhesus macaque and hanuman langur were grouped together as 'primate conflict', as many surveyed households were unable to distinguish the three species, and reported them as 'monkey' incidents. Canids (desert fox *Vulpes vulpes pusilla*, Indian fox *Vulpes bengalensis*, jackal *Canis aureus* and wolf *Canis lupus*) were often misidentified, and for our analysis we grouped these species together as canids. Canids were reported by people for causing both crop damage and livestock predation. We have separately looked at canids (CR) – jackal or fox reported against crop loss – and canids (LP) – jackal, fox or wolf reported against livestock loss. For damage, the 12 responses that we modelled were incidents attributed to chinkara *Gazella bennetti*, chital *Axis axis*, elephant *Elephas maximus*, gaur *Bos gaurus*, nilgai, canid (CR), primates, pig *Sus*

Table 4.1 Site characteristics

Characteristics	Kumbalgarh	Phulwari	Jaisalmand	Sitamata	Kanha	Tadoba	Dandeli-Anshi	Bhadra	Nagarahole	Bandipur	BRT
Park area (km²)	610	511	52	423	940	625	1,303	492	644	880	540
Dominant vegetation	Thorny scrub, dry deciduous forest	Thorny scrub, dry deciduous forest	Thorny scrub, deciduous forest	Thorny scrub, dry deciduous forest	Sal, moist deciduous, dry deciduous forest	Tropical dry deciduous forest	Tropical evergreen, semi-evergreen forests	Tropical moist deciduous, evergreen forests	Tropical moist, dry deciduous forests	Tropical moist, dry deciduous forests	Tropical dry, moist deciduous, evergreen forests
Rainfall (mm)	425–775[b]	600–875[b]	600–875[b]	625–900[b]	1,000–1,500[c]	975–1,375[a]	1,250–4,000[d]	2,000–2,540[d]	900–1,500[d]	625–1,250[d]	600–3,000[d]
Elevation (m)	11–1134	225–998	244–488	218–882	371–858	190–266	3–804	583–1,587	698–967	678–993	572–979
Total area surveyed in km²	3,084	2,022	622	778	1,159	1,374	1,859	1,807	1,391	1,313	1,079
Total grids cells	290	196	50	84	218	173	245	174	119	122	119
Grid cells surveyed	238	156	48	60	97	107	143	139	107	101	83
Villages surveyed	494	350	109	143	347	187	304	316	274	262	215
Total HH surveyed	1,047	683	221	283	735	596	468	471	400	370	263
Average HH members (range)	8 (0–32)	8 (1–29)	7 (1–26)	7 (0–26)	6 (0–26)	5 (0–16)	7 (0–55)	5 (0–30)	5 (0–50)	5 (0–60)	6 (0–16)
Education <8th Grade	76%	80%	74%	82%	39%	54%	50%	63%	58%	47%	64%
Average livestock (range)	2 (0–150)	3 (0–18)	2 (0–16)	2 (0–23)	7 (0–131)	4 (0–78)	5 (0–38)	4 (0–153)	3 (0–40)	4 (0–35)	3 (0–85)
Human population density in adjoining districts (persons per km²) ¥	Udaipur 262 Rajsamand 255 Pali 164	Udaipur 262	Udaipur 262	Udaipur 262 Chittorgarh 197	Mandla 121 Balaghat 184 Kabirdham 194	Chandrapur 94	Belgaum 356 Uttar Kannada 140	Chikmagalur 158 Devanagere 326 Shimoga 207	Kodagu 135 Mysore 443	Chamarajanagar 180 Mysore 443	Chamarajanagar 180
Livestock density in adjoining districts (total livestock per km²)¶	Udaipur 197 Rajsamand 243 Pali 187	Udaipur 197	Udaipur 197	Udaipur 197 Chittorgarh 184	Mandla 154 Balaghat 203 Kabirdham 174	Chandrapur 69	Belgaum 445 Uttar Kannada 97	Chikmagalur 182 Devanagere 371 Shimoga 203	Kodagu 84 Mysore 337	Chamarajanagar 194 Mysore 337	Chamarajanagar 194

Sources:

¥ – Census of India 2011; ¶ – Livestock Census of India 2007

(a) – Nagendra et al. 2010 (Vegetation); IMD website, last five years' data (Rainfall)

(b) – Robbins et al. 2007 (Vegetation); IMD website, last five years' data (Rainfall)

(c) – DeFries et al. 2010 (Vegetation); IMD website, last five years' data (Rainfall)

(d) – Karanth et al. 2013b (Vegetation); IMD website, last five years' data (Rainfall)

scrofa, sambar *Boselaphus tragocamelus*, canid (LP), leopard *Panthera pardus* and tiger *Panthera tigris*.

Top mitigation measures utilised by people to protect crops, livestock and property were recorded in all sites, and also used as predictors. These included four measures common to all sites for crop loss (added or improved fencing, added or improved scare devices, added or improved lighting and use of guard animals) and one for livestock loss (closer eye on animals).

Multiple spatial attributes of each study site were extracted and used as predictors. Land use land cover maps were used (250k BHUVAN, ISRO) to extract forest and grassland/scrub habitat, and QGIS version 2.2.0 – Valmiera (Quantum GIS Development Team 2014, qgis.osgeo.org) was used to extract distances and areas. The five selected landscape-level predictors were distance to forest cover, distance to water body, distance to reserve, percentage forest cover in a 3 km radius and/or percentage scrub and/or grassland within a 3 km radius (see Karanth *et al.* 2012, 2013a, 2013b).

We also assessed number of crops grown by households reporting crop loss and number of livestock owned for those reporting livestock loss. We documented 40 major crop types across 11 sites. We grouped these into eight broad categories – cereals, millets, vegetables, legumes and pulses, large palatable crops (sugarcane and banana), cash crops with canopy cover and small cash crops. All categories except small cash crops were used as predictors.

The study site itself used a covariate. We modelled the site as a factor variable, where one of the sites is taken as a reference and the other sites are modelled relative to this reference site. This allows us to account for potential local site-based influences across such a heterogeneity of sites not accounted for by other variables.

For each species, data were subset based on previous ecological knowledge and reporting by households. For example, leopard incidents were reported in all 11 sites, and therefore the full dataset was used. In contrast, elephant conflict incidents were reported in five sites, and for our analysis we only used these sites. Each dataset was tested for multicollinearity, and predictors with a Pearson's correlation coefficient > 0.5 were discarded (Karanth *et al.* 2010; Karanth *et al.* 2012; Karanth *et al.* 2013a, 2013b). The predictors were standardised by subtracting the mean and dividing by two standard deviations to enable direct comparison of beta coefficients within models (Gelman 2008).

For each species, an *a priori* set of models were defined, ranging from five models for primate, wolf and livestock-predation related to jackal/fox to six models for all other species. These were then fit into a logistic regression (Generalised Linear Model) framework due to binary response variables. A Corrected Akaike Information Criterion (AICc) was obtained for every model (Burnham and Anderson 2002). Each set of models were ranked based on AICc weights, and the top models in each set that together explained >95 per cent of the variability were selected (Supplementary Information). The AICc framework is an information theory approach that prioritises better fit models, but penalises over-specified models, and therefore serves as an indicator of optimal trade-off between parsimony and fit. Probability estimates for each reported species causing crop loss or livestock death was obtained by model averaging.

Results

Our analysis focused on understanding conflict incidents attributed to 12 species reported by 5,154 households across 11 study sites in India. We modelled species-specific reported loss and damage as a function of the varieties of crop grown or number of livestock owned, the study site, landscape characteristics and mitigation measures employed. We obtained one to three top ranked models for each species.

Crop cultivation and loss

Surveyed households reporting crop loss were relatively high in all sites, ranging from 58 per cent in Bhadra to 80 per cent in Jaisamand (Table 4.2). The number of crop raiding incidents experienced varied between 0 to 8 annually across sites. The highest number of incidents were attributed to wild pig in five sites (Kanha, Tadoba, Dandeli-Anshi, Bhadra and BRT, Table 4.2). Elephant incidents were reported most in Nagarahole and Bandipur. Nilgai was the main crop raider in Kumbhalgarh, Jaisamand, and Sitamata while canids ranked highest in Phulwari. Average reported loss across all sites was Rs 3,269 (average ranging from Rs 6,763 in Sitamata to Rs 38,692 in Bhadra, Table 4.2).

Cultivation of cereal (rice, maize, wheat, barley) was positively associated with chital, chinkara, gaur, nilgai, pig, sambar and canid (CR) raiding incidents. There were no significant trends for elephant and primate incidents (Table 4.3). Millet cultivation did not figure in the top models for chital conflict, and there was no significant trend for primate incidents. Chinkara and gaur conflict was negatively related to millet cultivation, while elephant, nilgai, pig and sambar conflict was positively associated with millet (Table 4.3).

Cultivation of legumes and pulses (includes nine crops) was associated positively with chital, chinkara, nilgai, pig and sambar conflict, and negatively with gaur raiding incidents (Table 4.3). Legumes were raided by chital, pig, sambar, nilgai and to a lesser extent chinkara, did not figure in the top models for primate incidents, and showed no trend with respect to elephant and gaur incidents.

Vegetables showed no strong associations for most species except for households reporting canid (CR), nilgai and sambar incidents. Cultivation of areca, rubber and coffee (plantation cash crops with canopy) were positively associated with primate incidents and no significant relationship with elephant incidents. Sugarcane and/or banana (large palatable crops) showed a positive association with canid (CR) and a negative association with gaur incidents while there was no significant association with elephant and sambar incidents.

The size of agricultural landholding was positively associated with chital, elephant, gaur and sambar incidents as predicted, and negatively associated with chinkara and canid (CR) incidents. There was no significant trend observed for other species (Table 4.3).

Table 4.2 Loss and mitigation across sites

Characteristics	Kumbalgarh	Phulwari	Jaisalmand	Sitamata	Kanha	Tadoba	Dandeli-Anshi	Bhadra	Nagarahole	Bandipur	BRT
HH reporting crop loss	78%	64%	80%	74%	79%	72%	66%	58%	59%	74%	67%
Average crop loss in Rs	10,768 (0–1,000,000)	4,625 (0–500,000)	7,110 (0–100,000)	6,763 (0–100,000)	4,324 (0–175,000)	14,159 (0–250,000)	9,934 (0–60,000)	38,692 (0–800,000)	21,521 (0–700,000)	22,015 (0–450,000)	22,888 (0–700,000)
Number of crop raiding incidents	0–6	0–7	0–4	0–6	0–6	0–8	0–5	0–7	0–6	0–5	0–6
Top ranked crop raiders (% of HH reporting)	Nilgai 97% Pig 40% Primate 11%	Canids 59% Chinkara 55% Nilgai 28%	Nilgai 99% Jackal 22% Pig 12%	Nilgai 91% Pig 33% Chinkara 17% Canids (CR) 17%	Pig 94% Chital 32% Primate 32%	Pig 99% Chital 45% Nilgai 42%	Pig 43% Elephant 19% Gaur 12%	Pig 87% Elephant 31% Primate 25%	Elephant 45% Pig 44% Chital 4%	Elephant 80% Pig 77% Chital 6%	Pig 98% Elephant 49% Primate 10%
Top crop loss mitigation measure (% of HH reporting)	Night watching 70% Fencing 59% Lighting 55%	Scare Devices 35% Night watching 31% Fencing 21%	Night watching 72% Scare Devices 57% Lighting 40%	Night watching 66% Scare Devices 59% Lighting 48%	Night watching 62% Scare Devices 46% Fencing 21%	Night watching 51% Scare Devices 33% Fencing 33%	Night watching 55% Scare Devices 44% Fencing 44%	Scare devices 37% Night watching 35% Fencing 36%	Night watching 31% Scare devices 27% Fencing 25%	Night watching 58% Scare devices 25% Fencing 35%	Night watching 57% Scare devices 36% Fencing 27%
HH reporting livestock loss	20%	11%	9%	7%	36%	17%	13%	16%	18%	15%	9%
Average livestock loss in Rs.	2,031 (0–100,000)	1,009 (0–100,000)	1,357 (0–100,000)	663 (0–25,000)	1,078 (0–75,000)	2703 (0–200,000)	2,954 (0–75,000)	7,370 (0–500,000)	12,352 (0–1,000,000)	2,190 (0–50,000)	2,249 (0–70,000)
No. of livestock raiding incidents	0–3	0–3	0–3	0–2	0–5	0–2	0–3	0–2	0–2	0–2	0–3
Top predators (% of HH reporting)	Leopard 66% Canid 21% Wolf 20%	Canid 43% Wolf 33% Leopard 26%	Leopard 84% Canid 21%	Leopard 71% Canid 19% Wolf 10%	Canid 48% Wolf 47% Tiger 38% Leopard 31%	Tiger 67% Leopard 32% Canid 7%	Tiger 82% Leopard 28% Canid 10%	Tiger 74% Leopard 24% Canid 9%	Leopard 73% Tiger 36%	Leopard 70% Tiger 41% Canid 4%	Leopard 87% Canid 22% Tiger 13%
Top livestock loss mitigation measure (% of HH reporting)	Closer eye 23% Fencing 14% Lighting 5%	Closer eye 9% Guard animals 7% Fencing 6% Night watching 6%	Closer eye 9% Night watching 5% Lighting 2%	Closer eye 13% Fencing 5% Lighting 3%	Birthing structures 45% Closer eye 44% Night watching 19%	Closer eye 5%, Fencing 3% Night watching 2%	Closer eye 9% Removal of dead and waste animals 4% Guard animals 1%	Closer eye 9% Guard animals 5% Reduced use of public land 2%	Closer eye 9% Guard animals 4% Scare devices 3%	Closer eye 3%	Closer eye 2%

Table 4.3 Model-averaged beta estimates with standard error for wild species

Covariates	Chital conflict		Chinkara conflict			Elephant conflict			Gaur conflict		Canid (CR) conflict	Nilgai conflict	
	5 wi = 0.8	6 wi = 0.15	6 wi = 0.48	5 wi = 0.41	4 wi = 0.11	3 wi = 0.44	5 wi = 0.33	4 wi = 0.23	4 wi = 0.94	5 wi = 0.04	4 wi = 1	4 wi = 0.69	5 wi = 0.31
(Intercept)	-2.51 (0.18)	-2.56 (0.18)	-2.87 (0.15)	-2.88 (0.15)	-2.86 (0.15)	-1.98 (0.17)	-1.93 (0.17)	-1.91 (0.17)	-2.31 (0.27)	-2.08 (0.20)	-1.71 (0.19)	1.24 (0.19)	1.24 (0.19)
Kumbalgarh											-1.82 (0.25)	0.05 (0.21)	0.04 (0.21)
Phulwari			2.05 (0.19)	2.03 (0.20)	1.98 (0.20)						1.34 (0.22)	-2.57 (0.23)	-2.56 (0.23)
Sitamata			0.19 (0.24)	0.23 (0.24)	0.12 (0.25)						-0.74 (0.27)	-0.60 (0.25)	-0.59 (0.25)
Kanha	1.31 (0.22)	1.39 (0.22)											
Tadoba	1.72 (0.23)	1.76 (0.23)										-1.96 (0.22)	-1.98 (0.22)
Bhadra	0.54 (0.24)	0.62 (0.23)				0.18 (0.21)	0.22 (0.21)	0.14 (0.21)	-0.55 (0.30)	-0.75 (0.29)			
Nagarahole						2.42 (0.25)	2.33 (0.25)	2.30 (0.26)					
Bandipur						2.52 (0.23)	2.39 (0.24)	2.39 (0.25)	-0.43 (0.34)	-0.48 (0.33)			
BRT						1.26 (0.25)	1.13 (0.26)	1.15 (0.26)					
Scrub within 3 km	0.58 (0.16)		0.70 (0.13)	0.68 (0.13)	0.69 (0.13)	0.97 (0.18)	0.94 (0.18)	0.95 (0.18)	0.64 (0.29)	0.58 (0.29)	0.31 (0.13)	-0.59 (0.11)	-0.60 (0.11)
Forest within 3 km		0.65 (0.16)				0.50 (0.12)	0.51 (0.12)	0.48 (0.12)					
Distance to water			-0.29 (0.14)	-0.29 (0.14)	-0.33 (0.15)				0.24 (0.20)		-0.30 (0.14)	-0.25 (0.11)	-0.24 (0.11)
Distance to Protected Area	-0.29 (0.13)				-0.11 (0.14)	-0.71 (0.12)	-0.73 (0.12)	-0.72 (0.12)	-0.83 (0.21)	-0.79 (0.20)			

Agricultural landholding size	0.32 (0.11)	0.32 (0.10)		−0.26 (0.22)	−0.32 (0.23)	0.25 (0.11)		0.26 (0.11)	0.94 (0.22)	0.92 (0.21)	−0.49 (0.22)	0.12 (0.13)	0.14 (0.13)
Scare devices	0.58 (0.13)	0.63 (0.13)	0.82 (0.15)	0.88 (0.16)	0.89 (0.16)	0.91 (0.12)	0.88 (0.13)	0.87 (0.13)	1.05 (0.22)	1.00 (0.22)	0.78 (0.14)	1.18 (0.11)	1.19 (0.11)
Guard animal	0.39 (0.15)	0.41 (0.15)			0.06 (0.18)						0.58 (0.16)	0.11 (0.14)	0.13 (0.14)
Lighting	0.19 (0.15)		0.36 (0.19)	0.42 (0.19)	0.39 (0.20)	0.76 (0.17)	0.74 (0.17)	0.73 (0.17)	0.94 (0.23)	0.89 (0.22)			
Fencing				−0.17 (0.17)	−0.17 (0.17)	0.78 (0.12)	0.82 (0.12)	0.79 (0.12)	−0.24 (0.21)	−0.26 (0.21)	0.59 (0.16)	1.23 (0.11)	1.24 (0.11)
Legumes and pulses	0.65 (0.15)	0.67 (0.15)			0.23 (0.15)			−0.11 (0.21)	−0.60 (0.39)	−0.55 (0.39)		0.56 (0.12)	0.58 (0.12)
Vegetables	0.18 (0.31)			−0.35 (0.22)	−0.38 (0.22)			0.26 (0.21)	−6.72 (7.15)		0.30 (0.18)	0.34 (0.18)	
Millets			−1.04 (0.27)	−0.95 (0.27)	−0.98 (0.27)		0.30 (0.14)	0.29 (0.15)	−0.87 (0.45)	−0.86 (0.44)		0.74 (0.17)	0.77 (0.16)
Cereals	1.12 (0.18)	1.14 (0.18)	1.63 (0.59)	1.70 (0.59)	1.62 (0.59)		0.12 (0.12)	0.14 (0.12)	0.84 (0.29)	0.82 (0.29)	1.40 (0.59)	1.31 (0.18)	1.32 (0.18)
Large palatable crops								−0.22 (0.15)	−0.41 (0.29)	0.99 (0.33)			
Large cash crops							−0.18 (0.15)	0.07 (0.12)					
Closer eye on livestock													
Number of sheep or goat													
Number of cattle or buffalo													
Sheep or goat grazed on community land													
Cattle or buffalo grazed in forest													

(continued)

Table 4.3 (continued)

	Pig conflict		Primate conflict		Sambar conflict			Canid conflict			Leopard conflict		Tiger conflict	
	5 wi = 0.73	4 wi = 0.27	6 wi = 0.62	5 wi = 0.34	5 wi = 0.5	6 wi = 0.41	4 wi = 0.09	1 wi = 0.44	5 wi = 0.43	4 wi = 0.1	5 wi = 0.87	4 wi = 0.11	5 wi = 0.85	4 wi = 0.15
(Intercept)	0.25 (0.16)	0.25 (0.16)	-2.18 (0.20)	-2.19 (0.21)	-2.75 (0.22)	-2.64 (0.21)	-2.75 (0.23)	-1.22 (0.15)	-1.21 (0.15)	-1.22 (0.15)	-2.11 (0.18)	-2.09 (0.20)	-2.66 (0.19)	-2.70 (0.20)
Bhadra	0.24 (0.18)	0.22 (0.18)	0.50 (0.24)	0.42 (0.24)									0.69 (0.24)	0.72 (0.25)
Bandipur	1.26 (0.21)	1.27 (0.21)												
BRT	0.83 (0.23)	0.83 (0.23)												
Kanha	1.16 (0.21)	1.16 (0.21)	1.30 (0.24)	1.34 (0.24)							-1.10 (0.27)	-1.08 (0.29)	0.88 (0.25)	0.92 (0.26)
Kumbalgarh	-1.84 (0.21)	-1.83 (0.21)	-0.37 (0.28)	-0.31 (0.29)				-1.67 (0.20)	-1.74 (0.21)	-1.72 (0.21)	-0.07 (0.23)	-0.12 (0.25)		
Nagarahole	0.28 (0.21)	0.27 (0.21)									0.42 (0.24)	0.46 (0.25)		
Phulwari	-2.96 (0.23)	-2.96 (0.23)	0.42 (0.25)	0.42 (0.25)				-1.01 (0.22)	-0.98 (0.22)	-0.98 (0.22)				
Sitamata	-2.19 (0.26)	-2.18 (0.26)												
Tadoba	1.32 (0.21)	1.32 (0.21)			1.23 (0.29)	1.06 (0.28)	1.20 (0.30)						0.83 (0.25)	0.90 (0.28)
Scrub 3km	-0.48 (0.11)	-0.48 (0.11)	0.59 (0.14)	0.55 (0.14)			0.10 (0.20)		-0.16 (0.17)	-0.15 (0.17)		0.06 (0.15)		
Forest 3km	0.33 (0.11)	0.33 (0.11)	0.19 (0.16)	0.20 (0.16)	0.62 (0.22)	0.61 (0.21)	0.64 (0.22)				0.70 (0.14)	0.62 (0.15)	0.75 (0.19)	0.74 (0.19)
Distance water	0.20 (0.09)	0.19 (0.09)							-0.28 (0.17)	-0.28 (0.17)	0.13 (0.14)	0.15 (0.14)		0.11 (0.17)
Distance pa			-0.14 (0.12)	-0.14 (0.12)	-0.50 (0.18)		-0.48 (0.19)				-0.15 (0.15)	-0.15 (0.15)	-0.32 (0.14)	-0.33 (0.15)

	(1)	(2)	(3)	(4)	(5)	(6)	(7)
Agricultural landholding size		0.10 (0.07)	0.00 (0.12)	−0.03 (0.13)	0.03 (0.14)	0.23 (0.15)	0.25 (0.16)
Scare devices	1.07 (0.09)	1.07 (0.09)			0.70 (0.19)	0.64 (0.20)	0.68 (0.20)
Guard animal	0.41 (0.10)	0.41 (0.10)	0.46 (0.12)	0.19 (0.13)		0.26 (0.22)	0.28 (0.23)
Lighting							−0.27 (0.24)
Fencing	0.90 (0.09)	0.90 (0.09)	0.62 (0.12)	0.58 (0.13)	0.73 (0.19)	0.66 (0.19)	0.68 (0.20)
Legumes and pulses	0.64 (0.10)	0.63 (0.10)			−0.49 (0.18)	0.68 (0.22)	0.69 (0.23)
Vegetables	−0.03 (0.13)	−0.03 (0.13)					0.49 (0.35)
Millets	0.60 (0.10)	0.60 (0.10)		−0.22 (0.17)	0.80 (0.21)	0.58 (0.33)	0.54 (0.33)
Cereals	1.22 (0.10)	1.22 (0.10)	0.22 (0.18)	0.21 (0.18)	0.71 (0.22)	0.72 (0.23)	0.72 (0.23)
Large palatable crops			0.48 (0.15)	0.52 (0.15)			−0.54 (0.46)
Large cash crops							
Closer eye on livestock	1.30 (0.16)	1.30 (0.16)	1.28 (0.16)	1.85 (0.15)	1.84 (0.15)	1.17 (0.18)	1.16 (0.18)
Number of sheep or goat	0.33 (0.12)	0.34 (0.12)	0.32 (0.12)	0.37 (0.10)	0.36 (0.10)	0.36 (0.12)	0.35 (0.12)
Number of cattle or buffalo	0.14 (0.13)		0.13 (0.14)	0.36 (0.10)	0.35 (0.11)	0.36 (0.12)	0.35 (0.12)
Sheep or goat grazed on community land	0.88 (0.20)	0.90 (0.20)	0.89 (0.20)				
Cattle or buffalo grazed in forest					0.34 (0.21)	0.50 (0.16)	0.51 (0.16)

Figure 4.2 Example of crop loss in India
Source: Krithi Karanth

Livestock ownership and loss

Livestock ownership ranged from 0 to 153 animals per household (Table 4.2). Most (51 per cent) livestock owned across all sites was cattle, 29 per cent was goat, 15 per cent was buffalo and 4 per cent was sheep. Less than 1 per cent of households reared other livestock like pigs, camels and horses. Cattle and buffalo were largely grazed in fields (54 per cent) and forests (29 per cent). Sheep and goats were grazed on community land and scrub hills (42 per cent), followed by forests (31 per cent of HH) and fields (27 per cent of HH).

Livestock loss was reported by fewer households across all sites, ranging from 7 per cent of surveyed households in Sitamata to 36 per cent in Kanha (Table 4.2). Households reported experiencing 0 to 5 incidents of livestock predation per year. Livestock loss was mainly attributed to leopard in six sites (Kumbalgarh, Jaisaimand, Sitamata, Nagarahole, Bandipur and BRT, Table 4.2). Tiger related incidents were highest in Tadoba, Dandeli-Anshi and Bhadra, while canids were reported most in Phulwari and Kanha (Table 4.2).

All reported conflict incidents were attributed to three species types – tiger, leopard and canids (LP). The number of sheep and/or goat owned by each household was positively associated with leopard and canid (LP) conflict, agreeing with our predictions (Table 4.3). Grazing of goats and/or sheep on community land

(HH reports of 'hills', 'open scrub' and 'grassland' combined) was tested against canid (LP) conflict, and the resulting association was significant and positive (Table 4.3). The number of cow and/or buffalo owned by each household was positively associated with leopard and tiger conflict as predicted, but showed no significant association with canid (LP) conflict (Table 4.3). Grazing of cow and/ or buffalo was tested and tiger conflict was positively associated, while leopard conflict showed no significant association.

Sites, reserves and landscape characteristics

We found that for all 13 species, the study site was strongly associated with con-flict (Table 4.3). We identified site level variations. Kanha, Tadoba and Bhadra were associated with higher chital related incidents while sambar was highest in Tadoba. Nagarahole, Bandipur and BRT with elephant, and Bandipur and Tadoba with pig incidents. Phulwari with chinkara and Kanha with primate related incidents. Tiger incidents were identified in Kanha and Tadoba. No sig-nificant trends emerged for other species.

We used distance to the reserve as a covariate for seven out of the twelve species, which are known to occur predominantly in forested areas (Karanth *et al.* 2012). We found that distance to reserve was negatively associated with sambar, elephant, gaur and tiger related incidents, as expected. There was no significant association

Figure 4.3 Example of livestock loss in India
Source: Krithi Karanth

for other species (Table 4.3). We predicted incidents reported for chinkara, nilgai and canid (LP) to be negatively associated with distance to water within the 10 km buffer outside the park. Proximity to water was positively associated with occurrence of elephant, gaur, pig and sambar related incidents (Table 4.3), as predicted. Distance to water negatively influenced conflict with chinkara, nilgai and canid (LP) as expected. There was no significant association of distance to water for other species (Table 4.3).

Among habitat characteristics, we predicted a positive association of deciduous and/or evergreen forest cover within 3 km of the household with higher conflict. For pig, chital, elephant, gaur, tiger and leopard conflict we found positive associations conforming to our predictions (Table 4.3). The percentage of scrub forest and grassland (including degraded scrub, scrub land, fallow land and grassland) within a 3 km buffer of the household was used as a predictor for seven species. Chinkara, canid (CR) and primate conflict incidents were positively associated, while unexpectedly pig and nilgai showed negative association (Table 4.3).

Mitigation measures

Six major mitigation measures were employed by surveyed households to protect their crops and livestock. For crop protection, night watching was the top-ranked mitigation measure in nine sites, with the exception of Phulwari and Bhadra, where scare devices were ranked higher (Table 4.2). Other top measures included fencing used in nine sites, and lighting used in four sites. Use of scare devices as a mitigation measure was significant and positive for all crop-raiding species. Fencing was positively associated with all crop-raiding species, except gaur, chinkara (both species with negative but insignificant betas) and chital (did not figure in its top models). Use of guard animals as a mitigation measure was tested against all crop-raiding species except elephant and gaur. It was positively associated with chital, canid (CR) and pig conflict, and there was no significant association with primate, sambar, chinkara and nilgai conflict. Use of lighting was examined for chinkara, chital, elephant, gaur and sambar conflict – it was positive and significant for elephant, gaur and chinkara conflict, and insignificant when tested against chital and sambar conflict. All mitigation measures used as predictors for a particular species, whenever significant, were positively associated with conflict.

To address livestock loss, households reported keeping a closer eye on animals as the top measure in ten sites except Kanha and it was positively associated with incidents attributed to felids and canids (Tables 4.2 and 4.3).

Estimating crop and livestock loss by species

A comparison of betas within the model-averaged estimates for each species showed that study site had the largest influence in all cases (Table 4.3). The relative importance of the other predictor categories – mitigation measures, crop category or livestock count and landscape variables – was species dependent.

The mean estimated probabilities for crop loss were much higher than livestock loss across all sites, as expected (Table 4.4). The mean estimated crop loss across all sites was highest for nilgai at >0.90 (in Jaisamand, Kumbalgarh and Sitamata) and for pig >0.90 (in Kanha, Bandipur, Tadoba and BRT). Least damage-causing species included gaur and sambar in Bhadra and canids in Kumbalgarh and Phulwari. The mean estimated probabilities for livestock loss were lower than crop loss. The highest estimated losses (>0.30) were for canids in Kanha and tigers in Tadoba. Additional site-specific details are in Table 4.4.

Discussion

We found characteristic patterns in occurrence of human–wildlife conflict incidents with differences emerging across species and sites. Overall, reported crop loss and estimated crop loss incidents were much higher than livestock loss incidents (similar to other studies including Naughton-Treves *et al.* 2005; Agarwala *et al.* 2010; Karanth *et al.* 2012, 2013a, 2013b; Karanth and Kudalkar, 2017). Most commonly reported incidents for crop loss related to pig, elephant and nilgai. Livestock loss incidents were most frequently reported for leopard, tiger and canids.

We find distinct patterns of raiding depending on the crop grown – with cereals raided by most species except elephants and primates. In contrast, millets were raided by four species, legumes by five species and vegetables by three species. These findings across 11 sites reinstates the importance of re-orienting cropping patterns or identifying new crop varieties as potential solutions to mitigating crop loss. Although some minimal levels of raiding will continue to occur, the scale and intensity of damage can be significantly assuaged by shifting from cereals to millets in areas of high conflict. This shift in crop cultivation will perhaps be more agreeable to policy makers who often highlight the regrettable loss of food security associated with the push to convert to cash crops in areas of high wildlife conflict (Godfray *et al.* 2010).

At a species level, it is very clear that different species are associated with crop loss at different locations, making it very difficult to institute broad-scale policies and highlighting the importance of identifying local-scale patterns (Barlow *et al.* 2010). Two interesting patterns emerged – the association of omnivorous canids (CR) with sugarcane damage, and the mild influence of crops on elephant conflict. The former is in line with the folk perception that jackals eat sugarcane and other crops (K. Karanth, personal observation in Madhya Pradesh and Karnataka; Shashank Dalvi, personal communication in Maharashtra), although the more likely reason could be the high density of mice in these fields (Arjun Srivathsa, personal communication in Karnataka). There is a need to investigate perception, as a false claims propagated by superstition could do much harm when in fact they are more likely helping farmers. If, for example, jackals do in fact feed on sugar cane, more targeted mitigation measures can be envisaged. Literature does show significant vegetative matter in jackal faeces, but not enough to associate with crop raiding or sugarcane.

Table 4.4 Mean probability estimates (with error) for study sites

Conflict species	Kumbalgarh	Phulwari	Jaisamand	Sitamata	Kanha	Tadoba	Anshi-Dandeli	Bhadra	Nagarahole	Bandipur	BRT	Mean	Range
Chinkara	0.29 (0.16)			0.47 (0.18)								0.48	0.01–0.96
Chital		0.77 (0.12)			0.61 (0.15)	0.58 (0.19)	0.32 (0.15)	0.31 (0.19)				0.46	0.08–0.97
Elephant							0.46 (0.20)	0.31 (0.22)	0.63 (0.18)	0.72 (0.17)	0.49 (0.26)	0.52	0.04–0.99
Gaur					0.20 (0.14)		0.32 (0.20)	0.16 (0.19)				0.23	0.01–0.99
Canid CR	0.12 (0.11)	0.12 (0.07)			0.37 (0.14)							0.50	0.02–0.99
Nilgai	0.95 (0.06)	0.63 (0.18)	0.97 (0.03)	0.94 (0.08)		0.70 (0.24)						0.83	0.08–0.99
Pig	0.66 (0.25)	0.35 (0.18)		0.62 (0.22)	0.95 (0.05)	0.92 (0.07)	0.87 (0.12)	0.83 (0.13)	0.81 (0.12)	0.93 (0.05)	0.90 (0.09)	0.76	0.03–0.99
Primate	0.17 (0.07)	0.31 (0.10)			0.45 (0.09)		0.20 (0.09)	0.26 (0.11)				0.26	0.06–0.73
Sambar						0.33 (0.16)		0.17 (0.12)				0.27	0.04–0.81
Canid LP	0.12 (0.11)	0.12 (0.07)			0.37 (0.14)							0.17	0.04–0.77
Leopard	0.16 (0.14)				0.15 (0.11)	0.06 (0.06)			0.15 (0.10)	0.12 (0.08)		0.13	0.03–0.98
Tiger	0.17 (0.10)		0.17 (0.12)			0.30 (0.15)					0.16 (0.09)	0.20	0.05–0.90

We also find decreased influence of crops in elephant conflict, which points to the possibility of other reasons. The narrative around elephant conflict has received much focus (Jathanna *et al.* 2015a, 2015b), and around the five major protected areas of Karnataka where elephants occur (Karanth *et al.* 2013a), there has been a steady shift to unpalatable cash crops. The absence of crops as a strong driver of crop conflict despite high levels of conflict, point to either increased effectiveness of mitigation measures, cultivation of unpalatable crops or both. In the Karnataka sites we find that a shift in cropping patterns has not translated to decreased levels of conflict. The estimated losses suggest that elephant conflict is proportional to elephant numbers in each of the five reserves. Elephants are large-bodied mammals – they are wide-ranging and cannot be restricted to wildlife reserves (Hoare 1999; Fernando *et al.* 2005; Jathanna *et al.* 2015a, 2015b; Lakshminarayanan *et al.* 2016). This is especially true at the boundaries of parks, and parks in Karnataka have hard edges, that exacerbate this conflict due to high visibility of elephants when they move across the landscape.

The association of a number of livestock with higher vulnerability to conflict incidents, although unsurprising, highlights the importance of the need for effective livestock protection measures (Michalski *et al.* 2006; Kissui 2008). Studies have shown that better corrals (bomas in East Africa) significantly reduce predation of livestock by wild carnivores (Breitenmoser *et al.* 2005; Ogada *et al.* 2003). Reduced grazing pressure in protected areas is also an important factor in reduced livestock conflict, and conflict will continue to occur with many people still choosing to graze their livestock in the forest and scrub areas where forage is freely available. This is also known to increase disease transmission between wild and domestic animals, as well as deplete food availability for wild animals (Bagchi *et al.* 2004; Baker *et al.* 2008; Dar *et al.* 2009).

The nature of influence of landscape predictors reiterates the importance of wildlife reserves as source populations for some conflict-prone species, especially forest-dwelling species. The legal sanctity of a protected reserve is often associated with more intact vegetation and less anthropogenic activity (Fernando *et al.* 2005). While leopard, canids, nilgai and pig are known to occur in disturbed areas, other species actively select less disturbed habitats (Karanth *et al.* 2012, 2013a). The combined influence of less conflict further away from protected areas, more conflict with greater forest cover, little or no influence of scrub habitat (except for leopard) and more conflict associated with greater natural cover (used specifically for species of the scrub), all point to proximal effects playing a major role in conflict. This has been supported by other studies such as Hoare (1999), Naughton-Treves *et al.* (2005), Sitati *et al.* (2005) and Azevedo and Murray (2007) who documented similar patterns in Africa and South America.

A uniformly strong positive association of all (except one, brush forest removal) mitigation measures with conflict points to a long history of conflict in most locations, complemented by (a) the lack of species-specific mitigation measures being employed, (b) the general ineffectiveness of these mitigation measures in protecting losses for households experiencing conflict and (c) the likely situation of post-conflict mitigation measures being employed instead of preventive measures of proven efficacy. A parallel study by Karanth and Kudalkar (2017) found that although up to 12 different mitigation measures were deployed by households around protected reserves in India, use varied by state. They found that mitigation use was driven by households' conflict history (more than 20 years for livestock and 10–20 years for crops), proximity to reserves, and crops or livestock owned. Overall, mitigation use was more likely for crops (88 per cent) compared to livestock (32 per cent) (Karanth and Kudalkar 2017).

Mitigation measures are usually unscientific, rarely tested prior to implementation, general in nature and insensitive to temporal shifts, calling for greater focus on improving them (Webber *et al.* 2007). Households incur a heavy cost for investment of time and resources in mitigation measures, and many of these costs are hidden and particularly worrisome if they are ineffective (Graham and Ochieng 2008; Barua *et al.* 2013).

Some limitations of our study perhaps include uneven (and sometimes small) sample sizes in some locations, non-accounting of the possibility that the household is located at a large distance from the farmland /grazing land, among others. Despite these limitations, the current study is one of the few that look at disaggregated multi-species conflict as opposed to lumping all species together to examine crop or livestock loss. Preliminary insights show both site-specific factors and species-specific characteristics have a significant role to play in conflict patterns that emerge.

We do find some similarities, with particular species such as pig and leopard which are universally reported across different sites, and also between closely-related species. These similarities underline the possibility of an effective country-wide framework to manage conflict for the most common species based on sound ecological knowledge while allowing enough flexibility for site-specific modifications (Barlow *et al.* 2010). Increasingly confrontational sociocultural values, heightening land matrix contrast around protected reserves (Tadoba), and spillover of conflict species due to successful protection (as in the case of Bandipur and Nagarahole) and variability in success between different states of the country in managing conflict, all point at the need for a central policy to deal with human–wildlife conflict (Treves and Karanth 2003). At present, there are individual state-based policies that vary greatly in their application (from species listed, compensation rendered etc.).

Attributing causal relationships between mitigation measures and the persistence of conflict is particularly difficult, especially without time series data showing changes in conflict with changes in intensity of mitigation measure usage. The positive association to conflict in most cases hints at *post hoc* usage rather than a pre-emptive application, with locations that have a long history of conflict. The persistence of conflict, despite these mitigation measures, points to their diminished effectiveness. Few studies evaluate the effectiveness of mitigation measures (Jackson and Wangchuk 2004; Woodroffe *et al.* 2005; Graham and Ochieng 2008; Gehring *et al.* 2010) and we find this to be of critical importance given the time and effort being invested in mitigation strategies.

Our study is perhaps the first of its kind to examine in detail the role that species and sites play in shaping the occurrence of crop and livestock related losses in diverse ecological and socio-economic settings across India. We find that understanding the role that different species play along with the history of conflict at a location, and the differences in economic/cultural/social perceptions of losses need to be integrated into conflict management practices. Karanth and Gupta (in review) in their analysis of state-wide compensation policies found huge variations across India. Among states 22/29 compensated for crop loss, 18/29 for property damage, 26/29 compensated for livestock depredation, and 28/29 compensated for human injury/death, with significant variations in compensation policies and procedures. Similarly, their study found that across India in 2012–2013, 81,100 total incidents were reported and compensated nationwide (73 per cent crop loss and property damage, 21 per cent livestock predation, 6 per cent human injury and <0.4 per cent human death). The average expenditures per incident were US$46 for crop and property damage, $68 for livestock, $103 for human injury and $3,188 for human death (Karanth and Kudalkar, 2017). It is important to note that the total number of incidents are higher than most countries in the world, and the associated compensation rates are among the lowest in the world. Therefore, we believe that such multi-species and multi-site comparisons are critical to developing locally relevant policies and management actions with respect to improving ongoing prevention, mitigation and compensation efforts (Jackson and Wangchuk 2004; Madden 2004; Lagendijk and Gusset 2008; Dickamn 2010; White and Ward 2010; Kansky and Knight 2014) and our study provides the necessary building blocks to do so.

Acknowledgements

We thank the Centre for Wildlife Studies, Wildlife Conservation Society (New York and India) for their institutional support. We are grateful to the Karnataka, Madhya Pradesh, Maharashtra and Rajasthan Forest Departments for providing support. We acknowledge advice from U. Karanth, R. Defries, E. Weinthal, A. Krishna, J. Shah, S. Nepal, L. Naughton-Treves, N.S. Kumar, P.M. Muthanna, P. Dhanwatey, H. Dhanwatey and A Srivathsa. We thank research staff N. Ballal, P.K. Prasad, S. Dasgupta, R. Patwardhan, A. Srimathi, S. Kotian and R. Jhaveri for their contributions. Grants from DST Ramanujan Fellowship, National Geographic Society, Rufford, Duke University, Columbia University, Indian Institute for Management Udaipur funded this work. In Madhya Pradesh we thank H.S. Pabla, J.S. Chauhan, H.S. Mohanta and R. Shukla for their support. We are grateful to the Karnataka Forest Department, especially B.K Singh. We express our sincere gratitude to the Rajasthan Forest Department, especially G.V. Reddy, S.S. Deora, S. Sharma, L. Lalsingh, G. Lal, Vaisaram and Ibrahim. We thank over 150 volunteers who assisted in implementing these surveys across India.

References

Agarwala, M., Kumar, S., Treves, A., and Naughton-Treves, L. (2010). Paying for wolves in Solapur, India and Wisconsin, USA: Comparing compensation rules and practice to understand the goals and politics of wolf conservation. *Biological Conservation*, 143(12), 2945–2955.

Azevedo, F.C.C., and Murray, D.L. (2007). Evaluation of potential factors predisposing livestock to predation by jaguars. *The Journal of Wildlife Management*, 71(7), 2379–2386.

Bagchi, S., and Mishra, C. (2006). Living with large carnivores: predation on livestock by the snow leopard (*Uncia uncia*). *Journal of Zoology*, 268(3), 217–224.

Bagchi, S., Mishra, C., and Bhatnagar, Y.V. (2004). Conflicts between traditional pastoralism and conservation of Himalayan ibex (*Capra sibirica*) in the Trans-Himalayan mountains. *Animal Conservation*, 7(2), 121–128.

Baker, P.J., Boitani, L., Harris, S., Saunders, G., and White, P.C. (2008). Terrestrial carnivores and human food production: Impact and management. *Mammal Review*, 38(2–3), 123–166.

Barlow, A.C., Greenwood, C.J., Ahmad, I.U., and Smith, J.L. (2010). Use of an action-selection framework for human–carnivore conflict in the Bangladesh Sundarbans. *Conservation Biology*, 24(5), 1338–1347.

Barua, M., Bhagwat, S.A., and Jadhav, S. (2013). The hidden dimensions of human–wildlife conflict: Health impacts, opportunity and transaction costs. *Biological Conservation*, 157, 309–316.

Breitenmoser, U., Angst, C., Landry, J.-M., Breitenmoser-Würsten, C., Linnell, J.D., and Weber, J.M. (2005). Non-lethal techniques for reducing depredation. In R. Woodroffe, S. Thirgood, and A. Rabinowitz (eds.), *People and Wildlife: Conflict Or Co-existence?* (49–71). Cambridge: Cambridge University Press.

Burnham, K.P., and Anderson, D.R. (2002). *Model Selection and Multimodel Inference: A Practical Information-Theoretic Approach.* New York: Springer Science and Business Media.

Census of India (2011). Office of the Registrar General and Census Commissioner, India; Ministry of Home Affairs, Government of India. http://censusindia.gov.in/ (last seen 20 September 2017).

Dar, N.I., Minhas, R.A., Zaman, Q., and Linkie, M. (2009). Predicting the patterns, perceptions and causes of human–carnivore conflict in and around Machiara National Park, Pakistan. *Biological Conservation*, 142(10), 2076–2082.

DeFries, R., Karanth, K., and Pareeth, S. (2010). Interactions between protected areas and their surroundings in human-dominated tropical landscapes. *Biological Conservation*, 143: 2870–2880.

Dickman, A.J. (2010). Complexities of conflict: The importance of considering social factors for effectively resolving human–wildlife conflict. *Animal Conservation*, 13(5), 458–466.

Fernando, P., Wikramanayake, E., Weerakoon, D., Jayasinghe, L.K.A., Gunawardene, M., and Janaka, H.K. (2005). Perceptions and patterns of human–elephant conflict in old and new settlements in Sri Lanka: Insights for mitigation and management. *Biodiversity and Conservation*, 14(10), 2465–2481.

Gehring, T.M., VerCauteren, K.C., Provost, M.L., and Cellar, A.C. (2010). Utility of livestock-protection dogs for deterring wildlife from cattle farms. *Wildlife Research*, 37, 715–721.

Gelman, A. (2008). Scaling regression inputs by dividing by two standard deviations. *Statistics in Medicine*, 27(15), 2865–2873.

Godfray, H.C.J., Beddington, J.R., Crute, I.R., Haddad, L., Lawrence, D., Muir, J.F., ... and Toulmin, C. (2010). Food security: The challenge of feeding 9 billion people. *Science*, 327(5967), 812–818.

Graham, K., Beckerman, A.P., and Thirgood, S. (2005). Human–predator–prey conflicts: Ecological correlates, prey losses and patterns of management. *Biological Conservation*, 122(2), 159–171.

Graham, M.D., and Ochieng, T. (2008). Uptake and performance of farm-based measures for reducing crop raiding by elephants *Loxodonta africana* among smallholder farms in Laikipia District, Kenya. *Oryx*, 42(01), 76–82.

Hoare, R.E. (1999). Determinants of human–elephant conflict in a land use mosaic. *Journal of Applied Ecology*, 36: 689–700.

IMD (2017) India Meteorological Department, Ministry of Earth Sciences, Government of India. www.imd.gov.in/pages/main.php (last seen 20 September 2017).

Jackson, R.M., and Wangchuk, R. (2004). A community-based approach to mitigating livestock depredation by snow leopards. *Human Dimensions of Wildlife*, 9(4), 1–16.

Jathanna, D., Karanth, K.U., Kumar, N.S., Karanth, K.K., and Goswami, V. (2015a). Patterns and determinants of habitat occupancy by the Asian elephant in the Western Ghats of Karnataka, India. *PloS One*. doi:10.1371/journal.pone.0133233.

Jathanna, D., Karanth, K.U., Kumar, N.S., Goswami, V., Vasudev, D., and Karanth, K.K. (2015b). Estimating abundance and densities of Asian elephants: Analytical issues and practical challenges. *Biological Conservation*, 187, 212–220.

Kansky, R., and Knight, A.T. (2014). Key factors driving attitudes towards large mammals in conflict with humans. *Biological Conservation*, 179, 93–105.

Karanth, K.K., and Kudalkar, S. (2017). History, location and species matter: Insights for human–wildlife conflict mitigation from 5000 households in India. *Human Dimension of Wildlife*, 22(4), 331–346.

Karanth, K.K., Nichols, J.D., Karanth, K.U., Hines, J.E., and Christensen, N.L. (2010). The shrinking ark: Patterns of large mammal extinctions in India. *Proceedings of the Royal Society B: Biological Sciences*, rspb20100171.

Karanth, K.K., Gopalaswamy, A.M., DeFries, R., and Ballal, N. (2012). Assessing patterns of human–wildlife conflicts and compensation around a central Indian protected area. *PloS One*, 7(12), e50433.

Karanth, K.K., Gopalaswamy, A.M., Prasad, P.K., and Dasgupta, S. (2013a). Patterns of human–wildlife conflicts and compensation: Insights from Western Ghats protected areas. *Biological Conservation*, 166, 175–185.

Karanth, K.K., Naughton-Treves, L., DeFries, R., and Gopalaswamy, A.M. (2013b). Living with wildlife and mitigating conflicts around three Indian protected areas. *Environmental Management*, 52(6), 1320–1332.

Kissui, B.M. (2008). Livestock predation by lions, leopards, spotted hyenas, and their vulnerability to retaliatory killing in the Maasai steppe, Tanzania. *Animal Conservation*, 11(5), 422–432.

Lagendijk, D.G., and Gusset, M. (2008). Human–carnivore coexistence on communal land bordering the Greater Kruger Area, South Africa. *Environmental Management*, 42(6), 971–976.

Lakshminarayanan, N., Karanth, K.K., Goswami, V.R., Vaidyanathan, S., Karanth, K.U. (2016). Determinants of dry season habitat use by Asian elephants in the Western Ghats of India. *Journal of Zoology*, 298(3), 169–177.

Livestock Census of India (2007). Details of Livestock (18th Livestock Census). https://data.gov.in/catalog/details-livestock-18th-livestock-census (last seen 20 September 2017).

Madden, F. (2004). Creating coexistence between humans and wildlife: Global perspectives on local efforts to address human–wildlife conflict. *Human Dimensions Wildlife*, 9: 247–257.

Michalski, F., Boulhosa, R.L.P., Faria, A., and Peres, C.A. (2006). Human–wildlife conflicts in a fragmented Amazonian forest landscape: Determinants of large felid depredation on livestock. *Animal Conservation*, 9(2), 179–188.

Nagendra, H., Rocchini, D., Ghate, R., Sharma, B., and Pareeth, S. (2010). Assessing plant diversity in a dry tropical forest: Comparing the utility of Landsat and IKONOS satellite images. *Remote Sensing*, 2: 478–496.

Naughton-Treves, L.M., Holland, B., and Brandon, K. (2005). The role of protected areas in conserving biodiversity and sustaining local livelihoods. *Annual Review Environmental Resources*, 30: 219–252.

Ogada, M.O., Woodroffe, R., Oguge, N.O., and Frank, L.G. (2003). Limiting depredation by African carnivores: The role of livestock husbandry. *Conservation Biology*, 17(6), 1521–1530.

Peterson, M.N., Birckhead, J.L., Leong, K., Peterson, M.J., and Peterson, T.R. (2010). Rearticulating the myth of human–wildlife conflict. *Conservation Letters*, 3(2), 74–82.

Robbins, P., Chhangani, A., Rice, J., Trigosa, E., and Mohnot, S.M. (2007). Enforcement authority and vegetation change at Kumbhalgarh Wildlife Reserve, Rajasthan India. *Environmental Management*, 40(3): 365–378.

Sitati, N.W., Walpole, M.J., and Leader-Williams, N. (2005). Factors affecting susceptibility of farms to crop raiding by African elephants: Using a predictive model to mitigate conflict. *Journal of Applied Ecology*, 42: 1175–1182.

Treves, A., and Karanth, K.U. (2003). Human–carnivore conflict and perspectives on carnivore management worldwide. *Conservation Biology*, 17(6), 1491–1499.

Webber, A.D., Hill, C.M., and Reynolds, V. (2007). Assessing the failure of a community-based human–wildlife conflict mitigation project in Budongo Forest Reserve, Uganda. *Oryx*, 41(2), 177–184.

White, P.C.L., and Ward, A.I. (2010). Interdisciplinary approaches for the management of existing and emerging human–wildlife conflicts. *Wildlife Research*, 37, 623–629.

Woodroffe, R., Thirgood, S., and Rabinowitz, A. (2005). The impact of human–wildlife conflict on natural systems. In R. Woodroffe, S. Thirgood, and A. Rabinowitz (eds.), *People and Wildlife: Conflict Or Co-existence?* (1–12). Cambridge: Cambridge University Press.

5 Thinking like an elephant, looking beyond protected areas

Tarsh Thekaekara

Introduction

Nature conservation is a growing global priority, with protected areas (PAs) being the backbone of the modern conservation movement, where 'natural habitats' are protected from people. There has been a rapid growth in both the number of and area covered by PAs over the last half-century, but this has been flattening out since about 2005 (Jenkins and Joppa 2009). Many large mammal ranges are larger than these protected areas, and some biologists suggest that this approach alone may not be enough to conserve the world's biodiversity (Chape *et al.* 2005; Rodrigues *et al.* 2004). Parks are often at odds with local communities who live in and around them and are a source of conflict (Brockington 2004). There is a move to look beyond these parks and take a landscape level approach that integrates both human and wildlife needs (Joppa *et al.* 2008), but the obvious challenge is then 'Human–Wildlife Conflict' (HWC), which

> occurs when the needs and behaviour of wildlife impact negatively on the goals of humans or when the goals of humans negatively impact the needs of wildlife. These conflicts may result when wildlife damage crops, injure or kill domestic animals, threaten or kill people.
>
> (WPC 2005)

The term has become central to the practice of wildlife conservation, and assumed to be inevitable as people and wildlife increasingly compete for space and resources (Madden 2004). There has been a deluge of literature on the subject, and a database search for 'Human Wildlife Conflict' yields 1,500 results, with almost three papers being added every week (Scopus search, August 2016).

India's growth in the PA network has been similar to the global trajectory. The post-Independence conservation movement aligned itself closely with the North American preservationist ideal (Lewis 2003; Rangarajan 2009), aimed at creating human-free 'wilderness' areas. But this presented a unique set of problems when applied to India. First is the significant population density of 440 people per km^2 (World Bank 2016), which is more than an order of magnitude larger than the USA. There are no human-free areas, with about 3 million people living in PAs, and many times this figure around the PAs, whose livelihood depends on resources within them (Lasgorceix and Kothari 2009). There has understandably been significant conflict between the conservation and human rights lobbies over the displacement and disenfranchisement of these people, manifesting itself as the 'tribal vs. tiger' debate that has been a part of the Indian conservation discourse for over two decades (Guha 1997; Kothari et al. 1995). Second, and perhaps less studied, is that as human population has grown, India has not witnessed the large-scale decimation of large mammals that occurred in North America or Europe. Two thirds of the world's 40 to 50 thousand Asian elephants and half of the world's 2,000 wild tigers live in India, and share space with people at very high densities. This could perhaps be explained by the deep-rooted religious and cultural associations with animals (Palmer and Finlay 2003).

Elephants in particular, in a crowded country like India, pose a significant challenge of 'Human-Elephant Conflict (HEC)'. The average size of a protected area is about 370 km^2 (UNEP-WCMC 2005), while the home range of a single herd of elephants is in the range of 400–800 km^2 (Sukumar 1992), and only 26 per cent of the species' range in India comes under legally protected areas (Rangarajan et al. 2010). They require large quantities of food and water, and have a considerable impact on the people with whom they share space. Every year about 350 people are killed by elephants, they damage over 300,000 hectares of crops leading to compensatory payments by the government amounting to about Rs 150 million, and damage 10,000–15,000 houses (Lenin and Sukumar 2012).

They are one of the most intelligent species by human indices of cognition. They are able to use tools, learn quickly and cooperate with each other in complex tasks (Plotnik et al. 2011), are one of the few animals that are self-aware and respond to the mirror test (Plotnik et al. 2006), and are even able to do basic arithmetic beyond what any other non-human species is capable (Callaway 2008). Given their intelligence, simple barriers like electric fences and trenches, though used extensively and successfully in the short term, have had very little long-term success in separating human–elephant spaces.

As a species, both literally and figuratively, they break through the boundaries of the protected area paradigm. Given these challenges, the policy space has seen significant progress in the last few years. 'Project Elephant', India's flagship elephant conservation programme launched in 1992, right from its inception, focused on 'Elephant Reserves' rather than just PAs. These encompassed both forests and the agricultural landscapes around them, with the project aims including the protection of elephants, their habitat and corridors, while also addressing issues of HEC. Despite these stated goals, little seems to have been done on reconciling the needs of people and elephants. In 2010 the central Ministry of Environment and Forest constituted an 'Elephant Task Force', of mostly academic scholars, to look into the long term conservation of elephants across India. They noted that it was 'not immediate extinction as much as attrition of living spaces and the tense conditions of the human–elephant encounter on the ground that require redress' (Rangarajan *et al.* 2010: 1) and made some significant suggestions on taking a more holistic approach that looked at 'Elephant Landscapes' much beyond the conventional protected areas, governed more democratically by local 'elephant reserve committees', incorporating 'Conflict Management Task Forces' (Rangarajan *et al.* 2010: 1). But with changes at the ministry, there appears to be no evidence of any of these recommendations being implemented.

In 2012, on account of mounting tensions between the interests of people and wild elephants in the South Indian state of Karnataka, the High Court constituted yet another expert Elephant Task Force, with a mix of natural and social scientists as well as conservation managers/practitioners, to look into the issue and make suggestions for lasting elephant conservation and management recommendations. The task force, after considerable deliberation, suggested a zonation exercise with three categories; Elephant Conservation Zones, where elephant conservation takes priority over competing livelihood goals; Elephant–Human Coexistence Zones, where both elephant conservation and human livelihoods have to be balanced and reconciled; and Elephant Removal Zones, where concerns of human safety and livelihood take precedence over competing conservation concerns about elephants (Sukumar *et al.* 2012).

While there was broad-based support for this approach, none of the experts could agree on how this would unfold on the ground in terms of actual maps. What is the process by which these maps are made? Where and how should the boundaries of coexistence be drawn (Madhusudhan, personal communication)? Protected areas and largely intact forests would presumably be the conservation zones, but almost all the PAs in India have people living in them, so in reality would function like coexistence zones. Do local communities outside PAs have a say in deciding whether their lands and homes become part of an elephant coexistence zone? Urban areas would perhaps be removal zones. In 2013, when elephants ventured into the 'electronic city' of Bangalore, a metro of over 8 million people, the obvious solution was to chase the elephants into the closest forests.[1] When they ventured into the heart of Mysore in 2013, a city of about 1 million, chasing them out was not an option because they would have trampled people and property, and they were captured.[2] But when elephants routinely come to the periphery of Gudalur, a town of about 100,000 people, they are not chased out. The people's welfare is not the only consideration; elephant conservation is also a priority.

Amidst all these cartographic challenges and expert task forces, the lived experiences of the elephants and people who share living space, arguably take a back seat. I have lived in the Nilgiri hills in the Western Ghats mountains in South India for most of my life, and have actively engaged with wildlife conservation and research since 2008, through a local conservation organisation I co-founded, the Shola Trust. Our work has been primarily at the interface of people and wildlife, mostly in the Gudalur Forest Division (Figure 5.1), a region dominated by tea and coffee plantations and about 300,000 people, but also with a network

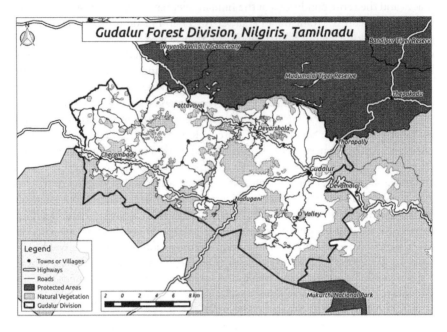

Figure 5.1 Map of the Gudalur Forest Division, including the key villages described in this chapter

of patchy forests and about 100 elephants. It is surrounded by more intact forests and PAs, and is a part of the Nilgiri Biosphere Reserve (NBR), declared in 1986 the first UNESCO Biosphere Reserve in India. The NBR consists of 5,500 km^2 of forests spread across the three South Indian states of Karnataka, Kerala and Tamil Nadu, containing seven PAs, Mudumalai, Mukurthi, Sathyamangalam, Bandipur, Nagarhole, Mukurthi and Silent Valley. The region now hosts one of the largest Asian elephant and tiger populations in India (Johnsingh *et al.* 2008) and consequently the world, and is a part of the Western Ghats – Sri Lanka bio-diversity hotspot (Myers *et al.* 2000). But the NBR is also home to an estimated 2 million people, all living in close proximity to and regularly interacting with these large and charismatic wild animals.

In this chapter I attempt to delve into a range of nuances around the issue people and elephants sharing space, and possibly challenge some of the dominant ideas about HEC being inevitable and that it 'occurs wherever these two species coincide' (Sitati *et al.* 2003). Given the Indian context, it is widely accepted that people and wildlife coexisting is an imperative more than an option (Narain *et al.* 2005; Rangarajan *et al.* 2010), but HEC remains the 'elephant in the room'. Using ethnographic descriptions of interactions between people and elephants, in two particular villages in the region, I discuss a range of factors that I believe are relevant to people and elephants sharing space.

Bharathan and friends at Thorapally

Bharathan was a large wild 'Makhna', a tuskless male elephant, and a bit of a local celebrity around Thorapally, a small town along the Mysore-Ooty highway, at the edge of the Mudumalai Tiger Reserve (MTR). The last decade has seen the village turn semi-urban, with farm lands giving way to hotels, resorts, restaurants and small shops catering to the growing number of tourists visiting the Nilgiri hills.

We first heard about him in 2013, and were waiting in the area one night, hoping to document his alleged unusual behaviour. The highway closed at 9.00 pm every night, and that was when Bharathan usually came out. We were sitting outside a brightly lit local restaurant when he suddenly emerged, coming out from behind the parking lot, towering over the neatly lined cars, calmly weaving his way through them. Our first instinct, from years of encountering wild elephants, was to run, but the locals all just continued to stand around, apparently unconcerned. He was a regular feature there, was possibly the only wild elephant in Mudumalai to have been given a name, and on seemingly friendly terms with the people of Thorapally. He continued walking past all the people standing around, not more than 15 metres from them, across the highway, and 50 metres along the road to a garbage dump where he proceeded to eat a mound of used banana leaf plates (that had been especially piled up for him). His hind quarters were on the road, blocking half of it, with a small crowd of tourists piling up on the other side, camera phones in hand. His rear end didn't make for good photographs, and the crowd soon started whistling and shouting, trying to get him to turn around. We were worried for the safety of the tourists and their ignorance of the danger of being in such close proximity to a large and dangerous wild elephant, and tried to warn them to move away, but with no results. The locals told us not to bother, Bharathan was used to all this and would not do anything. In keeping with their predictions, he completely ignored all the commotion building up. A young man from the crowd, tired of waiting for Bharathan to turn around, quickly ran across the road, and did the most incredible thing we have ever seen – tugged the huge elephant's tail and darted back. We were in shock; hundreds of people across India are killed every year in much less intimate encounters. Bharathan swung his hind leg out lazily (still only narrowly missing the foolhardy tourist), turned around briefly to look at the tourists, walked around to the other side of the pile of bananas and continued eating while keeping an eye on the troublesome crowd. Even the locals had not seen anything like it before. There were stories all around – of how he frequently outsmarted the jackfruit seller and stolen all the fruit, and how all his interactions with people were measured and thoughtful, not unpredictable and instinctive like other wild elephants.

No one seemed to mind having him around, but the story didn't end with him. About a year later a young tusker decided to follow Bharathan on his nightly forays into the town. The youngster was a lot less comfortable around people; he chased them, charged at (and damaged) a few cars, and broke down numerous fences and even walls of houses. There were rising protests in the area, with the highway finally blocked when the metal shutters of a vegetable shop were prised open and the contents emptied before anyone could do anything. In response, the Forest Department dug an 'elephant-proof trench' along the park boundary to keep the elephants in.

But that didn't stop the elephants. The trench could not be dug across the highway. Every night they would come walking along the highway right up to the check-post. The forest guard, not wanting to have the check-post broken down, would open it up and allow the elephants through. But the problem intensified as one more tusker joined them, and protests from the local people grew.

We were with the forest guard at the check-post one night, to get a better feel for the problem. He sat in the brightly lit hut by the side of the road, the forest to the north and the village to the south. He talked fast and passionately.

> You tell me what I can do? We, as the Forest Department have to protect all the animals in the forest. Down that side used to be bamboo forests before, where the elephants came all the time, and now people have taken it all. But then they protest when the poor elephants come out searching for food into land where they once roamed freely.[3]

Shortly after the road closed, we could see the looming elephant silhouettes in the distance, walking towards us along the highway. The smiling guard told us to 'get ready for some fun', and pointed to a pile of rocks he had collected, urging us to get some of our own. As they got closer they slowed down and inched forward, watching us closely. When they were within striking range he leapt into action, apparently forgetting the empathetic words about the 'poor elephants searching for food'. He hurled stones and abuses at them, shouting at the top of his voice. 'Why can't you just learn to stay inside the forest? Come and give me trouble every night, then after that the local people give me trouble every day. Why do you want to create all this trouble?' The elephants quickly retreated back along the highway, and calm returned.

The guard continued with his narrative seemingly unperturbed, about how it was all the people's fault and the poor elephants were being persecuted. After about 20 minutes, with the outline of the elephants still visible in the distance, a loud trumpet erupted just behind, literally shaking the walls of the hut. All of us instinctively ran out of the hut, towards the town. We turned back from a safe distance to watch the three males quickly making their way around the check-post, into the town. The guard smiled widely, almost proud of the elephants that had outsmarted us; 'Look at that . . . I thought there were only two of them, but they have got one more to help. No matter what we do, they will fool us and come across one way or another'.

I came back a few days later to talk to the people in the area, and everyone had strong opinions about the elephants. A restaurant owner was the biggest elephant supporter.

Have you seen anything like this anywhere in India with wild elephants? They are very peaceful, they just come and go without causing trouble to anyone. Only the foolish tourists disturb them and can cause some trouble.

But local farmers were less enthusiastic.

It's all fine for those hotel people. The elephants only eat the waste from the hotels and they get more money from all the people standing around and watching the elephants and buying tea. But what about us? They also destroy all our crops in the night. How will we survive? Some 20 or 30 years ago herds used to come by at certain times of the year and we used to chase them away. But it was never like this – where only males come, and that too almost every night. There is no way we can chase them off, they are not scared of us any more.

A local estate owner is more ambivalent:

There is of course a problem, but don't worry too much about the local people. See, this is quite a developed area, no one is completely dependent on agriculture like in the old days. Everyone has someone in the family who works outside or drives an auto or something. No one will starve because the elephants ate their crops. And besides, why do they all come out to watch the elephants? If they hate them they should all get together and make sure the elephants don't come out rather than just fighting with the forest guard. It's fun to all sit together and watch the elephants, everyone enjoys it.

I continued to visit the area on and off, and two years later, in 2015, there were still mixed feelings about them. The ambivalent estate owner was a lot more negative after a personal brush with a young tusker.

It was about 10 pm, and the elephant had come down from the main road. From the energiser sound we knew our electric fence had been broken. I went out to the verandah to shout out to the supervisor and workers to be careful, and saw the fellow standing right there! I slowly came back into the house, but kept watching him. He was looking straight at me, almost menacingly, and I felt a shiver going through me. I shouted to get him to move away, but instead he came charging straight at me! I ran back further into the house, and he stopped right at the front door. He looked so huge from close up, and could have definitely smashed down the house. He trumpeted loudly and seemed angry for some reason. Then, just out of spite, he went and smashed the car, turned back and glared at us, and walked away. We were really shaken. All this coexistence you talk about is not going to work.

The restaurant owners were still reasonably positive:

> It's not just Bharathan these days – there are more of them. But no one is excited about it like before. They come and go. Tourists like to watch them and they provide some entertainment. They have all learnt from Bharathan not to attack people, and there is not too much trouble.

The farmers were still upset with the elephants and that no one was interested in finding a solution. The people had self organised into an informal elephant committee to push the authorities to do something, but could not decide on particular demands. We were sitting in the tea shop, and everyone, including people passing by, stopped to join in the conversation about the elephant problem.

> Every time some incident occurs we protest and they send some *kumkis* [trained captive elephants] from Mudumalai. They stay here for two or three days, and then none of the wild elephants come out. But then they go back and the wild ones come the very next day.

Most of them agree that the trench was a bad idea.

> They used to come and go quietly in the past – just move through without most people knowing about it. Only once in a while there used to be trouble. But now they can only come along the highway into like the middle of town, and there are lot more problems.

And the compensation is also a sensitive issue, which an estate owner points out:

> The whole set up is basically flawed. I have title for my land, and can get compensation for any elephant damage. But the poor people, who comparatively lose a lot more when elephants damage their buildings or crops, are not eligible for anything since they don't have proper title. I never claim anything, to keep the peace. There is a basic justice problem if only well-off people like us can get compensation. Anyway the government can't afford to give compensation to absolutely everyone who has elephant trouble – it will cost *crores* [10 million] a year for just this place, let alone the whole country. Some insurance scheme needs to be looked into. You conservation people should organise it, the department will never do anything.

Most of the local people were resigned to the fact that elephants will come and go, and they would have to live together. The trench had been breached at various points, and everyone had given up on maintaining it.

Driving through the area at the end of 2015 we came across a herd of elephants around dusk, just inside the reserve. Something struck us as odd with them, and then we realised it was a seven-member, all-male herd – something very rarely seen in matriarchal elephant societies where the males are usually solitary, with young ones sometimes forming loose bonds with older adults. They seemed to be led by Bharathan, waiting for darkness and their night out in the town. A new guard was at the check-post, and he was very worried – seven males was more trouble than anyone could manage. There was a general concern among

Figure 5.2 People's interaction with elephants in Thorapally near Gudalur in the Nilgiri Hills, Tamil Nadu, India

(a) Bharathan on the only occasion he was seen clearly during the day time
(b) The youngest of the Thorapally tuskers after breaking through the school fence

Photos: Tarsh Thekaekara

the local people about these elephants, but the sense of inevitability of sharing space remained.

The O'Valley elephants and the people they encounter

In January 2012, I sat through the night with a group of self-appointed elephant chasers, in the Devamalai village. There had been no elephants in the area in the last 30 years, since when people moved down to the current settlement from the plantation's more remote living quarters. A narrow winding concrete road led up to the plantation from the highway, and the village had grown along it. Elephants first came in 2010, but were not considered a huge problem since the dominant land use in the area was tea and coffee estates. They came a few times during the year, stayed in the hills during the day and came down to the village at night to eat the few banana trees planted around people's homes. When they were around the nights would come alive, and no one in the village slept peacefully. The men all sat around a fire waiting to chase the elephants away from the village, and their feelings about the elephants were a mix of awe, excitement, fear and bravado.

> Last week the tusker put its trunk in through Selvan's window and took all the salt. It even went around to the bathroom and took the soap! I don't know why they like to eat soap. It tastes really bad. The whole family was really scared and didn't sleep all through the night. At least they have a *pucca* house that can't easily be knocked down.
>
> Just let the him try and put his trunk into my house and I'll show him. I'll chop the trunk right off with my machete. That will stop all of them from coming in and giving us all this trouble. Just wait and watch, I'm going to solve this problem once and for all.
>
> Shut up you stupid drunkard. You don't know the first thing about elephants. The trunk is the strongest part. Your small little knife will just bounce off its trunk without making a mark. And then it will knock your house down because you made it angry. You should go home and sleep after drinking, not hang around here talking nonsense. If it comes now you won't anyway be able to run off and escape.

A few hours later there were sounds of people shouting and fire crackers bursting. The elephants had arrived. All the male members of the village seemed to have gathered themselves into groups, running up and down the narrow road, some with burning torches, others with electric ones, throwing fire crackers and beating on makeshift drums. No one could actually see the elephants in the dark, but they could hear them, and were constantly speculating about what they were doing and where they were going.

An old lady, the wife of one of the elephant chasers, shook her head in despair,

> These men are all crazy. One group chases the elephants this way, another chases them back. There is no solution. They just all use this as an excuse to

stay up in the night and drink, and then no one will go for work tomorrow. If some five of the boys sit and plan how to chase the elephants the problem will be solved. Maybe the elephants just want to cross the road and go into the forest on the other side.

Everyone distinctly remembered when the elephants first came in 2010, starting with a small family-owned estate. No one in the house had heard anything that night, and they were surprised to find a pile of elephant dung on their front steps in the morning. We visited the place, walked around the house looking for signs, and retraced the elephants' path. They had walked along the electric fence for about 50 metres, till they found the one fence post where the electrified wires had mistakenly been secured to the inside of the post. The post had been stepped on and neatly knocked over, after which the elephants had all carefully stepped between the wires. They had walked all around the house, between flower pots, bending under a low hanging roof, passing by large glass windows and even walking up and then retreating back down a narrow stepped passage leading up to the kitchen. They then quietly went back the way they had come, over the fence and into the hills. They had not eaten anything around the house – not any of the flowers or the young mango (*Mangifera indica*) and dadap (*Erythrina lithosperma*) saplings, or even a clump of yellow bamboo (*Bambusa bambos*), all elephant delicacies. The only signs they left behind were the pile of dung and a knocked-over broom near the kitchen. Why they visited was discussed at length, and the conclusion that the locals settled on was that they had undertaken a mapping exercise, to learn about the houses in their new territory. With the little ones also tagging along, the matriarch ensuring they were on their best behaviour, careful not to disturb the humans.

But there were other elephants in the area that were less peaceful. In 2013 a young tusker had come to the same house, and walked around breaking all the windows on one side of the house. He had smashed both the plastic water tanks and almost rolled them into balls, and crumpled the television's dish antenna. These actions though, were tolerated, as brash youthful behaviour that was unavoidable, and that he probably would not have done all this if there were people in the house to chase him away. There was talk of applying for compensation, but again for reasons similar to those cited in Thorapally, the family decided against claiming it as poorer families in the area not eligible to claim compensation would get upset by the inequality.

A few months later there was also a 'five herd' that destroyed a house. They first pulled down the tin roof sheets, and then slowly started knocking parts out of the 18-inch thick stone and mud-mortar walls. The two elderly people inside, were hiding under the bed and screaming. The villagers all gathered together, shouting, beating makeshift drums and waving flaming torches. But the elephants would not move away from the house, and kept at it. One wall came down and the elephants started trying to enter the two-room house. Adrenalin seemed to kick in, and a few of the young men from the crowd rushed forward with flaming torches to save the elderly couple. The elephants finally backed off. The people were shifted to a neighbour's house, but were severely traumatised, with the old man unable to talk at all for two days. The elephants stayed around the house all night, and only left the next morning. All the locals had something to say about the incident, some opinions very different from others.

I watched them, all five walking in a straight line on that ridge. We were suddenly terrified. Till then we never knew how powerful these animals actually are and what they can do to us if they want. It was mostly fun games in chasing the elephants till now, we were not afraid for our lives.

People all say that they must have been brewing illicit alcohol in the house – that's the only reason elephants completely break down houses in that way. But that old man would never do that, and there was no alcohol in the house – you saw it yourself. Even then they never break down houses when people are inside and shouting. Some elephants are just bad. You know like in us humans there will always be some criminals? It's the same for elephants

The people must have done something wrong in their lives. There is no other explanation.

The family-owned estates were perhaps the most 'tolerant' of the elephants, particularly so Harikrishna and Sangeetha Mohan, at Heathfield estate, northwest of Devamalai, at the edge of the Gudalur town.

I keep our gate locked during the day to keep unwanted people out. But I leave it open at night, to allow the elephants to move in and out, without having to knock the gate down! . . . The herd comes right up to the verandah. Last week, there were seven of them, they ate up all the flowers, but didn't do any other damage. They are actually very peaceful animals if you don't trouble them.

We like to sit here inside and watch them when they are out in the verandah. And they know we are watching, but they don't mind. One youngster was playing around the car the other day. She put her forehead against the back of the jeep and started rocking it back and forth. It was in gear and the handbrake on, but we were still scared she would push it down the hill. That would have been a big loss – imagine telling the insurance company that an elephant pushed our vehicle down the hill. So we had to make some noise and chase them away. Otherwise we always try to be peaceful with them, and they are peaceful with us.

Sangeetha Mohan's 80-year-old mother, at a meeting where everyone was complaining about the problems caused by elephants, was even more empathetic about the elephants' right to be in the landscape:

Don't listen to all these people, my boy. The elephants are our Gods, don't forget that. The British came and stole all this land from the elephants and killed so many of them. Now the elephants are just coming back to their ancestral homes. They have every right to be here, irrespective of what all these people say. This land first belongs to the animals. You must make sure people all understand this, and at the very least allow the elephants to come through their lands. They have no real problems with elephants, they are just small minded.

By 2016, more than five years since the elephants started coming into the area, things seemed to have calmed down. None of the people in the Devamalai village chased elephants any more. All the bananas around people's houses had either been eaten by the elephants or removed by the people. The elephants came by in the nights and occasionally even in the day, but usually went unnoticed or without a significant reaction from the people. The people and elephants seem to have found a way to both not get in each other's way.

In the O'Valley region, to the west of Devamalai, the small farmers perhaps had the hardest time living with the elephants. The valley covered an area of about 65 km², and got its name from James Ouchterlony, who leased it from the Nilambur royal family in 1845 to plant tea and coffee (Muthiah 1993). As the 99-year leases began to expire, ownership of the land became unclear. The land-holders treated the leases as title, and the land was often sub-divided and sold on many times. It was impossible for the state government to take back all these lands but it was also unable or unwilling (see Krishnan 2009 for a detailed discussion on this) to grant title to all those with the expired leases and in possession of the land. The GudalurJanmom Abolition Act, 1967, was passed in the state parliament, exclusively to deal with these disputed lands. There were numerous pending court cases by different individuals, all the way up to the Supreme Court of India, with no resolution in sight.

The majority of the residents in the valley were 'Sri Lankan Repatriates', who were settled in the Nilgiris around the 1970s, when the government converted large tracts of forests to tea plantation to provide them with employment (see Bass 2013 for more on this). Many of them moved out of the estates onto these disputed lands, and established small homestead farms of their own. Given that historically they had little or no interaction with elephants, they found it particularly hard to cope, and also got no support from the state as they are considered illegal encroachers. A resident, during a heated discussion about the elephant problem at a tea shop in O'Valley:

You have to help us somehow. We live in constant fear. Elephants never used to be here before, but in the last few years they are always here. They come at night and break down houses. We can't go out to the toilet in the morning without fearing for our lives. We can't come back to our houses from the bus stand if it gets later than six in the evening. More and more people are getting killed every year. Either the government should give us land somewhere else or they should chase all these elephants back to Mudumalai.

Despite this being the majority view among the O'Valley residents, there are also minority views that are more positive. We noticed one old man at the periphery of the discussion, who didn't say much. When we were leaving, he called us aside.

This is all just big talk. Don't tell anyone I told you all this, or mention my name anywhere. But since you are a local and can do something about the issue I will tell you clearly the reality of the situation. I have been here for over 30 years – more than most of the other people.

Things have changed a lot and the problems have increased. The number of people has increased a lot, and the elephants are not afraid as much now, and boldly walk on roads, drink water from the *panchayat* tanks etc. In the early days this area was like a forest, and we used to be scared to come back in the nights. But now it is a town, and people think elephants should not be in a town, they should be able to come and go whenever they want.

The real issue is land. Everyone is scared they will say it is an elephant corridor and throw people out. But that is also not possible. The government only brought us to this area and didn't say anything when we started cultivating the lands.

You tell the government to give us all *patta* [title deed] for the land. Elephants have always been here, and they will always be here. People will learn to adjust. This chasing them into Mudumalai [a wildlife sanctuary in the Nilgiri Hills] is foolish, everyone knows it cannot be done.

'Chasing' wild elephants 'back' did indeed pose a challenge. It sometimes worked when elephants were immediately outside a PA boundary, but almost never worked in a landscape like Gudalur, or with elephants that never seemed to go into a PA and were around people all through the year.

In 2011 there was an attempt to chase a 'rogue' single tusker back into Mudumalai after it had killed three people over the span of two weeks. It was a huge operation; the tusker was at the boundary of three forest divisions – Gudalur and Nilgiris North and Nilgiris South, both to the east of Gudalur. The trained captive elephants (*kumkis*), their keepers (*mahouts*) and some support staff had to come from Mudumalai, 30 km away. It was fraught with problems from the beginning, with some 50-odd staff from the department, various big and small NGOs offering their help and advice, hundreds of local onlookers and a large number of tourists. The police force was called in to manage the crowds. With four forest bureaucracies having to work together, there was no chain of command or any one person responsible for the whole operation. The four *kumkis* and their *mahouts* did not know the area at all, and since it was along the slopes of the Nilgiri hills they were limited in their movement options. The two local

Forest Department staff who knew the terrain well were alcoholics, and avoiding the senior officers to hide their inebriated condition.

The operation started at 6 am, and the team only kept getting glimpses of the wild elephant. Of the four *kumkis*, two were scared of the wild tusker and would not lead the chase. Every time they got the tusker moving in a particular direction he would branch off into a forest patch and hide from the crowds. By 6 pm they had barely moved 700 m from where they started in the morning. The *kumkis* were tired, hungry and thirsty, and the *mahouts* angry at their superiors in the Forest Department for the lack of leadership and clear instructions on what had to be done. At the end of the long day they had to find 150 kgs of green fodder for each of the elephants, along with a place with plenty of water to tether them for the night.

The wild tusker was also highly agitated by the day's events. At 9 pm a local estate manager called us to say a very angry tusker was around and breaking things. We went there and could all hear the elephant but could not see him. He was also thirsty, and was breaking all the irrigation pipes on the estate looking for water. Between 12 am and 4 am it had broken another estate's gate, and walked straight through. At 8 am he was reported in another estate 4 km away, on an adjacent hill.

I met one of the officers in charge of the operation early the next morning, with the intention of informing him of the elephant's movements through the night. The elephant moved 700 m during the day and then 4 km through the night on its own accord, and the officer and his team who were chasing the elephant throughout this time ended up much further from Mudumalai than when they started. But he was well aware of the futility of the operation:

> We know very well this is all useless. But Gudalur is a highly problematic area. We cannot be seen to do nothing. So we put on this big show. The local people and politicians will all be happy for sometime till there is some serious incident again. This is only like a PR exercise for us. We know the elephant cannot be chased back into Mudumalai.

The chase continued the next day, but with some changes. The veterinary doctor went out early with one *kumki* and located the wild tusker. He then darted it with a mild sedative, and got two of the *kumkis* to come up on either side and guide it away, though still not getting it anywhere close to the PA.

When discussing this incident in 2015 in the context of a different chase operation, the range officer's take was interesting:

> You remember that single tusker near Silver Cloud in 2011? We've not had any trouble from him since, or even seen him in the area. We just need to teach them that they cannot go around killing people. We can't push all elephants to Mudumalai, but these are like classes for them. Just like we do awareness programmes and sensitisation classes for people, we have to do the same for elephants. They are very smart, they will learn quickly, and also pass the message to other elephants.

Figure 5.3 People's interaction with elephants in O'Valley near Gudalur in the Nilgiri Hills, Tamil Nadu, India

(a) Elephants near garbage dump at Devamalai
(b) The matriarch of the O'Valley herd

Photos: Tarsh Thekaekara

Coexistence narratives and on-the-ground 'HEC mitigation'

The question of how to deal with elephants in such landscapes is highly debated across India, from 'task forces' downwards – over 250,000 people in an area of about 500 km², interspersed with patches of forests and about 100 elephants. The majority view is perhaps that while sharing space is inevitable now, coexistence in untenable in the long term, and elephants have no future in these landscapes.

The first argument is around people and the negative impact elephants have on them:

> It's all fine for you as a conservationist to want to have elephants in that landscape . . . but what about the local people? They don't want to coexist with elephants, how can we force it on them? They suffer huge losses. Can the government keep on paying out compensation continuously? Irrespective of what we all would like, leaving aside the trauma that local people face, the financial cost of this coexistence is not viable.[4]

Then on the idea of 'natural' and negative impacts on elephants:

> There are hardly any forests around . . . the basic needs of the species cannot be naturally met there. They need food, water and adequate shade. They spend all day hiding in small forest patches, and then raid people's crops at night, and drink water from tanks built for local people's water needs. Is this really the natural living condition for a wild elephant?

Crop raiding has traditionally been assumed to be 'natural' and explained around the 'optimum foraging theory' (Sukumar 1994) where raiding high nutrient crops for a few hours is much more efficient for an elephant than foraging all day on low nutrition vegetation. But another side of the argument also exists:

> The crop raiding is not good for the elephants . . . Across history humans as a species have had very limited access to salts, sugars and fats. Now when they are abundantly available we over indulge, and obesity, hypertension and diabetes are rampant across the developed world. The identical thing is happening with elephants . . . in their natural environment, in feeding for 12–18 hours a day they get a range of micro nutrients, macro nutrients and exercise. In these landscapes they remain relatively stationary all day, then feed on agricultural crops for a few hours and get the needed macro nutrients. But no micro nutrients or exercise. Obesity is clearly visible, the crop raiders are huge! And we don't know about their other health problems. We have to keep them out of places like Gudalur for their own benefit!

There are then various narratives in favour of coexistence. On the relatively new phenomena of all male herds in human dominated landscapes:

> Look at it in terms of reproductive success. In the wild, young males only get to mate when they are large enough to take on the adult bulls, and this happens when they are around 25 years old. But you should see the size of these crop raiders. Ranga, the leader, is huge! And the youngsters also bulk up really quickly – almost full size in 15 years. And they've somehow managed to ensure they all come into *musth* [aggressive behaviour caused by large rise in reproductive hormones] at different times. So a 15 year old comes into

musth, goes back into the forest and is able to mate with females with very little competition. They can't survive in the agricultural landscape alone, so both the old and young bulls come together when they are there, and are solitary when they are in the forest looking for females. It all makes perfect evolutionary sense!

The 'deep ecology' logic is also applied to the elephants, particularly by Forest Department officials and wildlife activists. That animals have a right to be there, and are the victims of habitat destruction and degradation as humans encroach on forest land. So the least that can be done by people is to allow the animals to share space.

Central to both sets of arguments – that is, both for and against coexistence – are elephant numbers, which are highly disputed. The global narrative is clearly one of an endangered species as classified by the International Union for the Conservation of Nature (IUCN), based on the population dropping by more than 50 per cent in the last three generations (75 years). About 50–100 elephants are killed every year by people, with the gruesome train accidents catching global attention and keeping this narrative alive. But official figures for the elephant population in India show a consistent increase, from a little over 20,000 individuals in 2002 to almost 30,000 individuals in 2012 (Project Elephant 2016). And again, the figures are contested by various experts as the estimation methodology has been constantly evolving.

As a senior biologist put it:

> I will not say anything about numbers. Our previous estimation methods were very poor, and God only knows exactly how many elephants there were. So actually now only 'God' can tell us if the numbers have increased, it has nothing to do with science!

But the 'elephant numbers are increasing' narrative is clearly prevalent among the Forest Department officials and the local communities who share space with elephants, and some elephant contraceptive programmes were considered, but stopped by judicial intervention.[5] It is relatively clear that ranges have expanded over the last few decades at local scales. And while these debates about elephant rights, habitats and numbers continue at various levels, the Forest Department and other relevant institutions continue to implement a variety of 'conflict mitigation strategies'.

Barriers – elephant proof trenches (EPTs) and electric fences – are the most popular by both the Forest Department and NGOs. But they are very expensive, where the budget/length of fence/trench allocated to each forest division is invariably an order of magnitude less than what they think they require, and they remain effective for a very limited period in relation to the amount of money spent. The trenches are guaranteed to work in the short term, but the elephants invariably find a way across in less than a year, particularly in high rainfall areas, where the trenches fill up with eroded soil after the first monsoon. The electric fences also fail quite quickly, either because of being broken by elephants or when vegetation grows under the fence and comes into contact with the wires, causing a short circuit and damaging the energiser. They tend to work better at keeping elephants out, particularly around individual private landholdings, but less so in a communal context, around a village or in the commons, where no one takes particular responsibility for them. And they almost never work at the edges of parks to keep elephants in; local people themselves sometimes take down the fence in order to allow their livestock into the park to graze. But those not in favour of the coexistence agenda insist:

> Yes, EPTs and fences often fail, but that's because of corruption and lack of will; they are not done properly since half the funds are swallowed, and then they are not maintained year after year. This is what we must push for – better implementation. There is just no other option.

And the other side of the argument (during the same discussion): 'You can't have these utopian ideas. This is how the Forest Department will always function. Mitigation has to be planned keeping the context in mind'.

Compensation is the other key element of HEC mitigation that is being widely used, and also supported by a number of conservation groups. While this is often crucial for impoverished families who lose their year's agriculture to elephants in one night, this approach also has its shortcomings. While the prevalent view is that it could act as a perverse subsidy that disincentivises farmers from protecting their fields (Bulte and Rondeau 2005), another problem was raised by a forest official, that is perhaps more relevant to India, with limited funds for conservation and large areas of human-wildlife overlap:

> Forest officers' biggest headache is finding crores of rupees to pay compensation every year. Moreover all you people try to be very efficient and help every single farmer file claims. NGOs and all other departments should also help in paying compensation, elephants belong to all of India, not only to the Forest Department.

The pro-coexistence groups have their own set of mitigation measures that aim to 'solve' the problem of human–wildlife conflict. More 'organic' and community-based fences are being experimented with, particularly beehive and chilli fences, that act more as soft rather than hard barriers. They have met with some success, and seem to be growing in popularity (Hedges and Gunaryadi 2009). A mobile phone text message-based early warning system has also been implemented in one area, and informing people in advance about elephant presence is showing considerable promise in reducing human deaths in accidental encounters (Howard 2015).

Figure 5.4 The range of human–elephant interactions near Gudalur in the Nilgiri
Hills, Tamil Nadu, India

(a) Local people watching an elephant
(b) *Kumkis* chasing a wild tusker back to the forests
(c) Staff taking photos of elephants

Photos: Tarsh Thekaekara

All of these strategies are being used widely across India and the world, with varying degrees of success and failure. The literature is full of uni-dimensional studies that measure the effectiveness of one mitigation strategy or another, without considering the gamut of ecological, social, economic and cultural contexts within which each strategy is implemented. Various groups and individuals strongly advocate one approach over another, but the primary quest to find a universal solution to the HEC problem continues.

Conclusions

Almost any discussion around human–elephant coexistence has to start with the question of PAs; the role they are going to play in wildlife conservation in India in the years to come and human use of these landscapes. The preservationist ideal would push to keep these spaces exclusively for wildlife, and further expect local communities to be willing to share their agricultural lands with wild animals. This position is clearly problematic, but the issue is complicated and heavily debated already, and I refrain from an in-depth engagement with it in this chapter, aiming to keep the discussion focused on elephants. For the sake of simplicity, I am going to assume that the broad consensus is that some compatible human use within PAs should be permitted, in keeping with the Forest Rights Act. In parallel, I also assume that wild animals will continue to use areas outside of protected areas, and local communities will continue to tolerate wildlife on their lands in some form or the other. The key question I focus on is how this sharing of space will actually unfold on the ground, particularly with respect to elephants.

As India 'develops', where the life styles and aspirations of rural people change, sharing space with a species like elephants is likely to be a significant challenge. Through the ethnographic descriptions in this chapter, various nuanced strands of complexity emerge which I coarsely summarise below.

First, the baseline context for this landscape is that some plantation crops that are not browsed by elephants and other animals offer significant opportunities in areas of coexistence, allowing an agricultural livelihood for local communities that do not compete with wildlife. The local economy of the region revolves largely around tea, coffee and a few other plantation crops. Many regions across India, like Valparai further south in Tamil Nadu, Coorg further north in Karnataka or even Assam and other areas in the northeast, are all similar plantation landscapes where the coexistence discussion is vibrant. These landscapes all differ vastly from other agricultural regions where elephants directly feed on the major agricultural produce, and affect the core of the village economy.

Second, local communities' tolerance of elephants is a key factor in deciding whether coexistence is actually going to be tenable in the years to come. This tolerance seems to be influenced by a range of factors – different across localities, ethnic communities and historic interaction with elephants, differing economic contexts, individual differences and even time. My MSc thesis in 2010 looked at how tolerance varied with ethnicity, finding indigenous groups who had a long shared history with elephants were much more tolerant than the immigrant communities who moved into the landscape more recently (Thekaekara 2010). This idea resonated well with local policy makers, and we found it being repeated at various government meetings, to the point where statements like 'no tribals get killed by elephants' were routine, every indigenous person was expected to be highly knowledgeable and tolerant of elephants, and all problems of human–wildlife conflict were attributed to newer immigrants. This narrative of indigenous people and harmonious coexistence, though new in this landscape, has parallels with simplistic generalisations about indigenous communities being 'fallen angels' or 'noble savages' with respect to biodiversity conservation or natural resource management (Hames 2007). This rigid classification is of course problematic, not allowing for individual and temporal variability. As described above, this does indeed change over time, in both positive and negative ways. And in some cases, like the forest guard at the check-post, the same person can almost simultaneously feel positive towards the species and negative towards a particular individual elephant.

Third, there is a fascination with elephants that draws people to them, even in cases of conflict. While the situations I describe in this chapter only touch on this issue, in almost all encounters between people and wild elephants that I have come across, people gather in large numbers to watch, and undoubtedly gain something from the experience of watching and interacting with elephants. In some cases, there is the entertainment and 'fun' in people having a night out chasing the elephants together, but in other cases they are also just content to watch the elephants for extended periods of time. For tourists seeking wildlife experiences this is of course understandable and expected, and a key part of the conservation narrative. But I find even people who interact with wild elephants on an almost daily basis, often negatively, are still willing to invest their time in watching elephants. Tea estate workers and supervisors stop working for a while and invariably call their managers to come and join them. What to do about the elephants is almost secondary, the first reaction is usually to all stop and watch them. We routinely come across people who complain bitterly about elephants and the damage they cause, who could be classified as being highly 'intolerant'. Yet, they are more than willing to spend an hour or two watching elephants with us, constantly discussing the elephants' activities, the interactions they have had with people and their lives in this human-dominated landscape. These positive experiences people gain from elephants are almost never quantified or even recognised in all the studies on HEC.

And finally, on to the elephants themselves. It is widely recognised that they are highly intelligent and adaptive animals, with no easy solutions to keeping them out of human habitation or mitigating HEC. The majority of work done on studying elephants has been by biologists, where elephant behaviour is assumed to be triggered by deterministic processes like instinct, resource requirements, reproduction success and fitness. The methods used and questions asked are still very similar to those used by the pioneers in the field of ethology

(Tinbergen 1953), all geared to understanding the species as a whole rather than individual personalities. But the social sciences have also seen significant engagement with animals, particularly in the last decade with the 'animal turn' from the mid-1990s, that 'explores the complex nexus of spatial relations between people and animals' (Wolch and Emel 1998: 110). To study animals not just in terms of their influence on human societies and culture, but to examine the lived experiences of the animals themselves. This work differs from the natural science approach in that animals are assumed to be thinking, sentient beings with agency, where decisions are made based on thought and cognition, and not just on pre-determined evolutionary processes.

These fundamentally different epistemological approaches are of particular importance to the human–elephant interface. Pushing our understanding of elephants beyond the species-wide generalisation is perhaps the first step. To view elephants as thinking, sentient beings – individual personalities that are constantly learning, adapting, making decisions based on complex cognitive processes, and even teaching each other how to respond to various human conflict mitigation measures. Our work has also hinted that local people and field staff of the Forest Department are perhaps better placed to more intuitively understand and manage the complexity at the human–elephant interface, and that there are no blanket solutions to the problem. The way forward maybe to rethink the process of policy formulation, allowing it to be a more bottom-up process, including the various views of the people on the ground who deal with elephants on a daily basis rather than the current expert driven, top-down approach.

There is perhaps no permanent 'solution' to the problem of HEC, and it is better understood as a complex and dynamic interface that will require continuous innovation and adaptation by both humans and elephants, to reduce the adverse effects the two species have on each other. The emerging interdisciplinary field of 'ethnoelephantology' (Locke 2013), that uses 'multiple forms of expertise, variously considering ecological, ethnographic, and historical aspects of the human–elephant nexus', shows considerable promise.

Notes

1 http://timesofindia.indiatimes.com/home/environment/flora-fauna/Rampaging-elephant-herd-pushed-towards-Tamil-Nadu/articleshow/20751566.cms.
2 www.thehindu.com/news/national/karnataka/young-tusker-goes-on-the-rampage-in-elephant-city/article2087769.ece.
3 All quotes in the chapter are from ethnographic interviews and discussions, from notes made at the time and are translated/paraphrased from Tamil/Malayalam. Most quotes are anonymised, but in some instances, where the respondents were fully aware of my background and happy to be quoted, names have also been included.
4 All quotes in this section are from discussions with senior scientists, elephant experts and Forest Department officials.
5 http://timesofindia.indiatimes.com/home/environment/flora-fauna/SC-pulls-up-West-Bengal-for-planning-elephant-sterilization/articleshow/41565790.cms.

References

Bass, D. 2013. *Everyday Ethnicity in Sri Lanka: Up-Country Tamil Identity Politics*. Abingdon, Oxon: Routledge.

Brockington, Dan. 2004. 'Community Conservation, Inequality and Injustice: Myths of Power in Protected Area Management'. *Conservation and Society* 2(2): 411–432.

Bulte, E.H., and D. Rondeau. 2005. 'Why Compensating Wildlife Damages May Be Bad for Conservation'. *Journal of Wildlife Management* 69(1): 14–19.

Callaway, Ewen. 2008. 'Elephants Master Basic Mathematics'. *New Scientist*, 20 August 2008. www.newscientist.com/article/dn14569-elephants-master-basic-mathematics.html#.U_fL9tbALFY.

Chape, Stuart, Jeremy Harrison, Mark Spalding, and Igor Lysenko. 2005. 'Measuring the Extent and Effectiveness of Protected Areas as an Indicator for Meeting Global Biodiversity Targets'. *Philosophical Transactions of the Royal Society B: Biological Sciences* 360(1454): 443–455.

Guha, Ramachandra. 1997. 'The Authoritarian Biologist and the Arrogance of Anti-Humanism'. *The Ecologist* 27(1): 14–20.

Hames, Raymond. 2007. 'The Ecologically Noble Savage Debate'. *Annual Review of Anthropology* 36: 177–190.

Hedges, Simon, and Donny Gunaryadi. 2009. 'Reducing Human–Elephant Conflict: Do Chillies Help Deter Elephants from Entering Crop Fields?' *Oryx* 44(1): 139–146. doi:10.1017/S0030605309990093.

Howard, Brian Clark. 2015. 'Text Messages Prevent Deaths by Elephants in India'. *National Geographic News*, 29 December 2015. Accessed 15 January 2016. http://news.nationalgeographic.com/2015/12/151229-elephant-early-warning-text-system-india-tamil-nadu-conservation/.

Jenkins, Clinton N., and Lucas Joppa. 2009. 'Expansion of the Global Terrestrial Protected Area System'. *Biological Conservation* 142(10): 2166–2174.

Johnsingh, A.J.T., R. Raghunath, and M.D. Madhusudhan. 2008. *Suggested Extension for the Mudumalai Tiger Reserve, a Unique Tiger Landscape in India*. Mysore: Nature Conservation Foundation.

Joppa, Lucas N., Scott R. Loarie, and Stuart L. Pimm. 2008. 'On the Protection of "protected Areas"'. *Proceedings of the National Academy of Sciences* 105(18): 6673–6678.

Kothari, Ashish, Saloni Suri, and Neena Singh. 1995. 'Conservation in India: A New Direction'. *Economic & Political Weekly* 30(43): 2755–2766.

Krishnan, S. 2009. 'Of Land, Legislation and Litigation: Forest Leases, Agrarian Reform, Legal Ambiguity and Landscape Anomaly in the Nilgiris, 1969–2007'. *Conservation and Society* 7: 283–298.

Lasgorceix, Antoine, and Ashish Kothari. 2009. 'Displacement and Relocation of Protected Areas: A Synthesis and Analysis of Case Studies'. *Economic & Political Weekly* 44(49): 37–47.

Lenin, Janaki, and Raman Sukumar. 2012. 'Human–Elephant Conflict in India'. *Sanctuary Asia*. Accessed 20 September 2015. www.sanctuaryasia.com/magazines/conservation/5214-human-elephant-conflict-in-india.html.

Lewis, Michael L. 2003. *Inventing Global Ecology: Tracking the Biodiversity Ideal in India, 1945–1997*. New Perspectives in South Asian History 5. New Delhi: Orient Blackswan.

Locke, Piers. 2013. 'Explorations in Ethnoelephantology: Social, Historical, and Ecological Intersections between Asian Elephants and Humans'. *Environment and Society: Advances in Research* 4(1): 79–97.

Madden, Francine. 2004. 'Creating Coexistence between Humans and Wildlife: Global Perspectives on Local Efforts to Address Human–Wildlife Conflict'. *Human Dimensions of Wildlife* 9(4): 247–257. doi:10.1080/10871200490505675.

Muthiah, S. 1993. *A Planting Century: The First Hundred Years of the United Planters' Association of Southern India, 1893–1993*. Madras: East West Books.

Myers, Norman, Russell A. Mittermeier, Cristina G. Mittermeier, Gustavo A.B. Da Fonseca, and Jennifer Kent. 2000. 'Biodiversity Hotspots for Conservation Priorities'. *Nature* 403(6772): 853–858.

Narain, S., M. Gadgil, H.S. Panwar, and S. Samar. 2005. *Joining the Dots: The Report of the Tiger Task Force*. New Delhi: Government of India.

Palmer, M., and V. Finlay. 2003. *Faith in Conservation: New Approaches to Religions and the Environment*. Directions in Development. Washington, D.C.: The World Bank.

Plotnik, Joshua M., Frans B.M. De Waal, and Diana Reiss. 2006. 'Self-Recognition in an Asian Elephant'. *Proceedings of the National Academy of Sciences* 103(45): 17053–17057.

Plotnik, Joshua M., Richard Lair, Wirot Suphachoksahakun, and Frans B.M. de Waal. 2011. 'Elephants Know When They Need a Helping Trunk in a Cooperative Task'. *Proceedings of the National Academy of Sciences*, March. www.pnas.org/content/early/2011/03/02/1101765108.abstract.

Project Elephant. 2016. 'Project Elephant'. *Ministry of Environment and Forests, Government of India*. http://envfor.nic.in/division/introduction-4.

Rangarajan, Mahesh. 2009. 'Striving for a Balance: Nature, Power, Science and India's Indira Gandhi, 1917–1984'. *Conservation and Society* 7(4): 299–312.

Rangarajan, Mahesh, Ajay Desai, Raman Sukumar, P.S. Easa, Vivek Menon, S. Vincent, Suparna Ganguly, BK Talukdar, Brijendra Singh, Divya Mudappa, Sushant Chowdhary and AN Prasad. 2010. *Gajah: Securing the Future for Elephants in India. The Report of the Elephant Task Force, Ministry of Environment and Forests. August 31, 2010*. New Delhi: Ministry of Environment and Forests.

Rodrigues, Ana S.L., Sandy J. Andelman, Mohamed I. Bakarr, Luigi Boitani, Thomas M. Brooks, Richard M. Cowling, Lincoln D.C. Fishpool, Gustavo A.B. da Fonseca, Kevin J. Gaston, and Michael Hoffmann. 2004. 'Effectiveness of the Global Protected Area Network in Representing Species Diversity'. *Nature* 428(6983): 640–643.

Sitati, N.W., M.J. Walpole, R.J. Smith, and N. Leader-Williams. 2003. 'Predicting Spatial Aspects of Human–Elephant Conflict'. *Journal of Applied Ecology* 40(4): 667–677.

Sukumar, R. 1992. *The Asian Elephant: Ecology and Management*. Cambridge and New York: Cambridge University Press.

Sukumar, Raman. 1994. 'Wildlife–Human Conflict in India: An Ecological and Social Perspective'. In R. Guha (ed.), *Social Ecology* (303–317). New Delhi: Oxford University Press.

Sukumar, Raman, Ajay Desai, Sharachchandra Lele, C.H. Basappanavar, S.S. Bist, N. Ravindranath Kamath, B.R. Deepak, V.V. Angadi, M.D. Madhusudan *et al.* 2012. *Report of the Karnataka Elephant Task Force: Submitted to the High Court of Karnataka*. Government of Karnataka.

Thekaekara, Tarsh. 2010. 'Dissecting the "Human" in Human–Wildlife Conflict'. MSc Thesis, University of Oxford.

Tinbergen, J. 1953. *Social Behaviour in Animals: With Special Reference to Vertebrates*. New York: John Wiley & Sons.

UNEP-WCMC. 2005. 'World Database on Protected Areas (WDPA)'. www.wdpa.org/.

Wolch, Jennifer R., and Jody Emel (eds.). 1998. *Animal Geographies: Place, Politics, and Identity in the Nature-Culture Borderlands*. London: Verso.

World Bank. 2016. 'Population Estimates and Projections'. http://databank.worldbank.org/data/views/reports/ReportWidgetCustom.aspx?Report_Name=HNP-single-age-pop-proj-male2&Id=9289b975fd&inf=n&zm=n.

WPC. 2005. 'World Parks Congress Recommendation V.20: Preventing and Mitigating Human-Wildlife Conflicts'. IUCN.

6 Biodiversity in community-managed landscapes

A view of the potential and constraints in the *van panchayats* of the Kumaon Himalayas

Ghazala Shahabuddin and Rajesh Thadani

Introduction

During the last two decades, there has been considerable emphasis on community-based conservation in the context of forest restoration and conservation. Community-based conservation (CBC) emerged as a response to unequal access to resources imposed by centralised state control (Berkes 2009; Bray *et al.* 2003). CBC is considered to be more sustainable and effective than strict nature protection, the primary rationale being that communities are more efficient and equitable in undertaking collective tasks in comparison to state bureaucracies (Agrawal 2003). Local people are also perceived to be better conservationists due to their forest-based culture that creates sensitivity to ecological constraints and sustainability issues (Berkes 2009). Currently there are large areas of forests under management by local people, for instance, in the Indigenous Reserves of Brazil and sacred groves and Joint Forest Management tracts in India (Agrawal 2005; Banerjee 2007; Bhagwat *et al.* 2005; Schwartzman and Zimmerman 2005).

In such decentralised systems, cooperative management is undertaken through participation of local people in rule making, resource monitoring and allocation, rule enforcement and conflict resolution via their own institutions (e.g. Agrawal 2001; Agrawal 2003; Nagendra 2007). In many cases, the people co-manage ecosystems with the state but retain considerable autonomy with respect to day-to-day management. In a comprehensive review of the common property resources (CPR) literature, Agrawal (2003) found that sustainable governance of such resources can take place in situations of clear property rights and tenure, social homogeneity and compactness of the user-group, high social capital and strong leadership, among other factors. Frequently, strong local institutions are also linked to external interventions by civil society groups.

Yet, the ecological aspects of community-based institutions in forest conservation have been the subject of much debate and research (see reviews in Porter-Bolland *et al.* 2012; Shahabuddin and Rao 2010). In some cases, people have been found to sustainably manage forest resources under their control, given a certain degree of autonomy and secure property rights (Chhatre and Agrawal 2009; Nagendra 2007). However, others have found that community-managed forests can be subject to high subsistence pressures so that the needs of livelihood may overwhelm conservation goals, leading to ecosystem degradation (see for example, Baral et al. 2007; Garcia and Pascal 2005; Osuri et al. 2014). External forces, such as those related to markets and infrastructural development may undermine local conservation efforts (Rao et al. 2012).

The diversity of outcomes in ecological studies related to CBC indicates a need to examine simultaneously both the biological and social variables so that underlying social-ecological processes can be better understood. Such an approach is also necessary to confirm the patterns seen in large-N studies using site-based information from varied ecosystems spread across the globe (e.g. Chhatre and Agrawal 2008; Persha et al. 2011). Large-scale studies are additionally limited in their insights because ecological variables averaged over a large number of sites with differing ecology, forest types and social contexts may not always give clear and interpretable results. Large-N studies necessarily involve simplification of concepts such as tenure, autonomy, leadership, ecological health and governmental control as these are highly country- and ecosystem-specific. Thus in-depth micro-scale studies are valuable both for their process-based insights into social ecology as well as site-specific ecological understanding.

Here we attempt to explore the ecological aspects of CBC and link them to functioning of forest institutions in a setting that is characterised by high ecosystem dependence, and secure tenure rights but rapidly changing market and demographic contexts. Since 2011, we have been studying ecology and management of forests managed by two villages located in mid-altitudes of the Indian Himalayas. We specifically explore the *van panchayats* (forest councils; henceforth referred to as 'VP'), a decentralised system of governance, in which the ownership of the forest land stays with the government but day-to-day management is primarily undertaken by local people (Agrawal 2005). Today, 15 per cent of legal forest area of the hill state of Uttarakhand is managed under the VP system (Uttarakhand Forest Department 2009).

In this chapter, we first examine the functioning of the VP as an institution in terms of its effectiveness in rule creation, rule enforcement and conflict resolution, in two villages in the middle Himalayas. We then evaluate the ecological outcomes of forest management using biological indicators that reflect forest structure and function. We then draw links between socio-institutional variables that define the VP system and the observed ecological outcomes of management. Based on our findings, we comment on the existing potential for forest conservation in the future.

Our two study villages are heterogeneous, composed of groups representing a range of castes, classes, livelihoods and forest dependencies, allowing us to explore a variety of social-ecological constraints and conditions within the community. We therefore believe that this localised study, though narrow in geographic scope, can be valuable for understanding both the effectiveness of communal resource management as well as the underlying social processes that influence ecology.

Study area and methods

Ecological setting

The mid-altitudinal forest belt of the central Himalayas (1,500–2,200 metres above sea level) in the state of Uttarakhand in India is considered an ecoregion of high conservation importance by WWF International (2009) due to high faunal and floral diversity. The area experiences monsoonal climate, with an average annual rainfall of 1,200 mm, occurring from July to September. The forests within this altitudinal belt belong to two major vegetation associations – chir pine-dominated and banj oak-dominated, both classified as Himalayan moist temperate forest (Champion and Seth 1968; Figure 6.1 and Figure 6.2). The dominant species in the oak-dominated stands at this altitude is banj oak (*Quercus leucotrichophora*) which occurs along with associates such as burans (*Rhododendron arboretum*), angyar (*Lyonia ovalifolia*), kaafal (*Myrica esculenta*) and Indian horse chestnut (*Aesculus indica*). Chir pine (*Pinus roxburghii*) forests mainly exist as mono-dominant stands with scattered burans and kaafal trees. Chir pine is a relatively fast-growing early successional species that gives way to oak-dominated hardwood stands under natural conditions (Singh and Singh 1987; Singh and Singh 1992).

Figure 6.1 Banj oak forest showing a diverse understorey and tree species, thick canopy cover and presence of large trees

Photo: G. Shahabuddin

Figure 6.2 Chir pine forest with sparse understorey and low canopy cover
Photo: G. Shahabuddin

Social-ecological concerns

While both forest types are native to the study region, there is evidence that chir pine forests (henceforth referred to as 'pine' forests) are extending their range at the cost of the oak forests due to the types of forest management practised historically and the prevalent disturbance regime (Singh and Singh 1987; Thadani 1999). Pine is commercially important as it yields a fair quality construction timber as well as pine resin. Pine is, however, unusable for fuelwood or fodder. Pine is also more hardy and resilient to habitat degradation as its germination and growth can take place under much drier soil and higher light conditions (Thadani 1999). The spread of pine forests is locally perceived to be linked to higher temperatures and the receding of the ground water table, and overall is seen as detrimental to rural livelihoods. In contrast, banj oak is considered to be critical for rural livelihoods since it yields fodder for livestock, high quality fuelwood and leaf litter which is used for making agricultural compost. Banj oak forests are also widely perceived as being important to the hydrological regime in this region, associated with perennial water supply, high plant diversity and a moist micro-climate. However, oak forests are reported to be declining in both extent and in quality, due to over-use, pine invasion, climate change, infrastructural development and construction, as noted both locally and by scientists (Saxena and Singh 1984;

Singh and Singh 1992). The importance of banj oak forest for rural livelihoods and ecosystem services as well as its perceived vulnerability, led us to focus our ecological studies on this forest type.

Study villages

The two study villages, Meora and Badhet, were located 1.5 km from each other by road, within the banj oak altitudinal belt, i.e. 1,500–2,200 metres above sea level. Meora had a total of 51 households and a forest area of 20 hectares, while Badhet had 47 households and governs a forest area of 92 hectares (Figure 6.3). All households are dependent on forests for fodder, fuelwood, leaf litter (for composting) and non-timber forest products (NTFP) for both food and medicine. Resin collection represents a major source of cash income. While there are no landless people in either village, stratification does exist on the basis of caste. The primary livelihoods in the study area are rain-fed agriculture, horticulture (pears, apricots and apples), small-scale animal husbandry and tourism-related activities.

Methodology

Social research was mainly carried out through structured (43) and unstructured interviews (56) (for details see Table 6.1). Various age categories and both

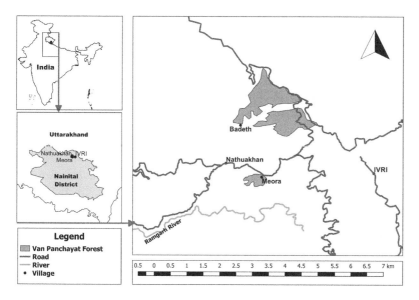

Figure 6.3 Map showing location of the two study villages within the state of Uttarakhand

Table 6.1 Details of social surveys

Gender	2011	2012	2013
Male	18	12	17
Female	21	5	26

Age	2011	2012	2013
11–30	11	0	6
31–50	14	10	29
51–70	14	7	8
Total numbers of interviews	39	17	43

Note: All interviews in 2011 and 2012 were unstructured, all interviews in 2013 were structured.

genders were represented somewhat equally in the set of respondents. Data was obtained on three main thematic areas through interviews: forest utilisation rules, actual usage patterns, and functioning of the VPs as community institutions including (a) process of rule/regulation creation, (b) forest protection and monitoring activities, (c) punitive action against offenders and conflict resolution and (d) management and restoration activities. In addition, issues of ecological and social change were also discussed with elderly villagers (>50 yrs). Field work was carried out during March–June of 2011, April–June 2012 and November–December 2013. While vegetation sampling was restricted to the dry season of 2011 and 2012, data on functioning of VP's was collected in November–December 2013, with indicators referenced to the period from January 2012 to July 2013.

Vegetation sampling was undertaken in the two VPs in order to study the ecological indicators related to forest use intensity, vegetation structure and regeneration. Circular study plots of area 100 m² were established using a uniform sampling design so as to comprehensively cover the oak forest patches present in both villages covering a total sampled forest area of 0.85 ha. Circular plots, of small size, have been found useful for quantification of forest structure and diversity in heterogeneous forest environments (Shahabuddin and Kumar 2005; Thadani and Ashton 1995). Within each circular plot, three kinds of vegetative measurements were made: forest structure (basal area, tree density, canopy cover); six signs of anthropogenic use intensity (lopping, fire incidence, grazing, leaf litter removal, coppice density, tree-cutting) and banj oak regeneration (density of various size classes of trees from seedling to adult stages). The details of how these indicators were quantified are given in Table 6.2. Table 6.3 gives the five categories into which all regeneration for oak was classified and the criteria thereof. Coppices were counted as a separate category because they are formed due to the lopping of young saplings, due to which multiple branches are formed and the tree attains the form of a low bush. Coppices are considered non-reproductive as they have a low probability of growing to adult size or producing seeds.

Table 6.2 Summary of variables used for assessing anthropogenic use intensity and values observed

S.No.	Variable assessed	Use intensity classes		
	Anthropogenic use intensity	Low	Moderate	High
1	Grazing	No signs	Moderate	Abundant
	% of plots	73%	14%	13%
2	Fire	No signs	–	Signs present
	% of plots	88%	–	12%
3	Lopping	No lopping	1–50% of trees lopped	51–100% of trees lopped
	% of plots	20%	21%	59%
4	Tree cutting	No stumps	1–5 stumps/plot	6–10 stumps/plot
	% of plots	35%	61%	5%
5	Leaf litter collection	Dry leaves and 1–6" humus layer present	Dry leaves only	Bare soil only
	% of plots	35%	54%	11%
6	Coppice density	None	1–20/plot	21–40/plot
	% of plots	19%	72%	9%

Table 6.3 Criteria for classification of size classes of banj oak

Seedling	0–30 cm in height
Established seedling	0–30 cm in height; multiple stems from root collar
Sapling	30 cm–2 m in height and <2.5 cm in DBH (diameter at breast height)
Coppice	30 cm–2 m in height; multiple stems from the root collar
Pole	>2m in height and 2.5–10 cm in DBH
Adult tree	>10 cm in DBH

Results

Norms and patterns of resource use

Each village has a legally allocated forest area for its own use. Villagers are heavily dependent on the forests for fuelwood, fodder, leaf litter and other NTFP. Our studies revealed that there are certain widely accepted regulations and norms of forest resource use in the study area. These are summarised in Table 6.4.

Fuelwood is collected and stored mainly during the winter months from December to March and most of this comes from banj oak and other hardwood species. Families reported collecting 2–3 bundles of about 40 kg each per week for their use. Some families do possess liquid petroleum gas (LPG) connections,

Table 6.4 Regulations and prevalence of extractive activities in the study villages

S.No.	Extractive activities	Actual occurrence
I	Prohibited activities	
1	Cutting of live trees	Prevalent
2	Cutting green branches	Prevalent
3	Use of fire (to enhance growth of grass)	Occasional
4	Free-range grazing of livestock	Occasional
II	Regulated activities	
5	Fuelwood-only fallen/dry branches and twigs	Not followed
6	Fodder grasses – during post-monsoon periods only	Followed
7	Pine resin collection only from trees >45 cm DBH	Not followed
III	Unregulated activities	
8	Fallen (dry) leaves – oak and other hardwood species	Comprehensive
9	Fallen (dry) pine needles	Prevalent
10	NTFP such as fruit of Myrica esculenta, mushrooms, lichen	Prevalent

subsidised by the government. However, these families use LPG sparingly due to the unpredictable nature of the supply, the expense involved and also their preference for firewood during the winter months. The larger landholders depend on their agricultural lands for some of their fuelwood supply but the smaller landholders are wholly dependent on the forest. In general, VPs have banned the cutting of live trees, except in special circumstances with permission from the VP, such as for cremations and weddings. Extraction of only dead branches and twigs is allowed for firewood.

Animal husbandry is, at best, a subsistence occupation in the study area. The number of cows and goats per household is quite low (1–4 cows and 2–5 goats at most). There are two sources of fodder: VP forests provide grass and leaves and agricultural fields provide crop residue. However, free-range grazing of livestock is banned. VP forests are opened up for grass-cutting for a short while during the post-monsoon months for collection of fodder grasses which are dried and stored till the following winter. Hardwood trees are lopped for leaves. However, in most cases, the collection from forests falls far short of local needs and villagers buy commercial fodder each year from nearby towns and other VPs that have a surplus to sell.

As an NTFP, pine resin collection is one of the most highly valued commercial activities and the resin is harvested during the dry season by means of removal and scraping of the bark. Pine resin collection is allowed from large trees only, i.e. those that are approximately 45 cm in diameter at breast height (DBH) or more, and only once each season (i.e. tapped from one point) by a specified number of collectors appointed by the contractor. Often trees are fired at the base to increase the resin flow, an activity that has been prohibited as fires tend to get out of control and damage tree regeneration. Firing trees repeatedly has been seen to cause tree mortality as well.

Resin collection is sub-contracted by the Forest Department (FD) to households from the local VP, who then hire migrant labourers for the extraction. Revenues from resin collection are paid to individuals within the VP who obtain the contract from FD, usually the same family every year. It was informally reported that Badhet VP earns about Rs 60,000–70,000 a year from resin contracts.

Leaf litter extraction is another very important activity for the locals and generally takes place from March until June, coinciding with the leaf fall of the hardwood trees during the spring and summer (Figure 6.4). Oak leaves have been found to retain a high percentage of nutrients in leaves at the time of leaf-fall and thus are favoured for making agricultural compost (Thadani 1999). Loads of 20–30 kg are collected and carried out, mainly by women, from the VP forests. Up to two such loads are carried by each household per week. This leaf litter is then used as bedding for livestock, composted with livestock dung and urine, and later applied in agricultural fields as organic manure. Leaf litter collection

Figure 6.4 Women collecting leaf litter from the oak forests for mulching
Photo: G. Shahabuddin

(for composting) is allowed without any restriction and the amount of collection in any given area depends on accessibility and need.

Other non-timber forest products (NTFP) are also extensively extracted by local people such as fruit of *Myrica esculenta*, lichens and mushrooms. One of the important NTFP are fallen pine needles, used mainly for packaging of fruit such as apricots and apples. There are no rules governing the collection of NTFP from the forests.

Most people in Meora perceived their VP forests as being insufficient for their daily needs of fuelwood and fodder and admitted to frequently extracting from other VPs due to lack of other options in the area. People in Meora, for instance, frequently collect fuelwood from the neighbouring VPs Simayal and Dadim. People in Badhet, however, do not visit other VPs as frequently, since they have access to a larger VP and in general own larger farmlands.

Functioning of the van panchayats

VPs were found to have a high degree of autonomy in decision-making, despite rules that require permission from the Forest Department for several activities, and clear property rights. The VP is headed by a local 'sarpanch' or village chief. In addition, there are eight other council members, each of whom is chosen from a different ward within the village, making a total of nine members in the VP core council. Table 6.5 summarises the various indicators of VP functioning as quantified during the study. Elections to the various positions within the VP are supposed to be held every five years and take place through the open ballot system. At the time of completion of the study (July 2013), however, no elections

Table 6.5 Indicators of functioning of van panchayats

S.No.	List of indicators of VP functioning (as of December 2013)	Badhet	Meora
1	Is there a guard appointed for protection?	No	No
2	If no guard, when was the system stopped?	1998	2009
3	When were the last elections held?	2006	2005
4	Number of council meetings of the VP (Jan. 2012 to July 2013)?	0	9
5	Number of general body meetings (Jan. 2012 to July 2013)?	0	4
6	Attendance level at VP meetings (Jan. 2012 to July 2013)	NA	5–10 people
7	Number of transgressions recorded (Jan 2012 to July 2013)?	No records *	No records *
9	Number of fining events out of transgressions detected?	2	0

10	Which are the major offences noticed?	Tree cutting, Lopping, Setting fire	Tree cutting, Lopping, Grass collection
11	Does the local forest guard attend meetings?	No	No
12	Any afforestation/water conservation work going on in the village?	None	Yes
13	Any participation of NGOs in NRM/ development work?	None	Yes
14	Collection of pine resin (commercial)	Yes	No
15	Records of revenue from pine resin collection	No	NA

* Occasional events are reported informally by people

had taken place in Meora since 2005. In Badhet, elections had been last held in 2006, were due in 2011, but had not taken place.

According to the rules, there should be one meeting of the core council every month and that of the general body (entire village) every three months. In Meora, meetings of the council were reported to be regular and frequent, with one taking place almost every month and the general body meeting every three months or so. However, participation in general meetings is very low, with about five to ten people attending on most occasions. It was reported that forest management issues are discussed but usually no decisions can be made due to lack of consensus. A few people from poor households said that they did not get to know about the meetings at all.

Badhet had had no meetings during the reference period of January 2012 to December 2013: either those of the general body or of the council. Earlier, most meetings in Badhet took place with only four to five council members, according to local respondents. Forest issues are also not a priority during the VP meetings. Issues of health, roads, educational facilities and other developmental issues generally predominate the discussions in Badhet. There has been investment in construction of a tarred road and temple in preference to investment in afforestation, forest protection or soil conservation activities.

When queried about the low level of participation and lack of meetings, some women felt that hardly any decisions are made during the meetings and therefore it was not useful to attend. Other individuals pointed to the arbitrariness with which decisions on resource use are made. One respondent said that he did not want to participate in the deliberations of the VP as personal interests and patronage of the elites usually stalled any consensus-based decision making.

We found a low degree of protection of the forests, as reported by most villagers. In order to ensure that rules are followed, a guard was appointed on a paid basis to patrol the forests in the past. However, the contributory system for payment of guards is reported to have broken down in both the study villages. Several people believe that guards do not stay in their jobs due to the fact that they are not paid adequately. On the other hand, others felt that hiring a local guard for protection had not led to a visible reduction in illegal activities, either by local villagers or external villagers. As one villager commented: 'There is not much discussion in VP meetings about monitoring; people are obligated to protect the forest themselves'. Consequently, in Badhet, there had been no system in place for patrolling and protection since 1998 (for 15 years). In July 2013, in response to a notice from the Forest Department, two guards were appointed to patrol the forest in Badhet. In Meora, there had been no appointed guard since 2009 (for four years). Patrolling duties are done informally by locals including council members, from time to time, however.

The outlined process of dealing with offenders is supposedly transparent, with names and fine amounts being recorded by the VP. From the discussions, however, it appears that it is usually outsiders who are fined. Most external rule-breakers are fined, and their equipment confiscated. During the reference period, no instances of fining had been recorded in Meora. In Badhet, two external offenders from Gadgaon, a neighbouring village, were fined in 2012 for extraction of leaf litter. Given that the practice of collecting biomass from other VPs other than their own is quite prevalent, the lack of fining events suggests laxity in protection and sanctioning.

At the discussions during the meetings in Meora, the prevalent perception was that much of the destructive activity was caused by four or five families within the village, who also did not attend meetings. There was talk of VP members known to stealthily release their livestock into the forest for grazing at night. Activities particularly destructive of the forest, such as lopping of green branches for firewood and fodder, were frequently attributed to migrant labourers.

Our data also suggests prevalence of elite capture of resources within the two villages. Several of our respondents showed discontent over allocation of live trees by the *sarpanch*, both past and present, for special occasions such as weddings and funerals. A local villager in Badhet pointed to instances of the *sarpanch* cutting trees in the event of a wedding, when others had been denied the same privilege only a short time ago for a funeral. Nepotism in allocation of contracts for resin collection is another instance. In Badhet, the son of the *sarpanch* was given the contract for three years in a row and further, was reported as having flouted the rules by tapping pine trees less than 45 cm in DBH. He was never fined. Further, there are no records of the actual revenues from pine resin collection in any given year, so the royalty to be paid to the VP could not be verified.

In response to the perceived decline in forest resources, there have been efforts by a local non-profit named Central Himalayan Rural Action Group (CHIRAG), which has been working in the region since 1986 to promote sustainable development. There has been regular afforestation through plantations and soil/water conservation to restore the health of the oak forests in the village of Meora, coupled with quantitative vegetation monitoring, since 1989. However, it is commonly believed by the villagers that the formal afforestation activities have not had results commensurate with the financial inputs or time spent. Most villagers believe that planted saplings are not capable of the same survival or growth rates as natural forest saplings. It is also reported that there is lack of sufficient protection by the local people. In the village of Badhet, CHIRAG has historically been unable to get the villagers to work together on plantation activities, reportedly due to deep caste-based fissures within the community, leading to lack of consensus in allocation of various duties and contracts relating to plantations.

There also appears to be considerable misgiving with regard to the governmental efforts in afforestation and water conservation. It was widely felt that the opinions of the VP and villagers is not taken before the governmental planning of water conservation or forestry projects. According to the new rules, a five-year working plan for the forests, designed by the villagers, has to be approved by the state Forest Department. The *sarpanch* felt that while the activities did bring some income to villagers, overall they were detrimental to the forest ecosystem. One instance is the planting of deodar (*Cedrus deodara*), poplar (*Populus spp.*) and shisham (*Dalbergia sissoo*) which are not native to this altitudinal belt.

The VP rules mandate the participation of forest guards in meetings and fining. However, there appeared to be low participation of the FD in the deliberations of the VP in Meora, and most people are not aware of the rules regarding the same. However, in Badhet, possibly due to the commercial value of pine resin collection, there is far more interest and involvement. For instance, the five-year working plan requirement was imposed only in Badhet.

Ecological assessment

Table 6.2 gives the various indicators of disturbance quantified in the field. In terms of compliance with rules governing grazing and use of fire in the oak forest, the field study shows a high level of compliance, with only 27 per cent of the area subject to a moderate or high level of grazing. No fire signs were seen in 88 per cent of the study plots in the banj oak stands. As mentioned earlier, use of fire is banned but fire is clandestinely set to pine forests to facilitate the tapping of resin and to increase grass growth. Such fires in pine areas often get out of control and enter the oak forest, so most of the fire signs were seen in areas of transition between oak and pine.

While we found high compliance with respect to grazing and fire, the rules related to branch lopping and tree cutting are not followed strictly with about 59 per cent of the plots showing intense lopping and 21 per cent showing moderate levels of lopping (Figure 6.5 shows a typical lopped banj oak tree). Limited cutting of live trees is regulated by the *sarpanch* through the permit system, as mentioned earlier. This is reflected in the density of large-tree stumps occurring in the forest – 61 per cent of the plots recorded 1–5 stumps and 5 per cent showed as many as 6–10 stumps per 100 m² (see Table 6.2).

Figure 6.5 A lopped banj oak tree
Photo: Vinay Nair

A high degree of damage is also caused by a variety of activities otherwise allowed, as seen in figures related to coppice density. Coppice density is a composite disturbance variable that combines the effects of damage to young saplings that can be caused by human trampling, accidental lopping during grass-cutting or sweeping of forest for leaf litter collection, all of which are allowed. The frequency and abundance of coppices in the study plots shows a high degree of disturbance – 72 per cent of oak plots recorded between 1 and 20 coppices; and 9 per cent recorded between 21 and 40 coppice individuals within the 100 m^2 area. Only 19 per cent of oak plots showed no coppices (Figure 6.6).

Figure 6.6   A heavily lopped forest patch showing oak coppice bushes and young pine
           regeneration
Photo: G. Shahabuddin

In terms of leaf litter removal, which is an unregulated activity, as many as 54
per cent of oak plots showed only a layer of dry leaves, indicating leaf litter collection until the previous dry season at least. A small fraction of plots (11 per cent)
showed only bare soil, indicating comprehensive collection of leaf litter annually,
for the past several years. Only 35 per cent of oak plots showed a healthy humus
layer, indicating that they had had no leaf litter removal for a few years.

The oak forest plots showed moderate canopy cover – an average of 61 per
cent. Almost 50 per cent of plots showed a healthy canopy cover of between
50 and 75 per cent and another 22 per cent of plots showed canopy cover between
76 and 100 per cent. In a study of banj oak-dominated forest, spanning over
93 plots at a similar altitudinal range, canopy cover ranged between 53 and 65
per cent (Thadani and Ashton 1995). Based on fieldwork in the 1980s, Singh
and Singh (1992) report a typical canopy cover of 77–80 per cent in oak forests. Thus it appears that the prevalence of lopping tree branches has affected
the canopy cover. Thirty per cent of oak forest plots show low values of canopy
cover (<50 per cent), which would be considered inadequate for this habitat,
probably caused by opening up of the canopy due to intensive lopping. Thadani
and Ashton (1995) show that maximal germination of oak acorns takes place
in intermediate levels of shade, i.e. 60–70 per cent canopy cover, and that both
higher and lower values than this can be inhibiting.

Average basal area of oak forest calculated in this study is 32.59 m² ha⁻¹. Thadani and Ashton (1995) recorded between 30.5 m² ha⁻¹ (in village forest). For protected private forest, 39.2 m² ha⁻¹ was recorded in 1995 (Thadani and Ashton 1995). Singh and Singh (1992) record an average basal area of as much as 40.9 m² ha⁻¹ for banj oak based on surveys over a larger area in Kumaon and this value has generally been accepted to be the healthy value in this forest type. Thus the basal area value shown by oak forest in our study is similar to that recorded for village forests 20 years earlier but much lower than what is expected for a protected forest.

Tree density in the VP forests average 670 adult trees per ha (trees >10 cm DBH). This is similar to the values obtained by Thadani and Ashton for private forests (602 ha⁻¹), sanctuary forests (656 ha⁻¹) and village forests (610 ha⁻¹) in 1995. It is higher than that seen in reserved forests under state control (481 ha⁻¹) by Thadani and Ashton (1995). Saxena and Singh (1984) recorded 586 trees per hectare in banj oak-dominated forest at similar altitudes. Based on fieldwork in 26 different banj oak stands, Singh and Singh (1992) recorded as many as 741 trees per hectare. Thus tree densities are not found to be affected by human use in these two villages

Examination of the size class distribution of oaks shows two distinct features (Figure 6.7). There is an almost complete lack of pole stage (sub-adult; 15 ha⁻¹) of trees and conversely a disproportionately high density of coppices (329 ha⁻¹). Since poles signify sub-adults that have a high probability of being recruited into the adult stage, their near-absence shows a declining adult population in the long run. Second, the high density of coppices (329 ha⁻¹) in comparison to both saplings (88 ha⁻¹) as well as poles (15 ha⁻¹) suggests a vegetation dynamic in which most oak saplings are being damaged (and turning into coppices) before they can reach the pole stage. Damage could be caused by direct cutting for fodder, trampling, inadvertent cutting during grass and leaf litter collection, fire or grazing incidents.

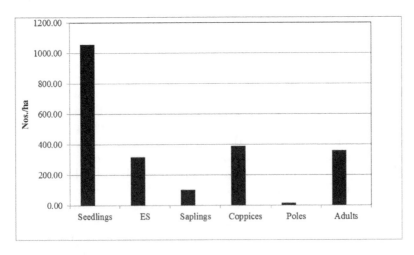

Figure 6.7 Density of regenerative size classes of banj oak in oak-dominated forest (ha⁻¹; ES – established seedling)

Links between socio-institutional and ecological variables

Our study indicates the low degree influence of the *van panchayat* system in forest management in this region. While there is relatively better self-regulation with respect to grazing and use of fire in oak forest, the rules related to branch lopping and tree cutting, do not seem to be followed very strictly. Many people do not appear to consider the *van panchayat* an important institution for resource management, as evidenced by the lack of sufficient protective activities and low extent of participation in its activities.

In the two VPs, it is not clear whether the regulated activities – such as extraction of large trees – are actually contained under sustainable limits. Interviews suggest that there do not seem to be any annual limits on cutting of trees. No one household can be refused permits without causing antagonism within the village. Second, almost all requirements for live trees are met clandestinely even if permits are not formally obtained from the VP, according to our field observations. In addition, leaf litter collection is not subject to any restrictions. Continual collection of leaf litter may lead to impoverishment of soil nutrients as a study shows that heavily extracted areas tend to have low nutrient status (Thadani 1999). Similarly, surveys have indicated lack of any regulatory mechanisms for collection of fruit of kaafal (*Myrica esculenta*) an important NTFP (pers. obs.).

Weak protection and self-regulation has thus evidently translated into mixed results on ecological outcomes of management. Our results thus suggest that some ecological variables are not affected and other features are at a disadvantage, due to the differential biological responses of species and variable uses by people, as seen in several other case studies (see review in Shahabuddin and Rao 2010). Tree density is not significantly different from values considered healthy for the forest type. However basal areas and canopy cover are reduced in comparison to protected forest, in the two VPs that were studied. However, the study of population structure of the dominant tree species banj oak confirm the widely perceived vegetation dynamic of compromised oak regeneration in the area, which, in turn, could encourage pine invasion. While a moderate degree of disturbance caused by lopping that opens up the canopy (Thadani and Ashton 1995), is favourable for germination of oak acorns, it is clear that the constraining factors for oak population has shifted to chronic damage at later juvenile stages. Invasion by pine saplings in degraded oak forest sites, where banj oak saplings are reduced to bushes, is commonly observed (for instance, see Figure 6.6). There are possibly other vegetational changes in our study site that have not yet been quantified, such as decline in density of large trees and decline in diversity of shrubs, herbs and epiphytes, which will be intensified due to pine invasion, as pine has naturally a low-diversity forest association in comparison to banj oak.

Some of the trends uncovered on ecological status were confirmed by our interviews during which people's perceptions were recorded. Density and diversity of trees and shrubs and diversity of native fauna are thought to have declined drastically during the last few decades. People also mentioned the multitude of herbs, creepers, epiphytes and grasses earlier abundant in the forest that have now largely dwindled. Results of such processes are visible in the intensively used

Figure 6.8 A degraded banj oak forest showing absence of shrubs/saplings, cleanly swept
forest floor, predominance of young trees and moderate canopy cover

VP forests, such as lack of duff layer, absence of understorey shrubs or saplings and
dominance of younger trees, though canopy cover is often retained (Figure 6.8).
Many perennial streams and lakes have gone dry due to over-use and diversion,
leading to water scarcity at this altitude and the disappearance of fish. Almost
every respondent commented on the spread of pine in the area at the cost of banj
oak, a process which was seen as highly detrimental to their livelihoods as well as
local ecology. One respondent in Badhet spoke of deteriorating soil quality due
to repeated fires, which was evidenced by the poor quality of grass available for
collection post-monsoon.

Discussion

Decentralisation and sustainable management

The situation in the *van panchayats* is favourable for sustainable management, with
legal rights entirely with the community and almost complete autonomy in rule
creation as well as its exercise. Rule-making autonomy and ownership over large
tracts of forests have been seen as critical and positive for ecological outcomes
(Chhatre and Agrawal 2009). However, despite such favourable conditions, the
VP system in the study area appears to have weakened. Forest protection is notably
compromised and rules of extraction are not strictly followed by the local people.
Participation in VP activities is considerably lower than before.

The weakening of the VP system has been attributed by some scholars to top-down interference by the state, such as in imposition of workplans after promulgation of Joint Forest Management (JFM) in the Kumaon area in the 1990s (Sarin *et al.* 2003). During this period, significant sums of money became available from government for forest protection and management. Such commercial inputs created divides, strengthened elite capture and alienated the common person (Sarin *et al.* 2003). Existing forest committees that were actively protecting forests were bypassed in favour of committees formed under new rules, to which funding was also diverted. Microplans for forest working were recast in favour of commercial operations rather than to regenerate biomass for subsistence (Sarin *et al.* 2003). More field work is therefore required to study the history of such processes in our study villages.

The role of emerging markets for various NTFP and the emergence of cash-cropping as an important income source could also be instrumental in the way people in our study area perceive and look after their resources today, in comparison to two decades ago (Agrawal 2001; Linkenbach 2007; Sarkar 2008). Both our study villages are well connected to markets and this may be responsible for some of the social change seen in the area. Commodification intensifies internal fissures and elite capture, as evident in the resin collection processes in our study villages. A review by Rao *et al.* (2012) finds a number of instances globally where powerful economic forces and the growing monetisation of livelihoods have changed harvesting rates, livelihoods and settlement patterns (Armenteras *et al.* 2009; Peralta and Mather 2000; Shahabuddin 2010; Weinstein and Moegenburg 2004). For instance, in Brazil, Peralta and Mather (2000) found major changes in an extractive forest landscape over a 15-year period. From 1975 to 1985, a mainly extractive economy had transformed to a settled agricultural pattern, leading to increased deforestation. Similarly, in the marine realm, authors have found that use of customary closures in fishing communities, depended on distance to markets, degree of dependence on the resources, modernisation indices and population size (Cinner *et al.* 2007).

In our study villages too, adverse ecological changes are attributed by people to climate change and direct human agency related to commodification and development. Several respondents talked about changing cropping patterns, increasing human population, road-building, inappropriate construction activities, demographic pressure and pine invasion as other anthropogenic causes of ecological change. For instance, some people spoke of pine having been planted even inside the *van panchayats* by influential elites pursuing short-term profits (from resin tapping). Sale of property to outsiders such as from Delhi and the building of concrete structures at the edges of the forest and on slopes are also thought to adversely affect groundwater recharge and surface water flow. When asked whether VPs could possibly take action to stall such changes, older villagers complained about the negligence of village chiefs and changing focus on fast-earned cash income rather than replenishment and conservation of forest resources. Incentives for forest conservation can be lost due to evident degradation, reducing returns from agroforestry and competing livelihood activities.

Potential for strengthening forest conservation

Despite the evidence for forest degradation within the VP forests, there is still considerable potential for use and restoration of the forest in a sustainable way. While oak regeneration is compromised, and canopy cover and basal area are lower than expected, tree density has remained relatively stable in our study villages over time despite the evident weakening of the VP system. Also it is also evident that banj oak forests are patchily used and that some areas, including village forests, private forests and government-owned tracts, have been relatively protected from damaging activities (pers. obs.). These patches can serve as sources for restoration of forest over the long term as they tend to be refuges for habitat-restricted flora and fauna. The juxtaposition of managed forests to strictly protected forest patches in the larger landscape mosaic may also be contributing to the role of managed forests in conservation of other taxa such as birds (pers. obs.).

With support from compensatory mechanisms, financing of protection and planting activities, and awareness programmes, village institutions can be strengthened. With increased technical inputs, it may be possible to bring in forest management measures that can help revive oak forest from coppices and native seeds. Further, governmental and non-governmental programmes for forest conservation need to have increased local participation, if they are to have a better impact. It is essential that substitutes for fuelwood and leaf litter and more productive agroforestry techniques be researched and implemented so that the primary extractive pressures on forest can be reduced. Further, alternative sources of income such as ecotourism need to be nurtured locally. Some initiatives have already been undertaken in the study area in this direction (pers. comm. with CHIRAG). Importantly, the VP system needs to be delinked from the Joint Forest Management model that causes considerable confusion with respect to ownership and accountability for forest protection.

Role of micro-scale studies in CBC

Chronic anthropogenic disturbance may be an important variable to consider when understanding the long-term impacts of forest use in forest-dependent communities (Garcia and Pascal 2005; Sassen et al. 2015). Such impacts, which are not easily visible, tend to be overlooked when studies are restricted to indicators such as remotely sensed forest cover (as in Somanathan et al. 2009), carbon storage (Chhatre and Agrawal 2009) or perceptions of locals on forest regrowth (Agrawal 2005). For instance, carbon storage based on basal area of trees or remotely sensed forest cover may not reflect other important ecosystem services such as the provision of a diverse set of goods to local people. Mono-cultural or mono-dominant stands may have basal areas or canopy cover as high as native forests, but may not be able to supply the diversity of goods necessary for subsistence. Measuring outcomes in terms of people's perceptions (e.g. Nagendra 2007) may also miss biological nuances as local people are likely to notice changes only in variables that directly affect their livelihoods. For instance, most local residents may not notice or comment on changes in faunal species populations as they are not of consequence to local diets or household economy.

Our results reiterate the fact that there can be effects of extractive use on forest ecology that can be ascertained only by small-scale, plot-based studies that take into account ecological variables that are specific to the given ecosystem. From the more practical perspective, by differentiating among the different extractive activities and their specific impacts, it is possible to develop more directed and focused strategies for forest conservation in this part of Uttarakhand, a historically important area for CBC.

Acknowledgements

We are grateful to Narendra S. Raikwal, Vinay Nair, Deb Sukla, Amogh D. Rai and Pankhuri Chaudhury for assistance with data collection and to Rajkamal Goswami for preparing the map. The study was carried out while G. Shahabuddin was employed as a professor at Bharat Ratna Dr. B.R. Ambedkar University, Delhi and she is grateful for the support. CEDAR and Ambedkar University financially supported the project. Thanks are due to CHIRAG for enabling meetings and discussions with local forest councils and local residents.

References

Agrawal, A. 2001, 'Common property institutions and sustainable governance of resources', *World Development*, vol. 29, no. 10, pp. 1649–1672.

Agrawal, A. 2003, 'Sustainable governance of common-pool resources: Context, methods and politics', *Annual Review of Anthropology*, vol. 32, pp. 243–262.

Agrawal, A. 2005, *Environmentality*, Duke University Press, Durham, NC.

Armenteras, D., Rodriguez, N. and Retana, J. 2009, 'Are conservation strategies effective in avoiding the deforestation of the Colombian Guyana Shield?', *Biological Conservation*, vol. 142, no. 7, pp. 1411–1419.

Banerjee, A. 2007, 'Joint forest management in West Bengal', in *Forests, People and Power: Political Ecology of Reform in South Asia*, eds O. Springate-Baginski and P. Blaikie, Earthscan, London and Sterling, Delhi, pp. 221–260.

Baral, N., Stern, M.J. and Heinen, J.T. 2007, 'ICDP life-cycles in the Annapurna Conservation Area, Nepal: Is development overpowering conservation?' *Biodiversity and Conservation*, vol. 16, no. 10, pp. 2903–2917.

Berkes, F. 2009, 'Community conserved areas: Policy issues in historic and contemporary context', *Conservation Letters*, vol. 2, no. 1, pp. 19–24.

Bhagwat, S., Kushalappa, C., Williams, P. and Brown, N. 2005, 'The role of informal protected areas in maintaining biodiversity in the Western Ghats of India', *Ecology and Society*, vol. 10, no. 1, art. 8. www.ecologyandsociety.org/vol10/iss1/art8/ (accessed 17 August 2009).

Bray, D.B., Merino-Perez, L., Negreros-Castillo, P., Segura-Warnholtz, G., Torres-Rojo, J.M. and Vester, H.F.M. 2003, 'Mexico's community-managed forests as a global model for sustainable landscapes', *Conservation Biology*, vol. 17, no. 3, pp. 672–677.

Champion, H.G. and Seth, S.K. 1968, *A Revised Survey of the Forest Types of India*, Natraj Publishers, Dehradun (reprint).

Chhatre, A. and Agrawal, A. 2008, 'Forest commons and local enforcement', *Proceedings of the National Academy of Sciences*, vol. 105, no. 36, pp. 13286–13291.

Chhatre, A. and Agrawal, A. 2009, 'Trade-offs and synergies between carbon storage and livelihood benefits from forest commons', *Proceedings of the National Academy of Sciences*, vol. 106, no. 42, pp. 17667–17670.

Cinner, J.E., Sutton, S.G., and Bond, T.G. 2007, 'Socio-economic thresholds that affect use of customary fisheries management tools', *Conservation Biology*, vol. 21, no. 6, pp. 1603–1611.

Garcia, C.A. and Pascal, J.P. 2005, 'Sacred forests of Kodagu: Ecological value and social role', in *Ecological Nationalisms: Nature, Livelihoods and Identities in South Asia*, eds G. Cederlof and K. Sivaramakrishna, Permanent Black, New Delhi, pp. 199–232.

Linkenbach, A. 2007, *Forest Futures: Global Representation and Ground Realities in the Himalayas*, Permanent Black, New Delhi.

Nagendra, H. 2007, 'Drivers of reforestation in human-dominated forests', *Proceedings of the National Academy of Sciences*, vol. 104, no. 39, pp. 15218–15223.

Osuri, A.M., Madhusudan, M.D., Kumar, S.V., Chengappa, S.K., Kushalappa, C.G. and Sankaran, M. 2014, 'Spatio-temporal variation in forest cover and biomass across sacred groves in a human-modified landscape of India's Western Ghats', *Biological Conservation*, vol. 178, pp. 193–199.

Peralta, P. and Mather, P. 2000, 'An analysis of deforestation patterns in the extractive reserves of Acre, Amazonia from satellite imagery: A landscape ecological approach', *International Journal of Remote Sensing*, vol. 21, no. 13–14, pp. 2555–2570.

Persha, L., Agrawal, A. and Chhatre, A. 2011, 'Social and ecological synergy: Local rule-making, forest livelihoods and biodiversity conservation', *Science*, vol. 331, no. 6204, pp. 1606–1608.

Porter-Bolland, L., Ellis, E.A., Guariguata, M.R., Ruiz-Mallen, I., Negrete-Yankelevich, S. and Reyes-Garcia, V. 2012, 'Community managed forests and forest protected areas: An assessment of their conservation effectiveness across the tropics', *Forest Ecology and Management*, vol. 268, pp. 6–17.

Rao, M., Nagendra, H., Shahabuddin, G. and Carrasco, L.R. 2012, 'Integrating community managed areas into protected area systems: The promise of synergies and the reality of tradeoffs.' Proceedings of Conference on *Protected Areas: Are They Safeguarding Biodiversity?* Zoological Society of London, London, 8–9 November 2012.

Sarin, M., Singh, N.M., Sundar, N. and Bhogal, R.K. 2003, *Devolution as a Threat to Democratic Decision-making in Forestry? Findings from Three States in India*. Working paper 197, Overseas Development Institute, UK.

Sarkar, R. 2008, 'Decentralised forest governance in central Himalayas: A re-evaluation of outcomes', *Economic & Political Weekly*, vol. 43, no. 18, pp. 54–63.

Sassen, M., Sheil, D. and Giller, K.E. 2015, 'Fuelwood collection and its impacts on a protected tropical mountain forest in Uganda', *Forest Ecology and Management*, vol. 354, pp. 56–67.

Saxena, A.K. and Singh, J.S. 1984, 'Tree population structure of certain Himalayan forest associations and implications concerning their future composition', *Vegetatio*, vol. 58, no. 2, pp. 61–69.

Schwartzman, S. and Zimmerman, B. 2005, 'Conservation alliances with indigenous peoples of the Amazon', *Conservation Biology*, vol. 19, no. 3, pp. 721–727.

Shahabuddin, G. 2010, *Conservation at the Crossroads: Science, Society and the Future of India's Wildlife*, Permanent Black, Ranikhet and New India Foundation, Bengaluru, pp. 118–138.

Shahabuddin, G. and Kumar, R. 2005, 'Effects of biomass extraction on vegetation structure, diversity and composition of an Indian tropical dry forest', *Environmental Conservation*, vol. 32, no. 3, pp. 1–12.

Shahabuddin, G. and Rao, M. 2010, 'Do community-conserved areas effectively conserve biodiversity? Global insights and the Indian context', *Biological Conservation*, vol. 143, no. 12, pp. 2926–2936.

Singh, J.S. and Singh, S.P. 1987, 'Forest vegetation of the Himalaya', *The Botanical Review*, vol. 53, no. 1, pp. 80–192.

Singh, J.S. and Singh, S.P. 1992, *Forests of the Himalaya*, Gyanodaya Prakashan, Nainital.

Somanathan, E., Prabhakar, R. and Mehta, B.S. 2009, 'Decentralization for cost-effective conservation', *Proceedings of the National Academy of Sciences*, vol. 106, no. 11, pp. 4143–4147.

Thadani, R. 1999. *Disturbance, Microclimate and Competitive Dynamics of Tree Seedlings in Banj Oak Forests (Quercus leucotrichophora) of the Central Himalaya, India*, PhD Thesis, Yale University.

Thadani, R. and Ashton, P.M.S. 1995, 'Regeneration of banj oak in Central Himalaya', *Forest Ecology and Management*, vol. 78, pp. 217–224.

Uttarakhand Forest Department 2009, *Uttarakhand Forest Statistics*, UKFD, Dehradun.

Weinstein, S. and Moegenburg, S. 2004, 'Acai palm management in the Amazon estuary: Course for conservation or passage to plantation?', *Conservation and Society*, vol. 2, no. 2, pp. 315–346.

WWF International 2009. WWF Global Ecoregions, Western Himalayan Temperate Forests. *Available* from http://wwf.panda.org/about_our_earth/ecoregions/westhima layan_temperate_forests.cfm (accessed 20 September 2017).

7 Rethinking landscapes

History, culture and local knowledge in the Biligiri Rangaswamy Temple Tiger Reserve, India

Nitin D. Rai and C. Madegowda

Introduction

State management of forests and biodiversity in India has had a contested history that initially involved British interests in timber, and subsequently independent India's state-making efforts at controlling land and forests. The resulting marginalisation of forest dwelling communities was premised on their role as users and thus the conflict between state imperatives and local desires. Gadgil and Guha (1992) have provided convincing accounts of the control of forests by the Indian forest administration. The curtailment of local access was based on the idea that the use of forests by local people has adverse ecological impacts. Colonial forest administrators based their impressions of local forest practices on received notions of wilderness. Such practices as fire, shifting cultivation and biomass extraction were variably restricted in state-controlled forests. Shifting cultivation and the extensive use of fire to clear forests was thought to be ravaging lush forests (Williams 2003). Draconian forest laws were passed to control forests and to check swidden farmers whose cultivation practice was blamed for much of the forest degradation. The power of this framing of the idea that local use is bad for forests continues to dictate conservation policy. The cordoning off of areas that are rich in biodiversity and the subsequent declaration of protected areas has been the focus of the state's conservation efforts.

Maps have played an important role in forest control, management and exploitation (Crampton 2009). The control of forests was enabled through a systematic accumulation of knowledge on forest management and the production of maps that showed only those elements that were of interest to the accumulation process. Maps contained topographic features and administrative borders that were necessary to manage and territorialise. The history of local people's residence, cultural relationships, ecological practices and knowledge was undermined, erased and unacknowledged in the management of the forest. Conservation plans were drawn up based on centralised ideas of measures that included fire suppression, tourism development, ban on forest produce harvest, and establishing inviolate areas. The marginalisation of indigenous communities and the erasure of local practice and landscape history is a carefully orchestrated exercise in vesting control of forests.

The cordoning off was possible in part due to the cartographic tools and techniques that independent India inherited from the British. The role of the state's scientific apparatus has long been acknowledged as being part of the process of establishing control. The use of maps, records and plans are central to this project (Peluso 1993). The British had left behind an immensely successful mapping enterprise that had produced large-scale topographic maps for the entire country that were the basis for planning. During forestry operations forests were divided into compartments, blocks, beats, ranges, divisions and circles. Maps played a crucial role in these demarcations. The reworking of the forest area into these units created a geography that was different from that of local users. The absence of local cultural features and names meant the slow erosion and negation of local presence from official documents and records. The subsequent displacement and sedentarisation of forest dwellers resulted in their invisibilisation and loss of customary connections to the forest. The scientific approach to forest administration was immensely successful in generating income for the state through timber production. The long-term impacts on livelihoods and culture of local, especially *adivasi*, people was dramatic and is only now beginning to be addressed.

The state's appropriation of forests has not gone unchallenged. There have been a growing number of local efforts to regain access and control over landscapes. Such efforts have taken a range of forms including using legal provisions, direct confrontation, everyday acts of resistance and building of a narrative that local people are good stewards of forests. The production of maps that demarcates indigenous lands to counter state maps has seen some resurgence. As Bernard Nietschmann (1995: 37) famously wrote, 'more indigenous territory can be reclaimed and defended with maps than by guns'.

In this chapter we describe an effort in a protected area that aims to produce a counter map that locates cultural sites and areas. The main purpose of the mapping effort was to produce an alternate idea of forest landscapes and rethink the place of local people in forest landscapes. We felt the need to facilitate nascent efforts of forest dwellers in seeking rights and restoration of customary practice. There is now a growing critique of participatory mapping and we would like to engage with this critique. Bryan (2015: 249) says that counter maps are 'defined by the forms of power and economy that they otherwise contest' and yet we agree that 'counter-mapping is a practice that we cannot say "no" to, and yet must call into question' (Wainwright 2008: 269). We describe a participatory mapping initiative in the Biligiri Rangaswamy Temple Tiger Reserve to demonstrate that mapping could play a significant political role in the assertion of rights and identity. We also call the readers' attention to the many critiques of mapping that suggest that the road to a counter map is unevenly paved.

The context

The Biligiri Rangaswamy Temple Tiger Reserve (BRT), covers an area of 540 km², and is located in the state of Karnataka, India and was declared a wildlife sanctuary in 1974 and a tiger reserve in 2011. 'Biligiri' (or white hill in the local Kannada language) refers to either the white rock face that constitutes the major hill crowned with the temple of Lord Rangaswamy, or from the white mist that covers the hills for a greater part of the year. Located at the confluence of the Western and Eastern Ghats, BRT is an area of high biodiversity. The western hills have an average elevation of 1,350 m while the eastern hills, forming a high ridge, have an average elevation of about 1,650 m and an average annual precipitation of 1,362 ± 159 mm (Setty *et al.* 2008).

BRT has a diversity of vegetation types including scrub, dry and moist deciduous forests, evergreen forests, shola and high-altitude grasslands, supporting a variety of fauna. BRT supports 776 species of higher plants (Kamathy *et al.* 1967), and 245 species of birds have been recorded here (Aravind *et al.* 2001). The forests form an important wildlife corridor between the Western Ghats and the Eastern Ghats, linking the largest populations of Asian elephant in southern India. The Soligas, a scheduled tribe, live in the Biligiri Rangaswamy Temple Tiger Reserve and surrounding hills of Chamrajnagar district. They have traditionally been shifting cultivators and dependent on the forest especially for tubers and honey. This use of the forest for livelihoods and cultural practice has resulted in a nuanced understanding of forest function and management. This local knowledge has not been incorporated into current management strategies of the sanctuary with the result that forest has undergone considerable change in species composition and stem densities (Sundaram and Hiremath 2012).

Myth has it that the ancestor of the Soligas, *Karraya* (from whom the Soligas claim descendence), was born in a bamboo cylinder. The name Soliga literally means 'from bamboo'. Soligas have different *kulas* (ancestral clans) with presiding deities, and each *kula* ascribed particular responsibilities. Thus the concept of *kulas* or clans evolved and out-marriage between *kulas* became the norm. The elders assert that there are no hierarchies among *kulas* as it is only a functional mode of allocating responsibilities for better administration. Marriages are only allowed between *kulas* not within each. In BRT the Soligas belong to six clans (Baleyaru, Teneyaru, Suriru, Beliru, Halaru, and Selikuru). The Soligas identify five types of sacred sites: *'devaru'* (god), *'marama'* (goddess), *'veeru'* (hero spirit), *'kallu'* (burial stones) and *'habbi'* (spring).

The establishment of the sanctuary in 1974 resulted in the displacement of the Soligas from their land and loss of access to their traditional agricultural practices. They were allowed to continue harvesting selected forest produce for sale and household use. Shifting cultivation and the use of fire was, however, banned. The Soligas were relocated to colonies close to roads and in areas that were considered marginal for wildlife such as scrub and arid areas near the boundary of the sanctuary. This displacement has disrupted their way of life both materially and culturally. To further exacerbate their problems an amendment to the Wildlife Protection Act in 2002 banned the commercial sale of forest product. This had adverse impacts on the health and wellbeing of the Soligas through the loss of their main cash-earning possibility (Madegowda 2009).

Counter mapping in the Biligiri Rangaswamy Temple Tiger Reserve

> A landscape ethnography emerges . . . which would read history back into the seemingly natural text of nature.
>
> (Arturo Escobar 1999)

The mapping of the cultural sites of the Soligas was initiated as part of our enquiry into the role of Soliga traditional institutions in conservation. A two-day workshop on the structure of customary institutions as well as on the cultural ecology of the Soligas resulted in a collaborative project that mapped their cultural sites using global positioning system (GPS) devices. The often unrecognised aspects of indigenous livelihoods are the cultural practices and traditional systems of justice and governance. The work included documenting practices and mapping cultural sites to explore how these might be used to claim rights as well as evolve systems of forest management. We mapped 593 sites in the 540 km^2 of the tiger reserve. The team consisted entirely of Soligas who received training in the use of GPS devices. The team relied on the expert knowledge of Soliga elders who located sites in interior forest. Often the location of certain sites was known only to a few Soligas, due to sites being clan-specific and now being visited less and less by Soligas due to their being relocated far from these sites when the protected area was established.

The Soligas have demarcated areas of forest known as a *yelle*.[1] Each *yelle* contains five sacred sites that are specific to a *kula* and are protected and guided by the presence of gods and spirits. *Yelle* are thus *kula*-specific boundaries within which forest areas have been named. *Yelle* demarcate areas of cultural significance and are not territorial. Ongoing interviews with the Soligas show that *yelle* are cultural spaces that housed the five sacred sites and that the *yelle* were subdivided among the clans based on requirement for the cultural practice of members of particular clans that did not have a cultural space close to their dwelling. Mapping has revealed that the entire forest area within the sanctuary is comprised of 46 *yelle*. Further, each patch of forest within each *yelle* has a name, making it possible for the Soligas to map orally the extent of each *yelle*. We have so far identified and mapped 1,127 forest patches as named by Soliga informants.

A preliminary version of the map showing the location of sacred sites for all clans was shared with Soliga elders, some of whom held customary office, and younger Soligas who are politically active in the indigenous rights movement. The reactions to the map were unanimously enthusiastic with all present seeking to widely distribute the map among government agencies, schools and in as many public fora as possible. The invisibilisation of Soligas within the landscape as a result of conservation and colonial forestry policy has systematically erased Soligas from maps, state documents and management plans. The mapping of their cultural sites on a map presented an opportunity for a renewed assertion of their place in the landscape.

Interestingly, while there was agreement on the need for a map of cultural sites, there was a difference in opinion on the mapping of *yelle*. Older Soligas, who were part of the customary institutions, saw the identification of *yelle* boundaries as an opportunity to rejuvenate the *kula* system with its traditional office and cultural practice. They hoped to see Soliga customary law reinstated. Soliga elders visualised the *yelle* as a boundary within which the five cultural sites – *devaru, kallugudi, veeru, samadhi* and *habbi* – were located. A few younger Soligas, aware of the legal provisions for claiming rights under the Recognition of the Forest Rights Act 2006 (FRA), were excited about using the sacred site maps as evidence to reassert local control in the landscape for livelihoods and identity. They did not, however, see value in drawing *yelle* as they felt that this might show demarcations within the forest rather than consolidation of rights over the entire forest. A few Soligas who do not have *yelle* near their village due to being displaced were also resistant to the idea of mapping *yelle* fearing that this might result in territorialisation of the forest and that they might be left with no access to the forest if clan-specific access rights were vested. The elders prevailed on the others suggesting that not demarcating *yelle* would attract reprobation from their gods. This silenced the detractors into agreeing to map the *yelle*.

With such a map, Soligas believe that they would be able to enter the forest unhindered and use the forest without the restrictions imposed by state policy, including the ban on NTFP collection. Soligas reiterated that the map demonstrated that Soligas have lived in the forest for long, managed the forest and named places within it. They noted that the naming of these places preserved these sites in memory as much as on the ground. Naming the forest they said was reflective of their ownership of the forest. The mapping process drew responses on the use and management of the forest in addition to locating Soliga cultural sites and practice in the forest. They recounted their use of the forest before displacement, such as the use of fire, the collection of various products and hunting practices which were permitted by the earlier ruler of the area and by the British. They contrasted the uses that the forest was being put to by them, the ruler and the British; for resources and cultivation, for hunting and for plantation activities and timber respectively.

The FRA aims to grant rights to tribal and other forest-dwelling communities to land for habitation and cultivation, forest produce, right to protect, regenerate, conserve or manage forest resources, and other rights customarily enjoyed by forest-dwelling tribes. The FRA also provides the unprecedented opportunity for collaborative forest management between forest dwellers and the state. Soligas have been energetic about claiming rights under the FRA to reassert their space in the management of the forest, gain access to their cultural sites within the forest and restore lost livelihoods. The provisions in the act that enable forest dwellers to claim rights to conserve the forest and to traditional and cultural practices are progressive and democratic. State authorities have, however, been slow in granting rights and have dissuaded Soliga efforts to claim rights.

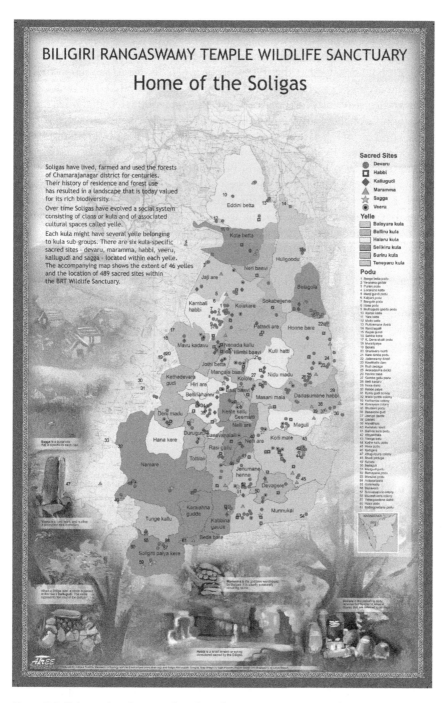

Figure 7.1 Soliga cultural sites within the Biligiri Rangaswamy Temple Tiger Reserve

The mapping effort coincided with the process to claim a range of rights under the FRA. Soligas were interested in the possibility that their situated knowledge might be used to manage the forest. Soligas have been particularly concerned about the spread of *Lantana camara*, an invasive species in the forest. They strongly believe that the spread of the species is due to the suppression of their management practices when the sanctuary was established. A major practice was the use of early season fires to keep the undergrowth open and maintain a savannah woodland. In the past they burnt the entire areas of the forest each year. The ban on the use of fire along with the ban on swidden cultivation has had enormous livelihood impacts. The ban on swidden cultivation reduced, and for some even eliminated farm production. The lack of fire use reduced the availability of tubers from the forest. The lack of fire and swidden agriculture has also over time changed the forest structure and composition. Soligas claim that the spread of the lantana is a result of these change in management practices. There is little being done to reduce lantana densities in BRT by the Forest Department. Lantana is only being removed on either side of roads to ensure visibility for tourists to view wildlife. Soligas argue that areas of the forest that are vulnerable to weed invasion should be targeted for *Lantana* removal. Soligas suggest that efforts to remove lantana should be focused on *hulu kadu* (savanna woodland) as *hulu kadu* was critical for wildlife as well as being susceptible to lantana invasion. Such local ecological knowledge is crucial for the long-term as well as adaptive management of the forest, which could combine well with more conventional scientific and state-mandated approaches. A map of the BRT representing Soliga vegetation categories was therefore produced to help with such management interventions. The map shows the Soliga names of the broad categories of vegetation and their extent in BRT in order to inform forest management.

The pulls and pitfalls of counter mapping

In an original analysis of counter mapping Nancy Peluso (1995: 403) states that

> local notions of territoriality . . . will further change as a result of mapping. Yet given the alternate futures – of not being on the map, as it were, being obscured from view and having local claims obscured, there almost seems to be no choice.

While the answer to the question of whether *adivasis* should map is an emphatic yes, we would like to draw attention to some concerns that need to be addressed as *adivasis* map their lands.

The BRT counter map was produced to challenge the forest administration's efforts to enforce inviolate protected areas and relocate people from these areas. The case for relocation of people is being made solely on the basis of the ecological argument that people's residence and use of forests will adversely affect wildlife densities. The map complicates this idea and makes the point that Soligas have historically been part of this landscape, and have a cultural as well as ecological relationship to the landscape that needs to be taken into consideration when conservation plans are being drawn up for an area.

The map of Soliga cultural sites and areas was an attempt to include indigenous people in the colonial and state map. We hoped that such an effort would complicate the dominant idea that conservation landscapes should be managed for biodiversity values alone. This dominant conservation approach has marginalised and displaced local people to produce 'inviolate' landscapes. We hoped that Soligas might be able to use the map as evidence for community rights over their customary area as well as produce a narrative of forests as socio-cultural and ecological landscapes. The mapping has had positive outcomes such as its being used as evidence during the process of claiming community rights to the forest. In the intervening years since the map was produced and during the presentation of this map and the mapping process at meetings and academic gatherings we have been asked various critical questions that have made us rethink our initial premises.

The literature on mapping has been growing, particularly papers by Nancy Peluso (1995), Joel Wainwright (2008) and Joe Bryan (2015). We now reflect on this effort noting that 'we must counter-map, and yet relentlessly critique those maps, always reading towards the concepts and strategies that will produce the strongest and most radically open, anticolonial modes of worlding the world' (Wainwright 2008: 272). Peluso (1995) made the first effort to direct these critical reflections by posing questions of counter mapping:

> How did the new maps reflect prior spatial configurations of power produced under colonial administration? How did mapping "reinvent" traditions relating to customary access to land and resources? And, how did the role of NGOs – to say nothing of academics and development agencies – alter community access to land and resources in all aspects of the mapping process, from their production to dissemination?
>
> (Bryan 2015: 255)

The political role that such a map plays was well understood by many of the Soligas who attended the meetings in which we discussed the map prior to mapping; a few Soligas who were aware of the territorial configurations of maps were worried about how demarcating clan areas on maps might create conflict among clans as *yelle* could be mistaken for territories rather than cultural zones. The state imaginary of these landscapes as territories could not be ignored. Such a dominant reading of maps conflicts with the social and cultural imaginary of the Soligas. The map has now been printed and has been in circulation for a few years and it might be time to assess the social and political outcomes of the map.

A major critique of counter maps are that they are linked to territorialisation given that they are 'destined to reproduce Cartesian understandings of space configured into nested scales of state sovereignty and private property' (Bryan 2015: 255). Jefferson Fox and colleagues note that participatory mapping has 'ironic effects' such as increased conflicts among indigenous groups, increased privatisation of land, loss of indigenous conceptions of space and increased regulation by the state (Fox *et al.* 2005). The question that we will now ask of this effort is if such a cultural map might still fall prey to the territorial imaginaries of the state and market?

This might very well be true for the many mapping initiatives that are now ongoing in India under the FRA during the process of granting community rights to forest land. Much of the mapping is being led by NGOs that have stated interests in ensuring property rights for local people. Such mapping brings forest dwellers directly under state control. The gains from mapping for local people such as better rights and governance could potentially be offset by the incorporation of customary practice and spatiality into the state machinery. Another often identified problem with mapping customary forest boundaries and land use is that maps tend to fix and simplify practices that are dynamic and complex (Roth 2007).

The BRT map is not territorial nor does it depict land use, but shows cultural connection to landscape. This might be the first step to an alternate spatiality that undermines state efforts to territorialise landscapes. The Soligas were clear that the lines that are described on the map are not territorial but cultural areas demarcated to house sites of cultural significance. Unlike most mapping efforts that are linked to restoring or granting rights, this one began as an effort to locate significant cultural sites and zones on a map. This is a departure from most counter mapping initiatives. The zones demarcate the areas linked (but not controlled) to clans of one indigenous community.

Our role as researchers and activists in this effort deserves some discussion. The technical expertise, the money to support the effort, the printing and dissemination of the final map were all enabled through funds obtained by our research institution, ATREE, from the Tata Trusts and the Ford Foundation. The map was envisaged first by researchers on the team and therefore does not reflect the imaginary of the Soligas. This explains to some extent the lack of enthusiasm that has been shown for the map subsequent to its publication and beyond its immediate use in the rights claiming process. For instance there has not been an aggressive distribution of the map despite copies being available for free.

A close reading of the literature on counter mapping suggests that the lack of ownership of the map by Soligas might be due to the following factors: the map does not translate into a direct territorial reconfiguration; the map records location of cultural sites and not the social process associated with either the mapping or the cultural norms associated with the site; and the map is Cartesian and therefore not easily interpretable. This throws up questions of how the mapping process might be made more inclusive of local perspectives and fully owned by local people. Sletto (2014: 369) suggests that rather than seeing the map as a 'product for instrumental ends' mapping should be viewed as 'social process'. The mapping process should also capture the memories, meanings and stories that are associated with the place being mapped. In BRT we recorded stories and memories associated with many of the sites that were mapped. While we produced the map as a product, the stories have not been shared. The rethinking of the map as a social process and practice will give powerful and new meaning to landscapes than the ones that the forest and conservation administration is now purveying. Soligas and *adivasis* need therefore to map relentlessly, imbuing each map with new and powerful meaning.

Note

1 While the word used often in conversation is *yelle* many respondents referred to this as *jaaga* which translates to place or land. In using the word *jaaga* a stronger association is made with the demarcated forest than the term *yelle*, which translates as boundary or area. *Soliga* respondents who used the word *jaaga* stated rather strongly that the forest was historically theirs and that they were being denied rights to their land. The word *yelle* seemed to be devoid of the weight and yearning for their ancestral land.

References

Aravind, N.A., Rao, D., and Madhusudan, P.S. 2001. Additions to the birds of Biligiri Rangaswamy Temple Wildlife Sanctuary, Western Ghats, India. *Zoos' Print Journal* 27(7): 541–547.

Bryan, J. 2015. *Routledge Handbook of Political Ecology*, edited by Thomas Perreault, Gavin Bridge and James McCarthy. Routledge, Abingdon, Oxon.

Crampton, J.W. 2009. *Mapping: A Critical Introduction to Cartography and GIS*. Blackwell, Malden, MA.

Escobar, A. 1999. After nature: Steps to an anti-essentialist political ecology. *Current Anthropology* 40(1): 1–30.

Fox, J., Suryanata, K., and Hershock, P. 2005. *Mapping Communities: Ethics, Values and Practice*. East West Center, Honolulu, HI.

Gadgil, M., and Guha, R. 1992. *This Fissured Land: An Ecological History of India*. Oxford University Press, Delhi.

Kamathy, R.V., Rao, A.S., and Rao, R.S. 1967. A contribution to the flora of Biligirirangan Hills, Mysore State. *Bulletin of the Botanical Survey of India* 9: 206–224.

Madegowda, C. 2009. Traditional knowledge and conservation. *Economic & Political Weekly* 44: 65–69.

Nietschmann, B.Q. 1995. Defending the Miskito reefs with maps and GPS: Mapping with sail, scuba and satellite. *Cultural Survival Quarterly* 18(4): 34–37.

Peluso, N.L. 1993. Coercing conservation? The politics of state resource control. *Global Environmental Change* 3(2): 199–218.

Peluso, N.L. 1995. Whose woods are these? Counter-mapping forest territories in Kalimantan, Indonesia. *Antipode* 27(4): 383–406.

Roth, R. 2007. Two-dimensional maps in multi-dimensional worlds: A case of community-based mapping in Northern Thailand. *Geoforum* 38: 49–59.

Setty, R.S., Bawa, K., Ticktin, T., and Madegowda, C. 2008. Evaluation of a participatory resource monitoring system for nontimber forest products: The case of *amla* (*Phyllanthus* spp.) fruit harvest by Soligas in South India. *Ecology and Society* 13(2): art. 19.

Sletto, B.I., 2014, Cartographies of remembrance and becoming in the Sierra de Perijá, Venezuela. *Transactions of the Institute of British Geographers* 39(3): 360–372.

Sundaram, B., and Hiremath, A.J. 2012. *Lantana camara* invasion in a heterogeneous landscape: patterns of spread and correlation with changes in native vegetation. *Biological Invasions* 14(6): 1127–1141.

Wainwright, J. 2008. *Decolonizing Development: Colonial Power and the Maya*. Blackwell, Malden, MA.

Williams, M. 2003. Deforesting the Earth: From Prehistory to Global Crisis. University of Chicago Press, Chicago.

8 Conservation and development

Beyond national parks and sanctuaries

Sushil Saigal, Swati Chaliha, Chetna Nahata and Sunpreet Kaur

Introduction

Being a megadiverse country that is also home to the world's largest population of the poor, the synergies and trade-offs between conservation and development are a major issue of debate in India. The idea of protection of the environment, including biodiversity, is enshrined in the Constitution of India (Articles 48-A and 51-A (g)). The Article 48-A lays down the state's responsibility for protection of environment and reads as follows: 'The State shall endeavour to protect and improve the environment and to safeguard the forests and wildlife of the country'. Article 51-A (g) mentions that environmental protection is a fundamental duty of every citizen of the country and reads as follows: 'It shall be the duty of every citizen of India to protect and improve the natural environment including forests, lakes, rivers and wild life, and to have compassion for living creatures'. Over the past several decades, especially since the 1970s, India has developed a fairly robust legislative and policy framework for conservation. The establishment of Protected Areas (PAs) has been the key strategy adopted by the country to translate the framework into actions on the ground. IUCN (International Union for Conservation of Nature) defines a PA as a 'clearly defined geographical space, recognized, dedicated and managed, through legal and other effective means, to achieve the long-term conservation of nature with associated ecosystem services and cultural values'. The Wildlife (Protection) Act, which came into force in 1972, was the first major legislative move by the central government of independent India to protect the country's biodiversity, and indeed the environment. This Act enabled the constitution and management of specified areas as PAs and prescribed activities that were allowed or disallowed. The two key categories of PAs established under the Wildlife Act were National Parks (NPs) and Wildlife Sanctuaries (WLSs). In India, the term PA became synonymous with the terms NP/WLS and these are still often used interchangeably.

The NPs and WLSs have attracted disproportionate attention for conservation, while there are many other lesser known categories of PAs, which have not been adequately studied to assess their role in conservation. The central government has played a proactive role in the establishment of these categories, especially since 1976 when 'Forests' and 'Protection of wild animals and birds' were added to the Concurrent List (List III) of the Constitution of India through the Constitution (Forty-Second) Amendment Act. These subjects were hitherto in the domain of the state governments.

These lesser known PA categories include those that have been established as a result of international initiatives, conventions or treaties, as well as those notified in accordance with domestic laws. Examples of the former include Biosphere Reserves (BRs), Ramsar Sites and World Heritage Sites (WHS). Examples of the latter include Conservation Reserves and Community Reserves under the Wildlife (Protection) Amendment Act, 2002; Biodiversity Heritage Sites (BHS) under the Biological Diversity Act, 2002; Eco-sensitive Zones (ESZs) and Coastal Regulation Zones (CRZs) under the Environment (Protection) Act, 1986 (amended 1991); and Critical Wildlife Habitats (CWH) under the Scheduled Tribes and Other Traditional Forest Dwellers (Recognition of Forest Rights) Act, 2006. In addition to PAs designated specifically for biodiversity conservation, large areas of India are notified as 'Reserved' and 'Protected' forests under the Indian Forest Act or relevant State Forest Acts, which are also of considerable conservation value. Since conservation is not stated as the explicit primary objective for designation of such forests, these have not been discussed in this chapter.

This chapter is an attempt towards documenting the experience with various lesser known categories of PAs (other than NPs and WLSs), and to analyse their conservation and development outcomes. The remainder of the chapter is divided into four sections. The first section explores the PA designations notified as a result of international initiatives, while the PA designations notified as a result of national laws are presented in the second section. The case study of Okhla Bird Sanctuary (OBS) ESZ is discussed in the third section. The key lessons that have emerged from the experience of lesser known PAs are discussed in the concluding section.

International categories

The objective of this section is to explore the conservation and development outcomes of different protection regimes notified in accordance with international initiatives, conventions or treaties such as Ramsar Sites, BRs and WHSs.

Ramsar Sites

Ramsar Sites are wetlands designated under the International Convention on Wetlands or the Ramsar Convention, adopted at Ramsar, Iran in 1971 (Ramsar 2014a). These sites are considered to be of international importance as they are representative of rare or unique wetland types, and crucial for conserving biological diversity. The Convention provides the framework for national action and international cooperation for the conservation and wise use of wetlands, which include areas of marsh, fen, peatland or water, whether natural or artificial, with water that is static or flowing, fresh, brackish, including areas of marine water the depth of which at low tide does not exceed six metres (Ramsar 2016).

There are over 2,000 Ramsar Sites in over 160 countries that are Parties to the Convention (Ramsar 2014b). The Ramsar Sites are designated based on a set of nine criteria, which emphasise the biodiversity value of wetlands (Ramsar 2014c). The Ramsar Convention is the only global environment treaty dealing with a particular ecosystem (i.e. wetlands) supporting distinct flora and fauna. India has designated 26 Ramsar Sites, out of which 24 have a management plan (Ramsar 2015). Although the Ramsar Convention recognises cautious management of the listed wetlands, many Ramsar Sites in India are facing various threats, including rapid urbanisation.

The plight of Deepor Beel, a Ramsar wetland on the outskirts of Guwahati city in Assam, is an example of how urbanisation is adversely affecting the wetland's biodiversity and other ecosystem services. This wetland is under serious threat due to leaching from the nearby Boragaon solid waste dumping site of the Guwahati Municipal Corporation. Moreover, industrial and sewer wastewater from the 'natural' channels of the River Brahmaputra feeding the wetland have led to wastewater accumulation and reduced the dissolved oxygen content of the wetland. Several colonies of Greater Adjutant Stork, an endangered bird existing in and around Deepor Beel, are being affected due to the degrading water quality and other ecological parameters. Unfortunately, the garbage dumps have become the main foraging grounds of the storks and use of pesticides in these dumps negatively affects this bird population (Konwar 2016). Although, following repeated objections from various environmental groups, the Guwahati Municipal Corporation agreed to shift the landfill site to another location in 2015 and alternative sites were also explored, no significant action was taken on the ground until June 2016 (Mr R Choudhury 2016, pers. comm., 18 July). The population of endangered Greater Adjutant Stork that resides in these areas constitutes more than half of the total world population. This fact alone should have led to greater conservation efforts but unfortunately the wetland continues to grapple with numerous challenges in spite of being designated a Ramsar Site (Jamwal 2015; Assam Tribune 2014; Times of India 2015).

East Kolkata Wetlands, a part of the delta system of the River Ganges and situated in the city of Kolkata, is another Ramsar Site that faces a similar plight due to urbanisation. Once known for the unique traditional practice of utilising wastewater through its fish ponds as a model of sustainable resource recovery, this wetland faces increasing stress due to poor land use planning and pollution (Mukherjee 2015). The ecology of the wetlands has undergone drastic changes in response to the changing salinity regimes. Over the years, the floral and faunal species diversity has reduced significantly. The wetland faces other risks from unsustainable ground water use and increased heavy metal content in the sewage. Thus, in spite of being a Ramsar Site, the East Kolkata Wetlands are among the most threatened ecosystems (Bhattacharya *et al.* 2012).

Figure 8.1 Greater Adjutant Storks (*Leptoptilos dubius*) on garbage dump at Deepor Beel, Guwahati, Assam, India

Source: Dr Raju Kasambe, 2015, via Wikimedia Commons. Used under Creative Commons Attribution-Share Alike 4.0 International license

Biosphere Reserves

The origin of the concept of BRs dates back to the UNESCO (United Nations Educational, Scientific and Cultural Organization) Biosphere Conference, which was held in 1968 (UNESCO 1993). The Man and the Biosphere (MAB) programme was launched in 1971 as a direct result of the conference (UNESCO 2016a). Various MAB projects focused on establishing a coordinated world network of sites representing the main ecosystems of the planet in which genetic resources would be protected, and where research on ecosystems as well as monitoring and training work could be carried out. These sites were named BRs (UNESCO 1973). In 1974, the criteria and guidelines for the choice and establishment of BRs were released by the UNESCO Task Force (UNESCO 1974).

The primary objective of BRs is to focus on overall preservation of plant and animal diversity within natural and semi-natural ecosystems, to provide areas for ecological and environmental research, and to provide facilities for education and training. BRs are natural and cultural landscapes extending over terrestrial and/or aquatic ecosystems. BRs are bio-geographic zones established to promote a well-balanced relationship between social and ecological systems, including conflict prevention and management of biodiversity.

Each BR fulfils three complementary and mutually reinforcing functions: sustainable conservation of the area, economic development of the local communities and promotion of research and information exchange. In order to undertake complementary activities of biodiversity conservation and sustainable management, BRs are demarcated into three inter-related zones. These zones are (i) natural or core zone, which is to be kept absolutely undisturbed; (ii) manipulation or buffer zone, which surrounds the core zone and where ecologically sound practices are permitted (e.g. research and ecotourism); and (iii) transition zone, which is usually not delimited and is a flexible zone of cooperation fostering economic and human development (MoEF 2007a).

BRs were thus envisaged as special environments for both people and nature, which could provide living examples of how human beings and nature can co-exist while respecting each others' needs. These areas are internationally recognised within the framework of UNESCO's MAB programme after receiving the consent of the participating country. The world's major ecosystem types and landscapes are represented in this network.

In India, the national Biosphere Reserve Programme was initiated in 1986 (MoEF 2007a) and a national MAB Committee was constituted as the apex authority to advise on UNESCO's MAB programme. However, no separate legal provision has been made for BRs, which are established within the framework of existing laws and policies. Therefore, the legal status of land included in the BRs is not affected and the zonation structure envisaged in the international documents is rarely, if ever, followed on the ground. There are 18 notified BRs in India, which overlap with other categories of PAs such as NPs and WLSs (MoEF 2016). This has major implications for the actual outcomes of the BRs, as illustrated by the following two examples.

The Nilgiri BR was the first BR to be established in India in 1986 (CPREEC 2015). It is located in the Nilgiri Hills range in southern India, which is a popular tourism site in the country (Daniels 1992). The designation of the area as a BR hasn't had any significant mitigating impact on mass tourism and its negative consequences for the environment as well as local communities. Many local communities are of the opinion that mass tourism has caused degradation of natural habitats and most of the economic benefits have been cornered by a small section of private hotel entrepreneurs or tour organisers with the locals mainly engaged in relatively less-paying hawking and vending jobs.

Located in the state of Uttarakhand in northern India, the Nanda Devi BR was established in January 1988 in the high altitude Himalayan region covering an area of 2,236 km^2 (Bosak 2008). The Nanda Devi BR area encompasses two NPs: the Valley of Flowers NP and the Nanda Devi NP. As the BR straddles two NPs, the stringent legal provisions related to NPs override the zonation envisaged for BRs. This has led to conflict with local Bhotia tribal communities, who perceive the imposed restrictions to be detrimental to their livelihoods and culture (Rao et al. 2000).

The experience of the Nilgiri and Nanda Devi BRs illustrates the vast difference between the global conceptualisation and local implementation of the BR concept. Although the BR concept envisages zonation with different levels of protection and sustainable use, it has been notional in practice with the actual activities being determined by the legal status of the land. For example, most extractive uses are prohibited in a NP.

Figure 8.2 Increasing inflow of tourists affecting the ecology of Nilgiri Biosphere
        Reserve, India

Source: Rajiv Ashrafi, 2016 (Flickr), via PhotoPin. Used under Attribution-NonCommercial-Share
Alike 2.0 Generic licence

World Heritage Sites

UNESCO adopted the Convention concerning the Protection of the World
Cultural and Natural Heritage in 1972 (UNESCO 2016b). It came into force
in 1977 with objectives to (i) define the World Heritage in both cultural and
natural aspects; (ii) enlist natural sites and monuments from the member
countries, which are of exceptional global value, the protection of which is
the concern of all humanity; and (iii) promote cooperation among all nations
and people to contribute to the protection of these sites for future generations
(UNESCO 1972).

As per the World Heritage Resource Manual, the World Heritage listing
requires that the quality and condition of a site should be maintained and, if
possible, enhanced in the future. Since these sites are of global importance, the
member countries are conferred the responsibility of achieving the conservation
objectives.

India has been an active member of the Convention since 1977 and has 35
World Heritage Sites, out of which 27 are cultural sites, seven are natural sites
while one site is of both cultural and natural importance (UNESCO 2016c).

Frey and Steiner (2011) opine that the World Heritage List has a strong
positive effect by (i) drawing global attention to prominent examples of our heritage and (ii) by promoting protection and conservation of the specified sites.

However, Jha (2005) found that the World Heritage recognition does not totally protect natural sites because a number of complex issues such as development, commercial interests, politics, ideology and the state of social order are involved.

This point can be illustrated through the case of Manas WHS in the state of Assam. It was declared a WHS in 1985 but faced major threats soon thereafter due to ethnic unrest and conflict in the region. In 1992, it was put on the list of 'sites in danger' and continued to be on this list until 2011 (UNESCO 2016d). During this period, it faced major challenges in the form of poaching and illegal extraction of various natural resources. The area also faced decline in its water sources leading to a shift towards a drier vegetation. Sarma et al. (2008) attributed these land-use changes to poor and ineffective habitat management activities. Although the ethnic conflict has subsided to a large extent, other significant challenges remain. In a survey conducted by WWF, titled 'Protecting People through Nature', Manas was listed among WHS facing threats from developmental activities (WWF 2016).

The case of Manas WHS shows that while designation of an area under an international category does lead to better recognition at national and international levels, it is not sufficient to ensure effective conservation and sustainable management on the ground. Further, the Manas WHS also had other international and national designations such as BR, Important Bird Area (IBA), NP, WLS, Tiger Reserve, and Elephant Reserve (UNESCO 2016d). Therefore, it is not clear what further value each additional designation adds to conservation and livelihood outcomes.

National categories

The objective of this section is to explore the conservation and development outcomes of various categories of PAs other than NPs and WLSs, which have been notified in accordance with national laws and regulations. These include BHSs, Conservation Reserves and Community Reserves, ESZs, CRZs, and CWHs.

Biodiversity Heritage Sites

BHSs are areas of high biodiversity value that are established under Section 37 of the Biological Diversity Act, 2002 (NBA 2015). These are well-defined areas that are unique and ecologically fragile ecosystems – terrestrial, inland waters, coastal or marine – having one or more of the following features: richness of wild as well as domesticated species or intra-specific categories, high endemism, presence of rare and threatened species, keystone species, species of evolutionary significance, wild ancestors of domestic/cultivated species or their varieties, past pre-eminence of biological components represented by fossil beds and having significant cultural, ethical or aesthetic values and are important for the maintenance of cultural diversity, with or without a long history of human association with them.

Biodiversity Management Committees (BMCs) are usually responsible for management of the BHSs. BMCs are established under Section 41 of the Biological Diversity Act, 2002 by a local body, such as gram panchayat (democratically elected local self-government at village level) or village council, within its area for the purpose of promoting conservation, sustainable use and documentation of biological diversity, including preservation of habitats, conservation of landraces, folk varieties and cultivars, domesticated stocks and breeds of animals and micro-organisms and chronicling of knowledge related to biological diversity. If a BHS extends to areas managed by more than one BMC, a committee known as the Biodiversity Heritage Sites Management Committee is constituted for managing the BHS (NBA 2008a).

The National Biodiversity Authority (NBA) issued the guidelines for the declaration of BHSs in 2009, almost seven years after the Act was passed. The progress of establishment of BHSs has been extremely slow with only seven sites notified up to June 2016. A major reason is that the process of formation of BMCs has itself been very tardy with non-uniform distribution. Although 37,769 BMCs have been reportedly constituted, nearly two-thirds (23,743) are located in just one state, Madhya Pradesh (NBA 2008b). Further, it is not known as to how many of these exist merely on paper and how many are functional.

Apart from the issue of absent or non-functional BMCs, another major issue is the lack of awareness among local communities. Although the guidelines for creation and management of BHSs clearly state that the BHS would not put any restriction on the traditional practices of the local communities, Negi (2015) in his study on the development initiative of a BHS in Uttarakhand found reluctance among local communities to declare their sacred natural sites as BHSs, fearing that this recognition would intrude on their own rights over the resources.

Overall, the concept of BHSs has remained a non-starter with only seven BHSs in existence even though 14 years have elapsed since the introduction of this new category of PA under the Biological Diversity Act, 2002. The total area covered under BHSs is a mere 55 km^2!

Conservation Reserves and Community Reserves

An amendment in 2002 to the Wildlife (Protection) Act (1972) created two new categories of PAs: Conservation Reserves (to be established in government-owned areas) and Community Reserves (to be established in areas where land is owned privately or by the community) (MOEF 2003).

These two categories of PAs were envisaged as buffer zones to or connectors and migration corridors between established NPs, WLSs as well as Reserved Forests. According to the Indian Forest Act, 1927, Reserved Forests are lands owned by the state governments in India where rights to all activities like hunting, grazing, etc. are banned unless permitted otherwise. The Conservation Reserves and the IUCN Category V PAs are similar and so are the Community Reserves and the IUCN Category VI PAs. Category V IUCN protected landscapes are generally not wilderness areas. They aim at overall protection of the area and its associated biodiversity. Category VI IUCN protected landscapes are unique in the sense that these focus on the sustainable use of resources as a means to achieve nature conservation with the preservation of associated cultural values (Arun Prasad n.d.).

The state government, after consultation with local communities, may declare any state-owned land adjacent to NPs and WLSs as a Conservation Reserve. The state government may declare any private or community land, where the community or an individual has volunteered to conserve wildlife and its habitat, as a Community Reserve to protect fauna, flora and traditional or cultural conservation values and practices. These areas do not necessarily have to be within any NP, WLS or a Conservation Reserve. There were a total of 67 Conservation Reserves and 26 Community Reserves notified in India by June 2016, which covered an area of 2396.31 km^2 (ENVIS 2011a; 2011b).

Jhilmil Jheel Conservation Reserve was set up in 2005 in the state of Uttarakhand. The Reserve is known for its swamp deer (*Rucervus duvaucelii*) population apart from a diversity of birds such as vultures (*Gyps indicus*), bristled grassbirds (*Chaetornis striata*) and peafowl (*Pavo cristatus*). However, the swamp deer population is declining due to their habitat fragmentation caused by encroachments by settlements in the corridor between the Reserve and the nearby Forest Ranges. Livestock of the nearby local communities graze in the Conservation Reserve resulting in competition for resources. Poaching is also one of the reasons for the declining swamp deer population. Therefore, the Conservation Reserve has not been able to fulfil its primary objective of providing a safe habitat and corridor for the wildlife (Tewari and Rawat 2013).

In Meghalaya, unlike in the other parts of country, most of the land is owned by village councils, communities or private individuals. Most of the Community Reserves formed in the country are located in Meghalaya. Interestingly, all these Community Reserves were constituted in 2014 (ENVIS 2011b). The Reserves have been reportedly successful in reducing human–wildlife conflicts, especially by empowering the local communities to take up conservation actions to protect the natural habitats of wild animals, such as elephants and Hoolock gibbons (Mawrie 2016).

The above two examples illustrate the mixed results of these new categories of PAs. As with many other categories of new PAs, the implementation of these on the ground has also been limited. Further, their distribution across the country is also uneven. Over 50 per cent (34 out of 67) of Conservation Reserves are located in the northern state of Jammu and Kashmir, while nearly 85 per cent (22 out of 26) of Community Reserves are located in the northeastern state of Meghalaya (ENVIS 2011a; 2011b). This imbalanced distribution of these PAs could probably be attributed to the political will or initiative of some individual(s) in key position(s) in these two states. There is probably also a fear among local communities that declaration of Conservation or Community Reserves could later result in the area being declared a NP or WLS, with attendant restrictions on the local communities' access and use of resources in the area.

These reserves also face a number of implementation challenges. For example, there is a requirement for the establishment of a 'Community Reserve Management Committee' (CRMC), which is the competent authority to prepare and implement management plans for the reserve and to take steps to ensure the protection of the wildlife and its habitat in the reserve. The nomination of the representatives in the committee is to be done from the local *gram panchayat* or *gram sabha*.

The *gram sabha* is the village assembly comprising all the people (adults) included the electoral rolls of the village or area covered by the *panchayat*. However, financial control is often a bone of contention. The source of funds to the CRMC to manage the reserve is another grey area. If CRMC is given a free hand to generate funds, some analysts fear that it might resort to certain revenue generation activities that might adversely affect the flow of ecosystem services from the reserve. Silence of the law regarding the *criteria* that must be fulfilled in order for an area to be declared a Community or Conservation Reserve is a much more fundamental question. Making the task of laying down any specific list of criteria even more difficult is the sheer diversity of places that could be declared Community or Conservation Reserves in India (Dutt, 2003).

Critical Wildlife Habitats

CWH, under the Scheduled Tribes and Other Forest Dwellers (Recognition of Forest Rights) Act (FRA) passed in 2006, have been defined as 'areas of National Parks and Wildlife Sanctuaries that are required to be kept as inviolate for the purposes of wildlife conservation'.

These habitats are notified after an open consultation with the state-level Expert Committee by the Ministry of Environment, Forest and Climate Change (MoEFCC) (until 2014, MoEFCC was named the Ministry of Environment and Forests (MoEF), but the new name has been used throughout the text to maintain uniformity). The main responsibility to determine critical habitats lies with the state-level Expert Committee, which consists of the following members: State Chief Wildlife Warden as the Chairperson; representative from MoEFCC, Government of India; representative from the Ministry of Tribal Affairs (MoTA), Government of India; two state-level experts in the field of wildlife; one local representative in the field of sociology/conservation or a representative from the *gram sabha*; and the Protected Area Manager. The Expert Committee also deals with issues of resettlement of the forest communities (MoEF 2007b).

As per the guidelines issued by MoEFCC, the state government should initiate the process for notification of a CWH by submitting an application on a case-by-case basis to the MoEFCC. These CWHs should be recognised with the aim of maintaining viable populations of faunal and floral species to conserve biodiversity and ecological systems in natural areas. The following extract from the guidelines explain the process of demarcation:

> . . . critical wildlife habitat area should be demarcated on the basis of species area curves specific for each bio-geographical area, as classified by the Wildlife Institute of India (Rodgers and Panwar, 1988). The size of the inviolate area within each critical habitat zone should be based on its potential to harbour viable populations of umbrella species (endemic species, top carnivores, mega-herbivores, indicator, wild relatives of species of economic value, endangered and threatened, and migratory species), which would serve to conserve the entire biodiversity of the area.
>
> (MoEF 2007b: 2)

Figure 8.3 A female (front) and male (back) Western Hoolock gibbon (*Hoolock hoolock*) from the Hoollongapar Gibbon Sanctuary in Assam, India

Source: Vijay Cavale, 2009, via Wikimedia Commons. Used under Creative Commons Attribution-Share Alike 1.0 Generic licence

As the initial guidelines issued in 2007 did not adequately address various practical issues involved in the notification of CWHs, revised guidelines were issued in 2011. However, the timeline suggested in the new guidelines was considered to be too short by many stakeholders. As the process involved two ministries – MoEFCC and MoTA – it made the process complicated and cumbersome with the potential for 'turf wars'. Another complicating factor was the declaration of approximately 31,940 km² in 28 existing and eight proposed Tiger Reserves as 'Critical Tiger Habitats' (Bhullar 2008).

Assam's Hoollongapar Gibbon Sanctuary was proposed to be the first CWH in the country in October 2011 (Bhattacharya 2010). The gibbon sanctuary is the only area in the country where seven primate species – Hoolock gibbons (*Hoolock hoolock*), Bengal slow loris (*Nycticebus bengalensis*), Assamese and rhesus macaques (*Macaca assamensis* and *Macaca mulatta*), pig-tailed macaques (*Macaca leonina*), capped langurs (*Trachypithecus pileatus*) and stump-tailed macaques (*Macaca arctoides*) – co exist (Behl 2011). However, its current status as CWH is unknown as there is no formal record of any identified CWH in India since the revised guidelines. Thus, CWH represents another new PA category that has remained a non-starter and no progress could be made even after ten years of the enactment of the FRA. This category is particularly interesting from a conservation perspective as it specifically mentions species-area curves as the basis of establishment of CWHs in different biogeographical zones.

Coastal Regulation Zones

India has a coastline of 7,516 km, ranging from Gujarat in the west to West Bengal in the east, and two island archipelagos (Andaman and Nicobar Islands and Lakshadweep Islands) (Venkataraman 2007). The coastal belt of India is characterised by diverse ecosystems including estuaries, coral reefs, mangrove swamps, creeks, backwaters, lagoons, cliffs and sandy and rocky beaches.

In order to regulate activities in the sensitive coastal ecosystems, a notification under the Environment Protection Act, 1986 was issued by the MoEFCC in 1991. This paved the way for establishment of CRZs. As per the notification, CRZs are defined as coastal stretches (including seas, bays, estuaries, creeks, rivers and back waters) up to 500 m from the High Tide Line (HTL) and the beach between the HTL and the Low Tide Line (LTL). The HTL is defined as the line on the land up to which the highest water line reaches during spring tide. However, the LTL has not been defined for the CRZ. LTL may be taken as the lowest low water line during the spring tide under average meteorological conditions and any combination of astronomical conditions (Thomas 2010). There are some additional conditions regarding water bodies joining the sea/ocean. The notification of 1991 included only the inter-tidal zone and land part of the coastal area and did not include the sea/ocean part. The notification specified various permissible and prohibited activities in CRZs (MoEF 1991).

In 2011, a new CRZ notification was issued. The definition of CRZ was widened to include the seaward side up to 12 nautical miles to include territorial waters as a protected zone (a unit used in measuring distances at sea, one nautical mile is equal to 1,852 metres.). This notification resulted in the creation of one of the most significant PA category in terms of area coverage.

The previous notification had a cap on the floor space index (FSI), restricted to the ground floor plus two floors, subject to a height limit of nine metres. FSI refers to the quotient of the ratio of the combined gross floor area of all floors, excepting areas specifically exempted under these regulations, to the total area of the plot. However, no restrictions are specified in the new notification, leaving development to be done in accordance with the extant planning and development rules. Facilities required for fishers' livelihoods – from fish drying to traditional boat-building yards – are included in the list of permitted activities in CRZ 2011, as against the 1991 notification (Narayanan 2011). As there is no authorised agency to demarcate the tidal lines (and hazard lines), the process and methodology to demarcate these continues to be ambiguous. Hazard line denotes the line demarcated by MoEFCC through Survey of India (SoI) taking into account tides, waves, sea level rise and shoreline changes during coastal planning, for the purpose of protecting the life and property of local communities.

As CRZ has major implications for coastal cities, ports, tourism and several other important facets of coastal life, a provision has been made for declaring different categories of CRZs (I–IV) with different levels of conservation conditions and rules. Further, some areas with special consideration have also been identified, i.e. CRZs within municipal limits of Greater Mumbai, Kerala and Goa. The provisions relating to Mumbai have predictably been most widely debated, given the sheer size of the population and high value of land.

Although CRZ has provided a strong legal basis for conservation of coastal ecosystems, its continuous dilution (e.g. there were 25 amendments between 1991 and 2009, mostly to make the CRZ notification less stringent), lack of clear environmental and social objectives, inadequate institutional structures (e.g. to demarcate tidal and hazard lines), lack of comprehensive coastal zoning, and insufficient baseline data and poor monitoring has prevented CRZ from achieving its potential outcomes (Panigrahi and Mohanty 2012).

Eco-sensitive Zones

The Environment (Protection) Act, 1986 (amended 1991) empowers the central government to impose restrictions related to certain industries, operations or processes in notified areas, which could only be allowed after following certain safeguards (Section 3(2)(v)). The first such areas, which were notified in 1989, were Murud Janjira (Raigad district, Maharashtra) and Doon Valley (Uttarakhand). Subsequently, Dahanu Taluka (Thane District, Maharashtra) was notified in 1991. Subsequently, these areas came to be known as 'eco-sensitive areas', 'no-development zones' and, increasingly, 'eco-sensitive zones' (MoEF 2002).

The challenges in establishing ESZs on the ground could be illustrated through the examples of Aravalli and Matheran, which are briefly discussed in this section. The Aravalli hill region in the states of Rajasthan and Haryana was declared an ESZ in 1992 (MoEF 1992). A number of restrictions were imposed, including on new mining operations. However, as a complete ban was not imposed, several mining operations continued. In 2009, the Supreme Court imposed a complete ban on mining operations in approximately 448 km² of the Aravalli hills in Faridabad and Gurgaon districts of Haryana, although mining continued in Rajasthan (Kapoor *et al.* 2009).

Matheran is located at a distance of around 100 kms from Mumbai. The first notification to declare Matheran as 'ecologically sensitive' was issued in 1998. Since the boundary of the proposed zone was a contentious issue among various state departments and stakeholders, the final notification to declare Matheran as ESZ could only be issued in 2003, five years after the first notification. Further, the area was reduced by more than half (214 km² as opposed to 498 km² in the initial notification) (Kapoor *et al.* 2009). The establishment of the ESZ resulted in a ban on various activities such as mining and quarrying, new tourism facilities, change of land use, construction near natural heritage areas, use of plastic bags, construction on slopes and felling of trees. The Matheran Monitoring Committee was formed in 2004. However, the term of the committee was not renewed. The zonal master plan was not prepared even after a decade (ENVIS 2014). According to one assessment, there were 584 illegal encroachments, especially due to increasing tourism (Parida 2016).

An important development took place in 2002, when the National Board of Wildlife (NBWL) recommended that 'lands falling within 10 km of boundaries of National Parks and Sanctuaries should be notified as eco-fragile zones'. The stated purpose of these zones is to regulate and manage certain activities

Figure 8.4 Matheran landscape, Maharashtra, India

Source: Elroy Serrao, 2015 (Flickr), via PhotoPin. Used under Attribution-Share Alike 2.0 Generic licence

to prevent ecological damage caused due to 'developmental activities' so that these act as 'shock absorbers' for NPs and WLSs (MoEF 2011).

Although there were provisions that allowed flexibility for making site-specific adjustments in the extent of area as well as regulation around different NPs and WLSs, this task was not accorded high priority by the state governments, probably because there were no clear guidelines from the MoEFCC. In 2006, the Supreme Court directed the MoEFCC to give a final opportunity to all states and union territories to provide their proposals for declaration of extent of ESZs (MoEF 2011). If the state governments did not submit ESZ proposals within the time given by MoEFCC, a 10-km radius around the each NP/WLS was to be declared as an ESZ. The Court also directed that all projects that were given environment clearance previously but fell within 10 km of PAs should be referred to the standing committee of NBWL for approval. In February 2011, the MoEFCC released guidelines and asked all states and union territories to submit site-specific proposals to set up ESZs around all NPs/WLSs, which should include their extent (MoEF 2011). It further clarified that the width of the ESZ and type of regulation may vary across different NPs/WLSs. The politics and issues related to ESZs around NPs/WLSs are best illustrated through the case of the Okhla Bird Sanctuary (OBS) located on the fringes of the national capital New Delhi.

Case: The Okhla Bird Sanctuary

Figure 8.5 Real estate developments within the confines of the Okhla Bird Sanctuary, India

Source: Srikaanth Sekar, 2016 (Flickr), via PhotoPin. Used under Attribution-Share Alike 2.0 Generic licence

The OBS is a 'man-made wetland' located at the border of the National Capital Territory of Delhi and the state of Uttar Pradesh. It is an IBA, part of which (around 3.5 km^2), located on the Uttar Pradesh side, was declared a bird sanctuary in 1990 (Sharma *et al.* 2015).

It is situated at the point where the Yamuna river enters the state of Uttar Pradesh, leaving the territory of Delhi (Figure 8.6). This sanctuary is an ideal habitat for birds, both resident and migratory. During winters as many as 324 species of birds have been recorded in the area (Okhla Bird Sanctuary 2016; Vishnoi 2015).

Apart from providing refuge to migratory and resident birds, the wetland performs several important functions for maintaining the ecological balance of the area, such as stabilising the water table. The sanctuary has great potential to attract national and international birdwatchers. However, rapid urbanisation in Delhi and the Noida region of Uttar Pradesh poses a serious threat to the sanctity of the sanctuary. Within the 10-km radius of the sanctuary, developmental activities such as construction of the Timarpur waste incinerator, Gautama Buddha Park, crematorium, roads, flyovers and metro rail lines, has put the sanctuary under threat. Industrial expansion in Delhi has also led to untreated sewage disposal, pollution and waste dumping in the Yamuna river that feeds OBS. Further, various anthropogenic activities like encroachment and construction, fishing, cattle grazing, poaching, destruction of habitat, lack of proper administration and management of the habitat are deteriorating the condition of OBS (Manral *et al.* 2012; Bhowmick 2015). The highly urbanised surrounding area, without a buffer

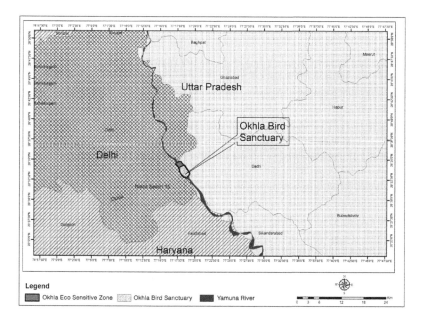

Figure 8.6 Imagery showing the location of the Okhla Bird Sanctuary

zone, is significantly changing the ecology and biodiversity of OBS. Further, the lack of coordination between two state governments – that is, Delhi and Uttar Pradesh – has hampered many initiatives.

The Noida administration approved about 50 developmental-cum-residential projects within the 10-km radius of OBS. These projects were initiated without the required approvals from NBWL. Following a petition in July 2013 against these building projects by a resident of Noida, the National Green Tribunal (NGT) directed that no construction activity will be permitted within a 10-km radius of the sanctuary and the construction already started will be rendered illegal and not issued 'Completion Certificates'. These certificates are required to occupy and use a building. The NGT further directed that in that 10-km radius of the OBS, no new project will be cleared unless NBWL issues a 'No Objection Certificate' (Banerjee 2014).

This, however, was a challenge as a 10-km wide ESZ would restrict developmental and real estate projects in the rapidly expanding urban area of the state of Uttar Pradesh. As the issue involved thousands of middle-class residents of the National Capital Region as well as billions of rupees of investment, it was discussed widely in the national media. It was perhaps the first time that the ESZ issue was debated so hotly in the country.

Interestingly, but perhaps not surprisingly, when the ESZ notification was issued in August 2015, the extent of the ESZ was reduced to a mere 100 metres on the eastern, western and southern boundaries and to 1.27 km on the northern boundary of the sanctuary (Indian Express 2015; Vishnoi 2015). This episode revealed that conservation issues become centre-stage and get media attention when these affect the middle class and other socially and economically powerful groups.

Conclusion

India has experimented with a wide array of PAs that have been constituted in accordance with international initiatives or domestic laws. However, most of the attention has been focused on NPs and WLSs, which are in fact treated as synonyms of PA. This chapter is a brief attempt towards a better understanding of the actual status and outcomes of lesser known PAs other than NPs and WLSs.

It appears that there is considerable difference between the global or national conceptualisation of PA categories and the actual implementation on the ground. For example, while the concept of BR envisages a zonation, it has at best been notional in practice. Some concepts such as CWH are easier to discuss on paper than to implement on the ground.

Many new PA concepts and categories have not taken off at all and their distribution across the country is usually skewed. This is perhaps due to lack of political will and corresponding availability of funds and institutional structures. For example, although the concept of BHS was introduced in 2002, only seven sites covering a mere 55 km^2 were constituted over the next 14 years. Some categories such as CWH have remained a non-starter due to lack of clarity regarding procedures and perhaps 'turf wars' between different stakeholder groups. The key lesson is that mere legislation is not enough, it needs to be backed with appropriate institutional structures, and a clear strategy. These, in turn, require political will and perhaps a few 'champions' in the right positions. It is perhaps due to this reason that around 50 per cent of Conservation Reserves and 85 per cent of Community Reserves are located in just one state, Jammu & Kashmir and Meghalaya, respectively.

There seems to be considerable overlap between different categories of PAs. For example, the Manas WHS is also a BR, IBA, NP, WLS, Tiger Reserve and Elephant Reserve. Further, the *de facto* management of most PAs is as per existing major PA categories (i.e. NP and WLS). Therefore, additionality in terms of conservation or livelihood benefits is doubtful.

Overall, it seems that various additional PA categories, which have been introduced in the past few decades, continue to play a marginal role in the conservation discourse in the country. They hardly get any attention unless socially and economically powerful groups are affected, especially in the metropoles, as vividly brought out in the case of a CRZ in Mumbai and an ESZ near New Delhi.

References

Arun Prasad, K.C.A. (n.d.). *Protected Areas of India vis a vis the Six IUCN Categories*. Teri University, Delhi. [online] Available from: www.teriuniversity.ac.in/mct/pdf/new/assignment/Assignment%20-%20K.C.A.%20Arun%20Prasad.pdf [Accessed 20 June 2016].

Assam Tribune. (2014). Green Tribunal bench warns GMDA, GMC. *The Assam Tribune*, 22 October. [online] Available from: www.assamtribune.com/scripts/detailsnew.asp?id=oct2214/city050 [Accessed 20 June 2016].

Banerjee, S. (2014). Okhla bird sanctuary case: Respite likely for Noida home-buyers, developers. *Down to Earth*, 12 August. [online] Available from: www.downtoearth.org.in/news/okhla-bird-sanctuary-case-respite-likely-for-noida-homebuyers-developers-45767 [Accessed 6 July 2016].

Behl, A. (2011). Critical Wildlife Habitat: Hopefully India's Hoolock Gibbon Sanctuary (Assam). *Wild Navigator*. [online] Available from: www.wildnavigator.com/critical-wildlife-habitat-hopefully-indias-hoolock-gibbon-sanctuary-assam/ [Accessed 28 June 2016].

Bhattacharya, S. (2010). Assam first to have critical wildlife habitat. *The Telegraph*, 3 October. [online] Available from: www.telegraphindia.com/1101023/jsp/northeast/story_13013100.jsp [Accessed 20 June 2016].

Bhattacharya, S., Ganguli, A., Bose, S. and Mukhopadhyay, A. (2012). Biodiversity, traditional practices and sustainability issues of East Kolkata Wetlands: A significance Ramsar site of West Bengal, (India). *Research and Reviews in Biosciences*, **6**(11), 340–347.

Bhowmick, S. (2015). Security to be beefed up at Okhla Bird Sanctuary. *The Times of India*, 24 September. [online] Available from: http://timesofindia.indiatimes.com/home/environment/flora-fauna/Security-to-be-beefed-up-at-Okhla-Bird-Sanctuary/articleshow/49090944.cms [Accessed 6 July 2016].

Bhullar, L. (2008). The Indian Forest Rights Act 2006: A critical appraisal. *Law, Environment and Development Journal*, **4**(1), 20–34. [online] Available from: www.lead-journal.org/content/08020.pdf [Accessed 28 June 2016].

Bosak, K. (2008). Nature, conflict and biodiversity conservation in the Nanda Devi Biosphere Reserve. *Conservation and Society*, **6**(3), 211–224.

CPREEC. (2015). *The Nilgiri Biosphere Reserve*. [online] Available from: www.cpreec.org/pubbook-nilgiris.htm [Accessed 20 June 2016].

Daniels, R.J.R. (1992). The Nilgiri Biosphere Reserve and its role in conserving India's biodiversity. *Current Science*, **64**(10), 706–708.

Dutt, B. (2003). Are community reserves the answer to conservation? *Down to Earth*, 15 August. [online] Available from: www.downtoearth.org.in/coverage/are-community-reserves-the-answer-to-conservation-13275 [Accessed 22 June 2016].

ENVIS Centre on Wildlife and Protected Areas. (2011a). *Conservation Reserves*. [online] Available from: http://wiienvis.nic.in/Database/cri_8229.aspx [Accessed 22 June 2016].

ENVIS Centre on Wildlife and Protected Areas. (2011b). *Community Reserves*. [online] Available from: http://wiienvis.nic.in/Database/cri_8228.aspx [Accessed 22 June 2016].

ENVIS Centre on Wildlife and Protected Areas. (2014). *Matheran: Ecologically Sensitive Hill Station of Maharashtra*. ENVIS Centre, Government of Maharashtra, Mumbai. [online] Available from: http://mahenvis.nic.in/pdf/Newsletter/nletter_Matheran%20-Ecologically%20Sensitive%20Hill%20Station%20of%20Maharashtra.pdf [Accessed 23 June 2016].

Frey, B.S. and Steiner, L. (2011). World Heritage List: Does it make sense? *International Journal of Cultural Policy*, **17**(5), 555–573.

Indian Express. (2015). Okhla eco zone property deals tied to outcome of proceedings: NGT. *The Indian Express*, 10 November. [online] Available from: http://indianexpress.com/article/cities/delhi/okhla-eco-zone-property-deals-tied-to-outcome-of-proceedings-ngt/ [Accessed 6 July 2016].

Jamwal, N. (2015). Disappearing lakes. *Deccan Herald*, 13 October. [online] Available from: www.deccanherald.com/content/506003/disappearing-lakes.html [Accessed 19 June 2016].

Jha, S. (2005). Can natural World Heritage Sites promote development and social harmony? *Biodiversity and Conservation*, **14**(4), 981–991.

Kapoor, M., Kohli, K. and Menon, M. (2009). *India's Notified Ecologically Sensitive Areas (ESAs): The Story So Far*. Kalpavriksh, Delhi and WWF-India, New Delhi.

Konwar, R. (2016). Photospeak: Scavenger in danger. *The Hindu Thread*, 6 June. [online] Available from: www.thehindu.com/thread/reflections/article8696423.ece [Accessed 19 June 2016].

Manral, U., Raha, A., Solanki, R. and Veeraswami, G. (2012). Hydrological characteristics and flood plain vegetation of human impacted wetlands: A case study from Okhla Bird Sanctuary, National Capital Region, New Delhi, India. *Asian Journal of Conservation Biology*, **1**(2), 110–119.

Mawrie, I. (2016). Community Reserves: A boon for both humans and elephants in Meghalaya. *The North East Today*. [online] Available from: http://thenortheasttoday.com/community-reserves-a-boon-for-both-humans-and-elephants-in-meghalaya/ [Accessed 22 June 2016].

MoEF. (1991). *Notification Declaring Coastal Stretches as Coastal Regulation Zone (CRZ) and Regulating Activities in the CRZ*. Ministry of Environment and Forests, Government of India, New Delhi.

MoEF. (1992). *Notification Restricting Certain Activities in Specified Area of Aravalli Range*. Ministry of Environment and Forests, Government of India, New Delhi. [online] Available from: http://envfor.nic.in/legis/eia/aravalli.pdf [Accessed 25 June 2016].

MoEF. (2002). *Eco-sensitive Zones Notifications.* [online] Available from: http://envfor.nic. in/legis/eco-senstive.htm [Accessed 25 June 2016].

MoEF. (2003). *The Wildlife (Protection) Amendment Act, 2002.* Ministry of Environment and Forests, Government of India, New Delhi.

MoEF. (2007a). *Protection, Development, Maintenance and Research in Biosphere Reserves in India.* Ministry of Environment and Forests, Government of India, New Delhi.

MoEF. (2007b). *Guidelines to Notify Critical Wildlife Habitat Including Constitution and Functions of Expert Committee, Scientific Information Required and Resettlement and Matters Incidental Thereto.* Ministry of Environment and Forests, Government of India, New Delhi.

MoEF. (2011).*Guidelines for Declaration of Eco-sensitive Zones around National Parks and Wildlife Sanctuaries.* Ministry of Environment and Forests, Government of India, New Delhi.

MoEF. (2016). *List of Biosphere Reserves, Their Area, Date of Designation, and Location.* [online] Available from: www.moef.nic.in/sites/default/files/BR%20List.pdf [Accessed 30 June 2016].

Mukherjee, J. (2015). Sustainable flows between Kolkota and its peri-urban interface: Challenges and opportunities. In A. Allen, A. Lampis and M. Swilling, eds., *Untamed Urbanisms.* Routledge, Abingdon, Oxon., 33–49.

Narayanan, S. (2011). New rules for coasts. *Down To Earth.* [online] Available from: www. downtoearth.org.in/coverage/new-rules-for-coasts-32983 [Accessed 1 July 2016].

NBA. (2008a). *Rules: The Gazette of India.* National Biodiversity Authority, Chennai, India. [online] Available from: http://nbaindia.org/content/17/20/1/rules.html [Accessed 30 June 2016].

NBA. (2008b). *Biodiversity Management Committees.* National Biodiversity Authority, Chennai, India. [online] Available from: http://nbaindia.org/content/20/35/1/bmc. html [Accessed 30 June 2016].

NBA. (2015). *Compendium of Biological Diversity Act 2002, Rules 2004 and Notifications.* National Biodiversity Authority, Chennai, India.

Negi, C. (2015). Developing sacred forests into biodiversity heritage sites: Experiences from the state of Uttarakhand, Central Himalaya, India. *Indian Journal of Traditional Knowledge,* 1(1), 96–102.

Okhla Bird Sanctuary. (2016). *Okhla Bird Sanctuary: Location.* [online] Available from: http://obs-up.com/location.php [Accessed 6 July 2016].

Panigrahi, J. and Mohanty, P. (2012). Effectiveness of the Indian Coastal Regulation Zones provisions for coastal zone management and its evaluation using SWOT analysis. *Ocean and Coastal Management,* **65**, 34–50.

Parida, U. (2016). In 9 years, number of illegal hotels have doubled in Matheran, finds municipal council. *The Times of India,* 26 March. [online] Available from: http:// timesofindia.indiatimes.com/city/mumbai/In-9-years-number-of-illegal-hotels-have-doubled-in-Matheran-finds-municipal-council/articleshow/51555927.cms [Accessed 30 June 2016].

Ramsar. (2014a). History of the Ramsar Convention. *Ramsar.* [online] Available from: www.ramsar.org/about/history-of-the-ramsar-convention [Accessed 21 June 2016].

Ramsar. (2014b). Wetlands of international importance (Ramsar Sites). *Ramsar.* [online] Available from: www.ramsar.org/about/wetlands-of-international-importance-ramsar-sites [Accessed 20 June 2016].

Ramsar. (2014c). The Ramsar Sites criteria: The nine criteria for identifying wetlands of international importance. *Ramsar.* [online] Available from: www.ramsar.org/sites/ default/files/documents/library/ramsarsites_criteria_eng.pdf [Accessed 20 June 2016].

Ramsar. (2015). *National Report on the Implementation of the Ramsar Convention on Wetlands.* Ramsar, Iran.

Ramsar. (2016). The list of wetlands of international importance. *Ramsar.* [online] Available from: www.ramsar.org/sites/default/files/documents/library/sitelist.pdf [Accessed 20 June 2016].

Rao, K., Nautiyal, S., Maikhuri, R. and Saxena, K. (2000). Management conflicts in the Nanda Devi Biosphere Reserve, India. *Mountain Research and Development,* **20**(4), 320–323.

Sarma, P., Lahkar, B., Ghosh, S., Rabha, A., Das, J., Nath, N., Dey, S. and Brahma, N. (2008). Land-use and land-cover change and future implication analysis in Manas National Park, India using multi-temporal satellite data. *Current science,* **95**(2), 223–227.

Sharma, N., Gaur, S., Dhyani, R. and Singh, A. (2015). Challenges of small protected areas in urban cities: A case study of Okhla Bird Sanctuary, India. *Environment, Development and Sustainability,* **18**(1), 295–310.

Tewari, R. and Rawat, G. (2013). Assessment of swamp deer habitat in and around Jhilmil Jheel Conservation Reserve, Haridwar, Uttarakhand, India. *International Journal of Conservation Science,* **4**(2), 243–249.

Thomas, K.V. (2010). Setback lines for Coastal Regulation Zone: Different approaches and implications. *CRZ – 2010 Draft: Responses and Challenges,* Goa, 2010.

Times of India. (2015). GMC to shift Deepor Beel dumping site. *The Times of India,* 24 March. [online] Available from: http://timesofindia.indiatimes.com/city/guwahati/GMC-to-shift-Deepor-Beel-dumping-site/articleshow/46667626.cms [Accessed 20 June 2016].

UNESCO. (1972). *Convention Concerning the Protection of the World Cultural and Natural Heritage.* United Nations Educational, Scientific and Cultural Organization, Paris, France. [online] Available from: http://whc.unesco.org/archive/convention-en.pdf [Accessed 18 June 2016].

UNESCO. (1973). Conservation of natural areas and of the genetic material they contain. *MAB Report Series,* 12. United Nations Educational, Scientific and Cultural Organization, Paris, France.

UNESCO. (1974). Task-force on criteria and guidelines for the choice and establishment of biosphere reserves. *MAB Report Series,* 22, United Nations Educational, Scientific and Cultural Organization, Paris, France.

UNESCO. (1993). *The Biosphere Conference: 25 Years Later.* United Nations Educational, Scientific and Cultural Organization, Paris, France.

UNESCO. (2016a). *MAB Programme.* United Nations Educational, Scientific and Cultural Organization, Paris, France. [online] Available from: www.unesco.org/new/en/natural-sciences/environment/ecological-sciences/man-and-biosphere-programme/ [Accessed 30 June 2016].

UNESCO. (2016b). *The World Heritage Convention.* United Nations Educational, Scientific and Cultural Organization, Paris, France. [online] Available from: http://whc.unesco.org/en/convention/ [Accessed 22 June 2016].

UNESCO. (2016c). *India: UNESCO World Heritage Centre.* United Nations Educational, Scientific and Cultural Organization, Paris, France. [online] Available from: http://whc.unesco.org/en/statesparties/in/ [Accessed 22 June 2016].

UNESCO. (2016d). *Manas Wildlife Sanctuary: UNESCO World Heritage Centre.* United Nations Educational, Scientific and Cultural Organization, Paris, France. [online] Available from: http://whc.unesco.org/en/list/338 [Accessed 22 June 2016].

Venkataraman, K. (2007). Coastal and marine wetlands in India. *Proceedings of Taal 2007: The 12th World Lake Conference*, 392– 400.

Vishnoi, A. (2015). Environment ministry likely to give go ahead to Okhla Eco-Sensitive Zone today. *The Economic Times*, 18 August. [online] Available from: http://articles. economictimes.indiatimes.com/2015-08-18/news/65530307_1_okhla-bird-sanctuary-draft-notification-esz [Accessed 6 July 2016].

WWF. (2016). *Protecting People through Nature*. WWF Switzerland. [online] Available from: http://assets.worldwildlife.org/publications/867/files/original/WWF_Dalberg_Protecting_people_through_nature_LR_singles.pdf?1459793033 [Accessed 24 June 2016].

9 Ficus to filter

Understanding complexities of market incentives for conserving biodiversity on private lands

Arshiya Bose

Ponappa grooms the tips of his moustache with beeswax. The mixture was prepared just the day before, by cutting off the wax caps of giant honeybee combs, clarifying with hot water and diluting with coconut oil. He sips coffee from a steel tumbler and looks out into his plantation. This morning the elephant herd has moved clumsily to the block near the irrigation tanks. This means that coffee picking can continue without disruption in the rest of the plantation. From the verandah, Ponappa can see the overhanging branches of a large ficus tree, or *atti* as it is known locally, heavy with honeycombs. Under the shade of the ficus's spreading canopy, robusta coffee plants flourish. Despite being over 50 years old, the plant's leaves boast resplendent green and the fruit, a profound red. The soil is rich in nutrients and rippling with moving creatures, as though waves in a deep ocean. It has been a modest season. Ponappa wonders whether this is because his coffee plants are past their prime. He could replace this 20-acre block with improved, high-yielding varieties but that would be expensive. More lucrative would be to raze this grandiose ficus and other large trees on his farm. They are the government's trees anyway. Clearing the shade and letting in sunlight would double coffee yields. Yes, Ponappa would have to negotiate with environmentalists who arrive each year to certify his coffee as 'shade-grown' or 'sun-kissed'. On second thoughts, perhaps that wouldn't prove such a tussle after all . . .

Across the Suez Canal, a senior conservationist at a world-renowned organisation enters a 'geeky chic' café in trendy East London. He asks for a 'Soy milk, single-estate, traceable, nature-friendly and ethically traded cup of filter coffee'. This is but a passé request at this café and so the coffee is fashioned onto the counter within minutes. The conservationist sits down, sips away and smacks his lips in guilt-free pleasure. His purchase of a single cup of coffee will protect a biodiversity-rich coffee forest many seas away in India. A poor, struggling farmer will be empowered to make ends meet. The conservation movement is now this advanced. Or is it?

Introduction

The intellectual journey of this story is rooted in emerging global discourses on conservation and markets. This chapter explores these discourses by analysing three spheres of relations that significantly influence the effectiveness of shade-grown certification. These spheres include: (a) relations between coffee growers, the Indian state and shade trees, (b) relations between coffee growers and global conservation ideals and (c) negotiations between private actors and the toggles of market-based conservation.

Conservation policy and action are increasingly focused on using markets to simultaneously address conservation and human needs. These emerging forms of market-based conservation are centred on ideas about providing natural resource users with tangible, economic incentives (most often, monetary incentives) to conserve nature. The promise of market-based approaches in categorically addressing the adverse social impacts of conservation while simultaneously producing positive conservation results is palpable in commitments by conservation organisations. Many prominent organisations have endorsed and oriented their core programmes towards such incentive mechanisms. Conservation International (CI) calls incentive agreements essential to 'making conservation people's choice' (CI 2013). The Wildlife Conservation Society is 'optimistic about paying for invaluable results' (Svadlenak-Gomez et al. 2007: 1).

In contrast, while the conservation landscape in India is brimming with initiatives that provide development benefits, alternative livelihoods, sustainable harvest rights and eco-tourism opportunities to forest-dependent communities, there are only a handful of conservation projects that provide monetary incentives. In many ways, the integration of conservation and human needs via markets – what seems in India, an extremely complex and almost unrealistic union – is being trumpeted by global conservation NGOs, international forums and scholarly and popular literature as the most logical next step in conservation thinking and practice.

It is a happy coincidence that this research story also involves coffee, my personal addiction, occupational hazard and a plant that has transformed the world (Allen 2000). The emerging narrative of market involvement in nature conservation is also visible in coffee production, albeit in reverse chronology. In coffee production, debates about environmental and social justice have been integrated into pre-existing market activity. Coffee production exists first and foremost as a market activity; a crop that is grown to be sold (in most cases). On the other hand, notions of market-based conservation are relatively unfamiliar in conservation thinking. However, the growing environmental impacts of coffee production, from conversion of tropical forests to adverse effects of agricultural intensification have contributed to the importance of conservation in discussions on coffee. Of particular relevance is the predicament around 'shade', which refers to the presence of native tree species used to shelter coffee plants from extreme climactic pressures. While such tree cover has undeniable value for biodiversity on coffee farms, coffee productivity is significantly compromised. This tug-of-war between profitability and conservation needs has preoccupied coffee growers and conservationists alike. One critical outcome has been the use of markets to address the delicate balance between shade and profitability and therefore, coffee becomes an ideal resting place for a study on economy and ecology.

The convergence of these seemingly independent discourses around a market-based narrative explains the intellectual roots of this research story. More compelling is the fact that this convergence occurs in the Western Ghats landscape,

Figure 9.1 Contrast between depleted tree cover (left) and restored tree cover (right) in shade-grown coffee plantations of Kodagu, India

Photo: Arshiya Bose

a region of intense conservation activity but little clarity and consensus on how to engage local stakeholders. The questions that ground this research study explore the connections between market-based conservation ideas as applied in coffee landscapes in India. Our curiosity concerns how such market-based ideas and practices unfold within Indian realities? What would be the dynamics of implementing market-based incentives for conservation and in what ways would such processes impact land-use and livelihoods? From the context of advocacy in India, do market-based incentives address human needs? What are these needs? How do people react to such incentives? How do natural resource users want to engage with conservation and what kinds of benefits do people expect, antici-pate or find acceptable?

I explore these questions mostly through the experience of certification for coffee in Kodagu district, Karnataka, India. Between 2010 and 2013, I carried out a wide range of interviews in Kodagu, primarily with planters but also with conservationists, foresters and members of the community who freely expressed their views on the politics of coffee cultivation in the region. I have included throughout this chapter a number of quotations from these interviews based on the notes made at the time. Whilst I have refrained from attributing quotations to a particular individual to protect identities of the interviewees, these quota-tions help to paint a general picture of local people's sentiments.

Market mechanisms for conserving biodiversity in agricultural landscapes

Market-based incentives have proliferated to address environmental degradation, including biodiversity loss in biodiversity-rich landscapes outside statutory pro-tected areas PAs.

The development of such mechanisms has paralleled increasing recognition about the functional role of biodiversity in farmlands, such as agriculturally important insects (Swinton *et al.* 2007; Turner and Daily 2008). The agri-environment schemes of the European Union (EU) Common Agricultural Policy that offer direct payments to farmers to modify their farming practices are good examples of large-scale market-based incentives in agricultural landscapes (Kleijn and Sutherland 2003).

Traditionally, normative frameworks for social justice, environmental issues and business ethics were vocalised by governments, labour unions and even religious institutions. However, in the current scenario of globalising economies, ideas and cultures in which social and environmental issues are transnational rather than national, regulation of these norms are increasingly provided by a new set of actors, such as NGOs, businesses and public-private partnerships (Giovannucci and Ponte 2005; Raynolds *et al.* 2007). In this 'regulatory wake' (Raynolds *et al.* 2007: 147), national and transnational actors promote new governance mechanisms or voluntary regulatory systems such as certification, eco-labelling and production standards. These voluntary systems act as market-based incentives which identify and reward commodities that are produced under acceptable social and environmental conditions (Muradian and Pelupessy 2005). NGOs have extended their roles beyond traditional advocacy for state regulations to engaging with business activities and private firms more directly. These new forms of governance, 'name and shame' bad practices and create incentives, through certifying and attesting labels for good practices (Raynolds *et al.* 2007: 149). Such regulatory systems have addressed environment, health, social justice aspects of production. For example, the Forest Stewardship Council (FSC) is an international not-for-profit organisation that accredits timber harvested from forests managed according to FSC's environmental standards (FSC 2013). Similarly, the Marine Stewardship Council (MSC) recognises and rewards sustainable fishing and provides 'eco-labels' on seafood that can be traced back through its supply chain to fisheries that have been certified against the MSC's standards (MSC 2013). As conscientious consumers embrace certification labels as guarantees of ethical practices, these voluntary regulatory systems have expanded across the globe, but most notably in Europe and North America (Linton 2005; Giovannucci *et al.* 2008). This is particularly valid for global agrifood systems, wherein governments were historically responsible for monitoring food safety and quality standards and providing an assurance to the public about the conditions of production. However, with a globalisation of the agrifood industry and the rise in private retailers setting their own standards, there has been a shift in governance from public to private actors, and indeed third-party certifiers (Hatanaka *et al.* 2005). The coffee industry has been one of the most active spaces for voluntary regulatory standards through certification oriented towards traceability, environmental sustainability, fair treatment of workers, quality and price security. Most of these regulatory regimes are third-party certifications, which are considered to be the most important in their potential to transform governance of global coffee chains (Muradian and Pelupessy 2005). A walk down an aisle of a supermarket presents a diversity of packages imprinted with imagery that is symbolic of the goals that they attempt to achieve; resplendent tropical birds, shade trees, faces of farmers and geographic origins. Intertwined with this imagery are the stamps of certification labels: Fair Trade, Organic, Bird-Friendly, Starbuck's C.A.F.E. Practices, UTZ-Certified and Rainforest Alliance (Bacon 2010; Jha et al. 2011). Some prominent certifications, relevant to the topic of this story, are briefly discussed below: Fair Trade, Organic, Rainforest Alliance, Smithsonian Bird-Friendly and UTZ-Certified.

The shade-grown coffee movement emerged in the 1990s as a response to the decline of North American migratory birds, the majority of which winter in tropical forests in Central and South America. Coffee can be cultivated under a wide spectrum of farming models. Current production systems range from:

a)   rustic farms with 71–100 per cent shade and greater than 50 species of trees;
b)   traditional polyculture with 41–70 per cent shade and 21–50 species;
c)   commercial polyculture with 31–40 per cent shade cover and 6–20 species;
d)   shaded monoculture with 10–30 per cent shade cover and 1–5 species to
e)   unshaded monocultures with zero trees and zero species richness.

(Perfecto et al. 2005)

In comparison to coffee grown under open sun conditions, farms that maintain shade cover and tree species diversity are shown to support greater biodiversity (Phillpott et al. 2007; Perfecto et al. 1996; Moguel and Toledo 1999; Greenberg et al. 1997; Perfecto et al. 2005; Perfecto et al. 2007). Shaded plantations also sequester carbon, retain soil moisture and buffer coffee plants against extreme climactic conditions, in particular drought and high temperatures. Shade coffee is also said to increase the effectiveness of microbial and parasitic organisms against coffee pests (Staver et al. 2001, cited in Muradian and Pelupessy 2005). Rice (2002: 234) uses the term 'coffee as habitat' to refer to biodiversity benefits that shaded coffee farms can provide for plants, insects and other arthropods, birds, mammals and, though fewer research projects have studied them, reptiles and amphibians. Numerous studies demonstrate that naturally shaded coffee plantations can serve as 'refuges for tropical biodiversity' (Perfecto et al. 2007), especially in regions with increasing fragmentation of forest areas. Nevertheless, there is an overall negative relationship between coffee productivity and shade cover where beyond a threshold of 48 per cent shade, there are decreasing coffee yields (Soto-Pinto et al. 2000). This pattern is argued to have created major incentives for the conversion of coffee farms from shade-grown to sun-grown. The terms 'technification' or 'intensification' are used to describe changed farming practices, including the development of coffee plants that are resistant to sun and/or the maintenance of limited and extractable shade trees (Perfecto et al. 1996). In this respect, market-based incentives have been designed to compensate for the loss in yield that would occur from maintaining shade trees for biodiversity habitats. Through such mechanisms, positive monetary incentives in the form of price premiums are provided to farmers to produce coffee (and indeed other agroforestry crops) through farming practices that have been specified by a third-party agency.

There are currently two certification schemes that take into account the importance of shade for biodiversity. These are the Smithsonian Migratory Bird Center's Bird-Friendly certification and Rainforest Alliance certification. Bird-Friendly coffee fosters farms that follow cultivation practices that are good for birds, i.e. maintaining stipulated standards for shade trees as well as organic farming practices (SMBC 2013). Bird-Friendly is considered the more rigorous of the two schemes because it combines both organic as well as shade criteria. However, its scope has been fairly limited in comparison to Rainforest Alliance, partially due to more stringent requirements, and Bird-Friendly certification has seen negligible movement in the Indian context.

The focus of this chapter is Rainforest Alliance certification, an initiative whose mission is to protect people and the environment by improving farm management. In their words, 'The mission of Rainforest Alliance is to protect ecosystems and the people and wildlife that depend on them by transforming land-use practices, business practices and consumer behaviour' (RA 2012: 1). Along with Bird-Friendly certification, Rainforest Alliance's standards are the only label that explicitly stipulates criteria on tree diversity and shade cover on coffee farms.

Although the participation in third-party certification is voluntary, coffee roasters and retailers increasingly adopt certification labels to enable their brands to be more competitive in the specialty niche market targeted towards conscientious consumers.

The growth of the certified coffee market is indicative of a shift from consumption in conventional markets where coffee is valued for its physical qualities to a specialty market where symbolic qualities associated with the process of production and trade are commoditised with a monetary value.

Although the structure of shade-grown certification differs considerably from other market-based incentives such as PES or direct payments, certification shares with these typologies an underlying premise of market-based environmental and social change. In this chapter, PES, shade-grown certification and market-based incentives are all considered as general terms to refer to a set of conservation tools that are based on the ideology of positive incentives. This is aligned with Sommerville *et al.*'s (2009: 34) revision of the definition of PES, where such schemes are defined as '(i) positive transfers to ecosystem providers that are (ii) conditional on the provision of the service (iii) where successful implementation is based on the consideration of additionality and varying institutional contexts'. The core and common ideology across such market-based incentives is that positive monetary incentives as opposed to negative incentives are most effective means to influence behaviour, attitudes and land-use practices for conservation purposes.

Given this landscape of ideas around certifications and market-based incentives, this research story asks two questions. First, how do natural resource users (in this case coffee growers) understand and engage in market-based mechanisms for conservation (in this case, certification)? Second, how is the reality of the way in which certifications work on the ground different from that set out in their design?

Local setting: Kodagu

The majority of the field-level observations for this story were made in Kodagu district, which is situated in the Western Ghats of India. Agriculture, in particular coffee cultivation, is a major land-use type covering an area of 1353.66 km^2 or 33.3 per cent of the district's total area. Apart from coffee, black pepper, rice and cardamom are important commercial crops in the area which contribute almost 40 per cent of annual farm-based revenue. State-managed forests comprise 38 per cent of the district's area (National Informatics Centre 2011). Urbanisation is seen as an increasingly dominant feature with considerable cultivated and uncultivated lands and wetlands being converted into towns and settlements under the combined pressures of land demand for tourism and population growth (Leroy et al. 2011). Coffee is one of the key drivers of the regional economy and the cultural identity of Kodagu (Ghazoul et al. 2009). Coffee production provides direct employment for about 500,000 people in India, 254,001 in Kodagu alone (Lee and Lee 2010). As of today, coffee in the district covers a total of 104,000 ha (75,500 ha of robusta [Coffea canephora] and 28,500 ha of arabica [Coffea arabica]), with a production of 120,916 metric tonnes (CBI 2013). A mosaic of forest ecosystems spread over 78 per cent of the district, with one national park, three wildlife sanctuaries, 1,214 sacred groves under informal community management and shaded-coffee plantations. Shade-grown coffee plantations comprise 33 per cent of the forest cover of the district (Bhagwat et al. 2008). According to earlier studies, the multi-storied coffee agroforestry system was developed and sustained by coffee growers based on their local knowledge of the benefits of shade trees for coffee plant health, soil, water and other aspects of coffee cultivation (Garcia et al. 2010). Shaded coffee plantations in Kodagu are shown to be important for the protection of species and habitats, especially outside statutory protected areas and often in human-dominated landscapes (Depommier 2003; Bhagwat et al. 2005; Garcia et al. 2010; Ghazoul et al. 2009). A survey by Desjeux (1999) found the tree densities on an estate range from 285 to 1,471 trees per hectare, a figure that is comparable to that of surrounding deciduous and evergreen forests. However, this unique coffee agroforestry system is undergoing transformation with regards to shade canopy density and diversity, linked to intensification of coffee production. According to existing studies, three major drivers of this ecological change are (a) loss of forest cover and expansion of commercial croplands, (b) reduced shade canopy on coffee plantations and (c) increase in exotic tree species.

A key player in the coffee agroforestry scenario in Kodagu was the project CAFNET, 'Connecting, Enhancing and Sustaining Environmental Services and Market Values of Coffee Agroforestry in Central America, East Africa and India', funded by the European Union and implemented by CIRAD, France. CAFNET in India was implemented in Kodagu by three local partners: University of Agricultural Sciences (UASB); Central Coffee Research Institute, Coffee Board of India; and the French Institute of Pondicherry from June 2007 to May 2011. The objective of this project was manifold but the overall aim was to document biodiversity, traditional agroforestry knowledge and dynamics of landscape change. The CAFNET project's final report corroborated scientific and agronomic studies elsewhere (see Soto-Pinto *et al.* 2000; Perfecto *et al.* 2005) that showed that the productivity of coffee was found to be less under conditions of high shade cover. In Kodagu, productivity was found to be 600 kg/acre under high shade and native tree cover (>70 per cent) and 890 kg/acre under low shade cover (<70 per cent), with no significant difference in quantity of inputs. Although coffee growers under high shade had invested lower input costs, they still faced a net loss of Rs 15.50 per kg relative to low shade (Chethana *et al.* 2010). The CAFNET project concluded that the marginal loss in productivity was not directly reimbursable through ecosystem benefits provided by native shade trees. This was because there is little information on the monetary value of ecosystem services, particularly with respect to yield such as pollination services or pest control services. Hence the project recommended that coffee growers be compensated through market-based incentive mechanisms. In this regard, shade-grown certification was identified and advocated as an appropriate tool to incentivise coffee growers to adopt or maintain sustainable farming practices, including supporting high shade cover and native tree species. From 2009 to 2010, CAFNET held a series of meetings in the district to generate awareness about shade-grown certification. The first farmer's group was formed in 2009 in a small village called Cherambane in Kodagu. Six coffee growers came forward with a willingness to adopt standards under Rainforest Alliance certification. Subsequently, despite the CAFNET project having ended, over 60 growers have been Rainforest Alliance-certified in Kodagu. Most stages of implementation of Rainforest Alliance certification are out-sourced to Ecom Trading Pvt. Ltd, a coffee exporter and buyer of certified coffee. In Kodagu, Ecom covers the certification fees and audit expenses on behalf of farmers but in return, farmers enter a contract wherein they are only able to sell certified coffee to Ecom. Ecom provides a premium for certified coffee that ranges from Rs 50 (US$1) to Rs 100 (US$2) per 50-kg bag of robusta and arabica beans respectively. The underlying premise is that this premium acts as a monetary incentive or catalyst for coffee farmers to abide by Rainforest Alliance's social and environmental standards. Rainforest Alliance says,

> We believe that the best way to keep forests standing is by ensuring that it is profitable for businesses and communities to do so. That means helping farmers, forest managers and tourism businesses realize greater economic benefits by ensuring ecosystems within and around their operations are protected, and that their workers are well-trained and enjoy safe conditions, proper sanitation, health care and housing. Once businesses meet certain environmental and social standards, we link them up to the global marketplace where demand for sustainable goods and services is on the rise.
>
> (RA 2012: 1)

Figure 9.2 Coffee plantation with silver oak (*Grevillea robusta*) cover
Photo: Arshiya Bose

Copious claims, modest realities: tracing the outcomes of incentive projects

Given policy discourses around certification and rationale for implementation, the big ticket question is: how is the reality of market-based incentives different from that set out in policy and theoretical ideas?

The crux of academic and policy narratives on market-based incentives is 'effectiveness'. The arguments for implementation are heavily premised on the belief that positive monetary incentives will bring about change. In comparison to Integrated Conservation and Development Programmes (ICDPs) or other forms of indirect incentives, direct incentives do not claim a space for uncertainty of outcomes. The conditionality of payments and design of performance-based rewards are argued to strengthen such mechanisms as institutions for change. Market incentives are posited to offset costs of conservation, in this case increased costs of cultivation or income lost through decreased coffee yields as a result of maintaining native shade trees and practising environmentally sustainable agriculture. In this research study, outcomes of shade-grown certification were explored through semi-structured and open-ended interviews as well as farmers' lived experiences. The value of understanding change through the lived realities of farmers, by studying how people conceptualise changes was preferred as a research approach (Bose *et al.* 2016).

Empirical observations show that shade-grown certification has very limited environmental and livelihood outcomes in Kodagu. The overarching story of change was that of 'business as usual' where coffee growers claimed to have experienced negligible changes in their farm management and cultivation practice, pricing and marketing of coffee and attitudes towards the environment. These findings were consistent both in the quantitative data collected on farmers' self-estimates of income, production costs, selling prices and tree density as well as qualitative data on experiences or narratives of change. In addition to 'business as usual', coffee growers also experience increased bookkeeping as an outcome of shade-grown certification. Finally, some farmers had experienced the objective of shade-grown certification to be solely the improvement of labour welfare rather than an integrated environmental and social welfare. The table below summarises observations on the outcomes of certification.

This comment by a certified coffee grower reflects a fairly widespread shared belief about the limited change in land-use and farm management practices as a result of shade-grown certification: 'Madam but my estate has always been eco-friendly. I didn't have to do anything new to get it certified'.

I find that although shade-grown certification has had limited environmental and social outcomes, it has had significant imprints. The key difference between outcome and imprints is that the latter are unintended and indirect impressions created by the experience of participating in shade-grown certification. In the case of Kodagu, coffee growers are intensely disenchanted with conservation initiatives, despite technically not having experienced project outcomes. In fact, this research shows how a lack of tangible conservation impacts can significantly influence how people perceive conservation. Coffee growers in Kodagu have participated in shade-grown certification, a process which has taken place with much fanfare and visibility in the public domain. They have been recruited by the certified buyer, pre-audited, audited, approved and rewarded through price incentives all to carry on business as usual. The fact that a public conservation project has not forced a change in farm management practices has been received as mysterious and with scepticism. This comment by a certified coffee grower provides evidence to this effect: 'Ayyo we have not done anything only. I'm thinking this certification is not at all concerned with shade conservation'.

In this case, shade-grown certification has not been perceived as a market-based tool for conservation. It has been understood as a market tool intended to serve the business objectives of coffee traders and exporters worldwide. The majority view of coffee farmers is that the lack of tangible changes to farm management incurred despite participating in a very public conservation project is indicative of an underlying purpose that has not been openly communicated.

I juxtapose these empirical findings of the experience of disenchantment from shade-grown certification with scholarship on the social impacts of conservation goals like PAs and ICDPs. In the case of PAs or ICDPs, unfavourable attitudes towards conservation projects is often a result of strict restrictions (in other words imposing a strong impact) on people's livelihood and land-use practices. In the case of a market-based conservation project in Kodagu, the lack of support for

Table 9.1 Summary of quantitative data on outcomes of shade-grown certification

Percentage of coffee growers that claimed negligible changes were required to qualify for certification	68.5% (n = 34)			
Percentage of coffee growers that experienced negligible changes in production costs	79.41% (n = 34)			
Percentage of coffee growers that experienced no change in coffee yields	96.71% (n = 31)			
Percentage of coffee growers that experienced no change in attitudes towards the environmental issues (including shade trees)	88.23% (n = 34)			
Comparison of native tree species density per acre (Mann-Whitney test, p = 0.0424)	Certified 68.03		Non-certified 109.4	
Comparison of silver oak density per acre (% of total shade trees) (Mann-Whitney test, p = 0.0995)	Certified 29.39		Non-certified 109.4	
Comparison of production costs per acre	Certified (robusta) (n = 24) Rs 28,210	Non-certified (robusta) (n = 20) Rs 25,780	Certified (arabica) (n = 8) Rs 32,810	Non-certified (arabica) (n = 8) Rs 41,880
Farmers' perceptions of changes to farm management as a result of shade-grown certification (n = 34)	Bookkeeping Occupational health and& safety Plastic disposal Cement drying yard Signboards Arranging audits	38% 20% 18% 9% 6% 3%		
Economic contribution of price premiums for shade-grown certification towards annual income (n = 36)	No contribution Somewhat Significant	65.22% 21.87% 12.91%		
Comparison of selling price per 50-kg bag of coffee	Certified (robusta) (n = 26) Rs 2,611.5	Non-certified (robusta) (n = 24) Rs 2,708	Certified (arabica) (n = 8) Rs 9,696	Non-certified (arabica) (n = 8) Rs 10,142
Comparison of yields per acre	Certified (n = 33) 1,265 kg		Non-certified (n = 30) 1,110 kg	

conservation efforts is rooted in mistrust emerging from a lack of restrictions on people's land-use practices.

The findings of this research from Kodagu in relation to the posited research question on the outcomes of market-based incentive initiatives also contributes to existing academic and policy debates on the role of additionality, opportunity costs and prioritisation of conservation efforts. The lack of additionality in Kodagu implies that the environmental (and social) requirements of the projects are lower than the existing land-use and livelihood practices. In the case of shade-grown certification, this disparity is clearest when comparing the shade requirements specified by Rainforest Alliance certification (e.g. 12 species per hectare) compared to existing tree diversity of over 22 tree species per hectare (CAFNET 2011). In this respect, it could be argued that direct incentives that maintain business as usual play an important role in halting further environmental degradation and biodiversity loss. However, empirical findings of this study critique this perspective in two ways. First, lack of additionality or maintenance payments to natural resource users can mask the politics and vested interests behind the design of the conservation project. For example, in the case of shade-grown certification, there is some evidence to suggest that the environmental and social standards have been deliberately maintained weak to serve business actors. Second, lack of additionality does influence the perceptions of landowners by augmenting mistrust and undermining local support for conservation.

Uncovering hidden imprints of shade-grown certification

This research story argues that although market incentives for conservation are promoted as standalone fixes designed to singularly address opportunity costs of conservation, such incentives are in fact embedded in a web of social and political relationships. This chapter further builds the chains of explanations by attempting to understand important actors across various scales, their vested interests and how these relationships shape subjectivities of coffee growers towards the conservation of shade trees. This chapter argues that conservation programmes, particularly those that are market-based such as shade-grown certifications are implemented in the wider context of disenchantment with conservation in Kodagu. This disillusionment with conservation is rooted in various political experiences but noteworthy are people's interactions with the Indian state, resistance to conservation processes that are perceived as imperialistic and the politics of partnerships with private actors.

Strategy and politics of state and shade

Shade-grown certification in Kodagu is advocated for by a mixed party of private actors such as coffee exporters, certification auditors, certification agencies such as Rainforest Alliance and UTZ-Certified and conservationists, comprising either groups or individuals who have publicly supported such initiatives. Both on paper as well as on the ground, certifiers and certified farmers do not explicitly engage with the Indian state regarding the certification process; neither the Coffee Board of India, Forest Department of Karnataka nor more generally, the State Government of Karnataka. Bypassing the involvement of the state in the management of natural resources is possible primarily because conservation of shade trees and overall biodiversity is being proposed on privately owned coffee farms, managed by individuals with clearly documented titles and land tenure security. Such arrangements are viewed optimistically by conservation actors at all levels – regional, national and global – who argue that weak, inefficient and corrupt states can seriously undermine conservation efforts (Laurance 2004; Ferraro and Simpson 2005; Smith and Walpole 2005; Peluso 1993). In fact, coffee growers in Kodagu also share similar views on incompetence of the state, as described subsequently in this chapter. However, this chapter argues that despite the ostensible 'rolling back of the state', shade-grown certification operates within a very prevalent mentality or experience of the state. This implies that although the state is not directly involved in market mechanisms for conservation, the experience of the state in other aspects of peoples' lives still strongly influences the views of coffee growers towards conservation on their private lands.

The presence of the state in peoples' everyday lives manifests in various ways, including in political struggles for autonomy and statehood. The demands for statehood, as argued by the Codava National Council (CNC), the largest political group in the district, are largely on the grounds that historically Kodagu has always been a separate state during the British and medieval periods until amalgamation with the Karnataka state in 1956. The CNC also argues for statehood on the assertion that 'The Kodagu race is most neglected by the Karnataka state', as written by N.U. Nachappa, President of the Codava National Council in a letter to the President of India in 2009. Leaders of the CNC, which is one of the primary movers of the demand for a separate state, argue that Kodagu has historically been an independent land in which the Kodagu people were the dominant landowners who had no 'obligations to external or superior forces' (CNC 2013).

> The Codava Land is geographically and culturally distinct from the rest of Kannada state. Its linguistic, agro-climatic and socio-economic characteristics are different. The Codava land was only incorporated in to the artificial entity of the so-called Kannada state with the advent of the state re-organisation and cannot be set to be fully integrated into the culture of the inheritor state of Kannada in Karnataka.
>
> (CNC 2013)

The demand for the protection of Kodagu identity through the reorganisation of the Karnataka state is intricately linked to people's perceptions of 'losing Kodagu identity due to the influx of other communities into Kodagu', arguably a result of economic opportunities in the district, including the expansion of the coffee industry (CNC 2006). Although the politics of statehood have been described simplistically, the purpose of addressing such issues in this chapter concerns the consequences of such tensions on people's views on conservation. For example, in response to a state proposal to create a National Park between the Pushpagiri and Brahmagiri Wildlife Sanctuaries, the President of the CNC submitted a letter to the Chief Minister of Karnataka stating,

> The proposed National Park definitely is a proposal to clear primary jungle in the first instance and denude the real forest growth thereafter and in between allow the visitor watch the denizens of forest in their free movement in other words the concepts of national park is to obliterate the biodiversity of a naturally thick forest and in course of time ruin the entire environmental magnificence.
>
> (Nachappa 2006)

The above comment provides a broader context of tensions, which are reflected in extreme mistrust of the state and severe opposition to the creation of additional state-managed PAs within the district. While mistrust of the state's intentions behind creating PA enclaves is a major driver of opposition, an equally important factor is the widespread belief among people that the state is incompetent at managing natural resources. A shared perception of the Forest Department is that it is ineffective at conserving wildlife in existing PAs and forests areas. Discussions about conservation throw up a few repeated narratives about how 'The Forest Department has planted only teak for timber (*Tectona grandis*) when they should in fact be planting fruit trees for elephants'.

The following statements illustrate such negative perceptions even further:

> First retain forest in the forest area. If there is forest, there will be no need for elephants to come out. If I was an elephant even I would love to live in my dark green plantation that has water rather than teak, acacia or subabool. Is that a forest?
>
> One thing I fight for is against the government. These guys, I tell you are a bunch of jokers. Now the elections are coming up so the current government has been issuing cutting orders like anything because they want to make their loot. The Forest Department is anti-forest.
>
> I plan to take my micro-glider and scatter jackfruit seeds in the forest as food for elephants.

Coffee growers no doubt share hesitation about the competency and political desire of the state to manage forests in the district effectively. In principle, it is likely that most would agree that compared to the state, people of Kodagu would be better environmental stewards (for e.g. 'I am a better environmentalist than the Forest Department'). Although the above comments provide refer to state-managed forests and PAs, such sentiments spill over to privately owned coffee plantations, over which the state can make no explicit claims. Disenchantment with the state's ability to manage forests is translated into a widely shared feeling that conservation efforts should focus on improved management of state forests before addressing biodiversity loss on coffee farms. For example, coffee growers commented:

Why do you put blame on the private man? You are trying to put spokes in my wheel instead of a smuggler's wheel. I don't see any trees regenerating in the forest. What have they done for the elephants? There has been a drought in Karnataka. Have they made any arrangements for elephants in the forest? Whereas I have got a tank, the elephants come and enjoy a bath in my estate.

Why don't you ask the Forest Department about conservation? First let them protect the forest. I am already doing environmentalism.

The core of disillusionment with the state and arguably the biggest driver of opposition towards conservation on private lands concerns legal rights to trees. Depending on land tenure, landowners can receive either the full commercial value of the trees harvested (such as in the case of 'redeemed' lands) or are compelled to pay a *seignoriage* value to the Karnataka Forest Department (such as in the case of 'unredeemed' lands) (Uthappa 2004). In both redeemed and unredeemed lands, coffee growers have to obtain permits from the Forest Department, a process that is often cumbersome and expensive owing to a series of 'bribes'. Some species of trees, particularly those of high timber value, such as tosewood (*Dalbergia latifolia*) and teak (*Tectona grandis*), are more strictly protected and can be sold only through auctions controlled by the Forest Department. In contrast, no prior permissions nor 'calisthenics' are required to harvest exotic species such as silver oak (see Karnataka Preservation of Trees Act 1976: GoK 1976; Nath et al. 2011). Nath et al. (2011: 107) assert that farmers describe difficulties in maintaining high tree diversity due to 'protectionist policies' behind land and tree tenures, which demand heavy duties and permits for felling, transport and selling of native timbers. Lack of ownership has encouraged farmers to plant exotic trees, such as silver oak instead (Elouard et al. 2000; Ambinakudige and Sathish 2009; Garcia et al. 2010). A number of coffee growers involved in this research project too asserted that ownership of tree rights would lead to judicious rather than indiscriminate removal of shade trees from coffee farms. Their arguments mirror the story of numerous case studies where tenure security has led to more sustainable natural resource management (see Agrawal and Ostrom 2001; Ribot and Peluso 2003; Uthappa 2004; Larson et al. 2008). Planters who subscribed to the view said,

If I had the right to cut my trees I would plant in a way that I could maintain shade but definitely cut the tree once its mature. Every tree has a life and when it reaches optimum maturity the quality of the wood deteriorates. A good, solid rosewood tree can fetch you six to seven lakhs.

Nowadays planters see trees with dollar signs on the trunk. It is because we are not allowed that we cut trees.

The demand for the rights to harvest trees is embedded in a broader context of actions that reflect widespread dismissal of the forest and conservation. For coffee growers, such actions include the removal of native shade trees, either through weeding out at a sapling stage or more covertly through girdling. Many coffee growers, whose land tenure permits them to harvest trees, apply for permissions and remove up to a hundred trees a year. After such removal, native trees are very rarely planted back into the estate for the purpose of shade.

At one level it could be argued that the demand for tree rights and removal of shade cover is indicative of the economic trade-offs inherent to keeping shade trees on plantations. However, it could also be argued that the demand for tree rights and resistance to conservation of shade trees on private lands is symbolic of a larger ideological and political struggle for political autonomy in Kodagu. The struggle over tree rights is not merely a struggle over the potential income from timber but also a dialogue about property rights.

Similarly, the resistance to retain, plant or conserve shade trees on private coffee farms is not merely the resistance to decreased coffee productivity from excess shade. It is also the resistance of trees and conservation of natural resources as property of the Karnataka state, from which the people of Kodagu want statehood. Shade trees are then, not just used to shade coffee plants from the sun, they are used as a symbolic tool in this everyday political resistance. They represent, as James Scott (1985: 38) said, a contestation over the 'appropriation of symbols, a struggle over how the past and present shall be understood and labeled, a struggle to identify causes and assess blame, a contentious effort to give partisan meaning to local history'.

In the case of Kodagu, the CNC's role is in the space of institutionalised politics concerned with formal, legal or *de jure* changes to governance of the district with regards to existing relations with the Karnataka state government. However, the disavowal of shade trees is a covert form of everyday resistance, unspoken and uncoordinated but arguably equally effective at negating the state's claim over property on private coffee farms. The lack of support for conservation of shade trees is as Scott (1985: 290) argued, 'implicit disavowal of public and symbolic goals' or an attempt to 'mitigate or deny claims made by superordinate classes' in a context where conservation of forests (including native forest trees on private farms over which the farmer has limited ownership) are explicitly activities of the state: 'To resist a claim or an appropriation is to resist, as well, the justification and rationale behind that particular claim' (Scott 1985: 297).

The underlying tone and framing of language with which coffee growers describe their views on shade trees, the state and conservation activities, including shade-grown certification, reveals implicit, yet strong political content. For example, some coffee growers made the following comments when asked about their views on shade trees, particularly tree rights:

> I don't cut junglweood with the purpose of making my income from it. But why should I keep it if I don't own it?
>
> The government doesn't like Kodagu. That's why we are the only district where we can own the land but not the trees on the land so I am forced to remove shade trees. I don't want any government property!

> Government cannot make a categorical statement saying it is their trees. See the situation now is that people cut trees left right and centre. That is not how it should be.

The experience of the lack of ownership of trees for an individual coffee farmer has also reinforced notions that trees can be maintained as shade on estates only if something tangible can be obtained, as is evident in comments such as,

> We get nothing out of junglewood so we are not planting it. Or we remove it at sapling state and planting silver oak instead. It is not the desire to keep silver oak but the lack of reason to keep junglewood that is causing the problem. We know that silver oak has a slight detriment to coffee but at least we own our silver trees.

This is a scenario different to the act of resistance in rejecting shade and is often more applicable to certain species of trees. For 'junglewood' or native species of commercial timber value, such as rosewood (Dalbergia latifolia) or white cedar (Dysoxylum malabaricum), coffee growers admit their frustration about not being able to harvest mature trees for their timber value. Those farmers whose land tenure does allow them the rights to trees have to invest time and money to run around filling out paperwork and securing proof of permission, making it only barely profitable to cut the tree.

> We remove junglewood trees at the sapling stage itself because once it grows tall it is expensive to maintain and we get nothing out of it. These damn things (referring to Dalbergia latifolia) are valuable but you can't cut it.

A significant ecological consequence has been the increasing rarity of trees without substantial timber value.

Save for a handful of timber valuable species and a few coffee growers, the role of shade trees has been that of a bargaining tool with the Indian state. The removal of shade and rejection of conservation efforts to conserve shade contain political motivations. Such everyday resistance is an implicit statement that the ownership of shade trees should belong to people. More broadly, the message is that the people of Kodagu should have the power to make decisions about natural resources and property, both individual as well as common. When conservationists dismiss farmers' lack of support for conservation as indifference, this inhibits a deeper insight into the historical and political tensions. An understanding of the context of shade trees within larger political struggles in Kodagu allows for a more holistic understanding of why conservation initiatives, such as shade-grown certification, fail to foster local stewardship. 'To allow the government's tree to flourish on my land would be like allowing the government into my home' and that would be akin to recognising the control the state has over the property of its subjects.

Rejection of conservation as imperialism

This chapter has thus far unpacked the politics of shade so far as interactions between the state and coffee growers and implications for notions concerning the conservation of native tree species. This section considers subjectivities towards shade conservation as a product of imperialism. Imperialism, in this context is defined as the 'unequal human and territorial relationship, usually in the form of an empire, based on ideas of superiority and practices of dominance, and involving the extension of authority and control of one state or people over another' (Gregory *et al.* 2011: 373).

Coffee growing is central to the cultural identity of the people in Kodagu. Knowledge about all elements of coffee production, including environmental aspects such as managing soil, water and shade trees is considered 'traditional knowledge' that 'flows from these cultural roots' (Neilson and Pritchard 2007: 311). In contrast, the rules and regulations of shade-grown certification are perceived to be 'foreign', intellectually conceived of and developed in Western countries without the participation of Kodagu producers who are required to abide by them. An implicit assumption in such processes that are designed far away from but implemented in Kodagu is that local agricultural practices and environmental and social sustainability are subservient to those designed in the global North (West 2010; Neilson and Pritchard 2007). In this respect, coffee growers in Kodagu commented as follows:

> We don't need someone else to give us *gyaan* (translated from Hindi as knowledge or information) or guidelines. We have always grown our coffee like this. Only now it may be a little more organised.
>
> These people learnt agriculture from us and now they are teaching us.
>
> Others have signed up because they are impressed with the way they speak and because there are a lot of white people explaining what certification is. I don't need to listen to them to maintain my standards.
>
> It is not because of the certification premium or guidelines that I take care of my estate. It is because I feel it is important for my coffee to look after the soil. The same goes for looking after my workforce. I take care of my people because I want them.

However, I find that while the social and environmental norms have not been experienced as excessive or imposing, they have been experienced as irrational and imperialistic. Therefore, in addition to critiquing the roots of certification as Western, this research argues further that such roots create a sense of disenchantment that further alienates coffee growers from conservation efforts. Such disenchantment is evident in comments such as the following:

> These foreigners keep hatching schemes to interfere with coffee production.
> (An interviewee, referring to a discussion
> with Europe-based ecologists)

Putting up signboards saying 'Rainforest Alliance certified' is for white man's benefit. Why should I go through all the hassle?

Intrinsic to the disenchantment of coffee growers with romanticised Western ideologies embedded in certification rules and regulations is their lack of concrete participation. The findings of this research complement a study carried out by Ninan and Sathyapalan (2005) on farmers' 'willingness to pay for conservation', which emphasised that people's support and positive attitude was contingent on their participation in the strategic design of conservation initiatives right from the outset. Neilson and Pritchard (2007) also concluded, although theoretically without any explicit empirical evidence, that an externally imposed conservation project would be less likely to receive widespread support. The nature of these sentiments deviates in principle from allied debates on local community participation in PAs and conservation through restricted access. In latter debates, participatory decision making is seen a critical safeguard for the livelihoods and rights of often impoverished and marginalised natural resource users. In Kodagu, arguments for participation are for participation's sake since as of now farmers have experienced few livelihood-related restrictions as a result of shade-grown certification. In this landscape, coffee growers feel strongly about rules, rule makers and rule making and an experience of disempowerment and distance from decision making is only expected to lead to growing disenchantment and the weakening of sentiments of environmental stewardship. Planters in Kodagu say,

> Rainforest Alliance is not understanding the local problems. Their labour requirements in this certification are oriented towards ill treatment of labour in Africa. Our problems are labour shortage. If they don't let us participate then how will they know what our problems are?
>
> See, if we can jointly discuss how to conserve the environment, then I am all game. But the problem is all these environmentalists sit in air-conditioned ivory towers and don't consult the farmer. See the amount of garbage in cities. Have you seen how they have ruined their cities? You might find some garbage lying around in Kodagu but it is probably not as dangerous as garbage in Japan. There, every garbage is dangerous unless correctly disposed. So first they should consult us. Then we can plan the environment.
>
> Do they think I am too dull to be consulted?
>
> It is important to know what the goal of this project is. There is distrust in the village because of the lack of knowledge. More trust would make it a partnership. Right now it is one-way traffic.

In addition to disenchantment about the process of certification as exclusionary, coffee growers in Kodagu hold strong perspectives on the consumers for shade-grown certified coffee. At first glance, it appears surprising that coffee producers in Kodagu would raise questions about a system in which seemingly conscientious consumers are connected to conscientious producers through conscientious coffee businesses.

This discussion on 'distant action' and symbolism of sustainable coffee is significant because it describes global processes and then analyses these within the Kodagu context. Analyses of distant action and symbolism resonate within the Kodagu landscape in slightly different ways from those discussed above. Coffee growers in Kodagu very vividly imagine a niche for 'Kodagu coffee' and symbolically Kodagu identity. Farmers even strategically use shade-grown certification as a means towards achieving this larger vision. However, they strongly disassociate from connotations of economic and social justice emblematic of sustainable coffees, particularly representations of coffee farmers as vulnerable and impoverished. For example, coffee growers in Kodagu describe their disagreement with the symbolic meanings of shade-grown certification in the following ways:

> I don't want people to buy my coffee because I am poor. I want them to buy it because it is of good quality.
>
> I am not poor and backward like coffee farmers in Africa.
>
> These foreigners buy our coffee because they think we are poor and starving. They will get a shock when they come to my house.
>
> We are not farmers. Please call us planters. You can call people in South America and Africa farmers.

The dissonance with shade-grown certification for its exclusion of coffee growers and use of symbolism and values with which planters in Kodagu do not fully relate is strengthened by people's experiences with certification audits. The certification process itself involves coffee growers in Kodagu being audited and assessed by 'outsiders' who are unfamiliar with the evolution of local agricultural practices and associated politics. Despite being 'Indian', auditors are considered to be unknowing of the local culture and social practices and not qualified to assess sustainability of plantations given their own lack of agricultural expertise. Farmers perceive not only the attitudes of auditors to be authoritarian and arrogant but the entire certification process itself. Coffee growers claim they are expected to suddenly 'fall in line' or do all sorts of 'calisthenics' in order to arrange for certification audits.

> Bird-friendly coffee, sun-kissed, rain-kissed coffee! They are coming and telling me how to look after my labour. I am telling them not to come back again. Instead of paying those fools Rs 50,000, I prefer to pay my labour that money. Buyers should come and see the estates themselves rather than sending a certifying agency. They are trying to pull wool over a lot of people's eyes.

In order to qualify for Rainforest Alliance for the first time, a farm has to be audited by the auditing agency and successfully comply with at least 80 per cent of the total criteria of the standards and 100 per cent of the mandatory criteria. Auditors can use their discretion on assessing compliance of these criteria. In order to be re-assessed for certification annually, the auditing agency carries out random and surprise visits to the farm. Ecom, the certified coffee buyer, is informed about the surprise visit either a day or a few hours in advance and the coffee growers are very rarely informed in advance. The surprise auditing is stressful even for Ecom, who basically pay for the audit fees. An employee at Ecom described the audit as follows:

> One evening I got a call from IMO saying that they were going to audit a farm in Sakleshpur area. I was at home in Virajpet. By the time I reached the farm the auditors had reached and already left because the owner was not there. They had called him and asked him to let the audit happen but his phone was unreachable and his labourers didn't let the auditors enter the estate. So we tried to explain to the auditors that even if they had informed us three days in advance we could have ensured a successful audit. Even three days is a surprise visit. If a planter has cut down all his shade trees they will not grow back in three days. This audit is major tension for us.

This kind of 'snoopy-tom' work, as audits are referred to, is received with considerable opposition as is evident in the statements below:

> I am not a fan of this snoopy-tom work that they do around estates.
> Tell me, why should I not be present when they are speaking to my labourers? They come to my estate and then tell me to get out. Last time, one of the labourer's children was playing on the estate while his mother was picking and the auditors accused me of child labour. If you don't consult with me, talk with dignity, how will you understand the situation?
> The conditions of certification are more important than price premium. They should not control us.

The experience of certification audits in Kodagu is not unique in its emphasis on audits. Lyon (2009: 223) comments that the 'Northern bias of certification standards includes burdensome recordkeeping requirements and expenses associated with certification'. Tad Mutersbaugh's work with organic coffee producers in Oaxaca, Mexico describes similar scenarios where the certification is described as 'Organic coffee is documents!' (Mutersbaugh 2004: 545) and 'If we don't have documents, our work in the field doesn't serve us' (Mutersbaugh 2004: 545). Mutersbaugh (2004: 533) suggests,

> These standards are found to embed contradictions between inclusiveness and transparency that lead to difficulties in field-level implementation: in essence, practices required to make organic production legible to transnational certifiers often have the opposite effect of making certification unintelligible at the village level.

It could be argued that disenchantment with shade-grown certification as imperialism in Kodagu is rooted in tensions discussed in this section, Western notions of sustainability and lack of participation, excessive use of symbolism and imagery that is perceived as unrepresentative. Tensions concerning conservation thus emerge from a combination of these factors, but an overall experience of 'unevenness', whether due to sentiments of 'West versus us' or lack of participation. An understanding of these tensions offers an understanding of the failure to create an 'intimate government', what Agrawal (2005) defines as the construction of shared interests and the ability to overcome 'action at a distance', 'government at a distance' or 'market governance'. If shade-grown certification were to instead 'disperse rule' and involve coffee growers in decision making about certification standards, strengthen ways to self-regulate or jointly regulate, it might have led to changes in land-use practices and behaviour such that coffee growers were more mindful of native shade trees and the consequences of their removal (Agrawal 2005). At present, disenchantment with conservation and efforts to conserve shade prevail.

> Environmentalists make too big an issue about shade.
> Environmentalists are mentalists!

Conclusions

The arguments to pay increased attention to market-based incentives in conservation policy and practice reason that direct incentive approaches are institutionally simple. Such arrangements involve straightforward transactions between natural resource users and incentive providers and do not require the complicated add-ons associated with indirect approaches. In contrast, indirect incentives like ICDPs, provision of alternative livelihoods or access rights to forest and natural products involve a whole host of institutional issues that need to be addressed in order for the conservation project to be effective. For example, ICDP projects around PAs frequently require state or conservation agencies to establish Village Development Committees (VDCs), self-help groups (SHGs) or other village-level committees to manage the funds distribution and community engagement in the ICDP project. In a second example, the success of sustainable use programmes rests critically on land tenure and access rights. The resolution of tenure insecurities and conflicts is therefore an essential prerequisite to such conservation efforts. It is because indirect approaches are so explicitly implemented within a larger institutional climate that in comparison, direct incentives are considered less complex. This particular story aims to engage with theoretical assumptions by asking if and how market-based incentives are embedded within local and global processes and, influenced by historical, social and political dynamics, are able to modify land-use practices. In this concluding section, we also explore this politics by analysing three spheres of relations that significantly influence the effectiveness of shade-grown certification: (a) relations between coffee growers, the Indian state and shade trees (b), relations between coffee growers and global conservation ideals, and (c) negotiations between private actors and the toggles of market-based conservation.

Although market-based approaches operate on the premise of the withdrawal of the state in conservation practice and policies, the presence of the state in other aspects of everyday life continues to be powerful, particularly concerning tenure security and access to natural resources. Tensions between the people of Kodagu and the Indian state have ecological implications that spill across the boundaries of state-managed PAs into privately owned coffee farms where there is conflict over the ownership of trees. Protectionist state policies concerning the ownership and rights to extract trees from private coffee farms have led to widespread rejection of forests and conservation. As a result, coffee growers whose land tenure permits them to harvest trees often remove up to hundred trees a year, rarely planting back into the plantation. Many, whose land tenure disallows harvesting, heavily weed out seedlings and sapling or covertly remove trees through girdling. The active involvement in protests for the demand for tree rights is indicative of the seriousness of this issue for many coffee growers.

The story of everyday resistance towards conservation efforts, PAs or species is increasingly discussed in literature on conservation effectiveness. Harkness (1998) explains how villages in northern Yunnan, China rushed to destroy trees that they had previously protected after their community-managed forest was established into a state-owned nature reserve. Closer to Kodagu, in many parts of India, such conflicts over forest have been described as symbolic of larger political conflicts. For example, Deb Roy and Jackson (1993) describe how extremist groups fighting for autonomy in Assam became actively involved in conflicts and protests concerning the establishment of Manas National Park. In parts of Maharashtra and Chhattisgarh, conflicts between tribal communities and the state over legal rights to community-managed forests became an integral element of the movement over tribal homeland (Gadgil and Guha 1992; Gadgil and Guha 1994).

An understanding of the context of shade trees within larger political struggles in Kodagu, allows for a more holistic understanding of why conservation initiatives, such as shade-grown certification, fail to foster local stewardship. As one coffee grower commented, 'To allow the government's tree to flourish on my land would be like allowing the government into my home', and that would be akin to recognising the control the state has over the property of its subjects.

Empirical findings in Kodagu also illuminate political tensions and unevenness between coffee growers and global conservation ideals, which are perceived as imperialistic. Shade-grown certification is seen as a distinctly Western project, designed and conceived of in countries of the global North and bereft of the participation of coffee producers. In a landscape where coffee production is central to identities, the exclusion of local communities in the design and implementation of certification standards is seen as an indirect way of undermining local agricultural practices as subservient. The disillusionment with global conservation ideas is evident in the following comment from a certified farmer: 'These people learnt agriculture from us and now they are teaching us'.

In this respect, the subjectivities of coffee growers in Kodagu are analogous to Crystal Fortwangler's work on the creation of PAs in the US Virgin Islands, where an employee of the United States National Park Service is quoted as saying,

The problem with park management is that they think locals don't understand or appreciate the environment. We do. We grew up here knowing how to conserve. We had to conserve and be resourceful. What we do not appreciate is being disrespected.

(Fortwangler 2007, as cited in Igoe and Brockinton 2007: 443)

These findings also parallel Sarah Lyon's (2009) research with a Mayan community in the highlands of Guatemala and Paige West's (2010) work with the Gimi people in Papua New Guinea, both of which also raise questions vis-à-vis the origins of shade-grown certification. The geographical and conceptual distances between the two social worlds, the local and global, produce rules and regulations that are shaped by Western ideals, arguably North American (Lyon 2009) fantasies of a coffee farm as a forest – untouched and traditional, teeming with endangered wildlife species, and coffee farmers as fervent conservationists, willing and excited to protect biodiversity. Lyon (2009) and West (2010) find that such fantasies have directly influenced the creation of rigid rules and regulations that are experienced as excessive by local farmers.

In Kodagu, coffee growers feel strongly about rules, rule-makers and rule-making, and market-based incentives such as shade-grown certification that are implemented as global blueprints across social-ecological systems of great variability are expected to lead to growing disenchantment and weakening sentiments of environmental stewardship. For example, farmers in Kodagu ask, 'See, if we can jointly discuss how to conserve the environment then I am all game' but 'Do they think I am too dull to be consulted?'

A related set of implications of the absent participation of producers between the design of global conservation ideas and their application is that coffee growers in Kodagu strongly disassociate with symbolism used to promote certified coffee. Producers in Kodagu react with dissonance to representations of coffee farmers as weak and impoverished and express disagreement with the symbolic meanings of shade-grown certification. In contrast, Kodagu producers imagine a niche for Kodagu coffee, culture and identity and engage with shade-grown certification as a tool to achieve this larger vision.

Market-based incentives are enmeshed within a historical, social and political context that strongly influence the response and effectiveness of these incentives. The findings also propose strong arguments for the fact that the incentives for unsustainable land-use practices, including agricultural intensification and removal of native trees from coffee farms, are not necessarily solely economic. Therefore, the ability of economic incentive measures to address historical, political and social explanations for land-use practices is limited.

This study from Kodagu emphasises the effects of local contexts and questions the effectiveness and local support for globally designed and motivated interventions. A fundamental weakness of global blueprints, such as global social and environmental standards for coffee production, is that these are disembedded and therefore neither address local context drivers of environmental problems nor enable any local support. In reflecting, as Martin *et al.* (2008:5) have, this study from Kodagu argues about the risks in market-based strategies that ally dispro- portionately with economists who emphasise efficiency, rather than equity and legitimacy. Therefore, it is crucial for conservation organisations, policy makers and scholars writing about direct incentives to acknowledge the importance of local contexts, perceptions and particularities in shaping outcomes. Part of this process would include expanding the kinds of knowledge to capture the nuances, richness and specificity of local land-use practices and cultural and political his- tories as part of the conservation design and decision-making process. While this has been accepted to some extent in discourses about community-based conservation, emerging market-based strategies fail to explicitly integrate such knowledges into design and implementation.

There are no straightforward answers or lessons from this research story that can either concretely prove or disprove various claims about the effectiveness of direct incentives in changing land-use and livelihood practices. The outright superiority or rejection of market-based incentive models cannot be established through the argu- ments presented in this case study from Kodagu. However, this was not the primary objective of this study. Nevertheless, this Kodagu study illuminates the coexistence of contradictions, disconnects and inherent unevenness in the nature of relations, whether between coffee growers and conservation initiatives, global ideas and local realities, or private actors and conservation ideals that altogether leave conserva- tion discourse and practice precariously balanced. This study also emphasises ways in which theoretical ideas and policy discourses assume, simplify and depoliticise the practice of such market approaches. Finally, it reveals critical flaws in such con- servation approaches by providing empirical evidence that questions assumptions, demonstrates the limitations, shows complexities and emphasises the importance of locally meaningful conservation ideals.

* * *

Ponappa, the coffee grower in Kodagu and the conservationist in the 'geeky- chic' café in East London are connected through chains of explanations. As the conservationist knocks back the dregs of his cup of sustainable coffee, Ponappa prepares to raze the government's ficus trees. The two individuals are connected, albeit not in ways that are most immediately obvious. A butterfly flapping its wings in East London does by no means cause a storm in the Western Ghats. These connections and causes and effects are much more subtle. They lie under the labels of 'sustainable', 'shade-grown', 'biodiversity-friendly', 'ethical' and 'win-win'. Yet, the impacts are cyclonic nonetheless.

References

Agrawal, A. (2005) Environmentality: community, intimate government, and the making of environmental subjects in Kumaon, India, *Current Anthropology*, 46(2): 161–190.

Agrawal, A. and E. Ostrom (2001) Collective action, property rights, and decentralization in resource use in India and Nepal, *Politics & Society*, 29(4): 485–514.

Allen, S.L. (2000) *The Devil's Cup: Coffee, the Driving Force in History*, Canongate Books, Edinburgh.

Ambinakudige, S. and B. Sathish (2009) Comparing tree diversity and composition in coffee farms and sacred forests in the Western Ghats of India, *Biodiversity and Conservation*, 18(4): 987–1000.

Bacon, C.M. (2010) Who decides what is fair in fair trade? The agri-environmental governance of standards, access, and price, *The Journal of Peasant Studies*, 37(1): 111–147.

Bhagwat, S., C.G. Kushalappa, P.H. Williams and N. Brown (2005) The role of informal protected areas in maintaining biodiversity in the Western Ghats of India, *Conservation Biology*, 19: 1853–1862.

Bhagwat, S., K.J. Willis, J.B. Birks and R.J. Whitaker (2008) Agroforestry: a refuge for tropical biodiversity, *Trends in Ecology and Evolution*, 23(5): 261–267.

Bose, A., B. Vira, B. and C. Garcia (2016) Does environmental certification in coffee promote 'business as usual'? A case study from the Western Ghats, India, *Ambio* 45(8): 946–955.

CAFNET (2011) Coffee Agroforestry Network India Final Report, College of Forestry, Ponnampet.

CBI (2013) Database on coffee, *Coffee Board of India*. Retrieved 30/12/2017, from www.indiacoffee.org/indiacoffee.php?page=CoffeeData.

Chethana, A., N. Nagaraj, P. Chengappa and C. Gracy (2010) Geographical indications for Kodagu coffee: a socio-economic feasibility analysis, *Agricultural Economics Research Review*, 23(1): 97–103.

CI (2013) Economic incentives, *Conservation International*. Retrieved 20/12/2016, from www.conservation.org/learn/culture/communities/Pages/incentives.aspx.

CNC (2006) *Social, Political and Constitutional Rights and Entitlements of the Codavas*, Madikeri.

CNC (2013) Codava National Council. Retrieved 18/12/2016, from www.codavanationalcouncil.com/.

Deb Roy, S. and P. Jackson (1993) Mayhem in Manas: the threats to India's wildlife reserves, in E. Kemf (eds.) *The Law of the Mother: Protecting Indigenous Peoples in Protected Areas*. Earthscan, London.

Depommier, D. (2003) The tree behind the forest: ecological and economic importance of traditional agroforestry systems and multiple uses of trees in India, *International Society for Tropical Ecology*, 44(1): 63–71.

Desjeux, Y. (1999) *Contribution des arbres d'ombrages des caféiers à l'approvisionnement en bois de feu des petits planteurs du Coorg (Karnataka, Inde du Sud)*, Mémoire de fin d'études, ENITA, Bordeaux.

Elouard, C., M. Chaumette and H. de Pommery (2000) The role of coffee plantations in biodiversity conservation, in P.S. Ramakrishnan *et al.* (eds.) *Mountain Biodiversity, Land Use Dynamics, and Traditional Ecological Knowledge*, Oxford and IBH Publishing, New Delhi, 120–144.

Ferraro, P.J. and D.R. Simpson (2005) Protecting forests and biodiversity: are investments in eco-friendly production activities the best way to protect endangered ecosystems and enhance rural livelihoods?, *Forests, Trees and Livelihoods*, 15: 167–181.

Fortwangler, C. (2007) Friends with money: private support for a national park in the US Virgin Islands, *Conservation and Society*, 5(4): 504–533.

FSC (2013) Forest Stewardship Council: who we are. *Retrieved 23/12/2017*, from https://ic.fsc.org/about-us.1.htm.

Gadgil, M. and R. Guha (1994) Ecological conflicts and the environmental movement in India, *Development and Change*, 25(1): 101–136.

Garcia, C., S.A. Bhagwat, J. Ghazoul, C.D. Nath, K.M. Nanaya, C.G. Kushalappa, Y. Raghuramulu, R. Nasi and P. Vaast (2010) Biodiversity conservation in agricultural landscapes: challenges and opportunities of coffee agroforests in the Western Ghats, India, *Conservation Biology*, 24(2): 479–488.

Ghazoul, J., C. Garcia and C. Kushalappa (2009) Landscape labelling: a concept for next-generation payment for ecosystem service schemes, *Forest Ecology and Management*, 258(9): 1889–1895.

Giovannucci, D. and S. Ponte (2005) Standards as a new form of social contract? Sustainability initiatives in the coffee industry, *Food Policy*, 30(3): 284–301.

Giovannucci, D., A. Byers and L. Pascal (2008) Adding value: certified coffee trade in North America, *Munich Personal RePEc Archive*, MPRA Paper No. 17174.

GoK (1976) Karnataka Preservation of Trees Act of 1976, Department of Parliamentary Affairs and Legislation, Government of Karnataka.

Greenberg, R., P. Bichier, A.C. Angon and R. Reitsma (1997) Bird populations in shade and sun coffee plantations in central Guatemala, *Conservation Biology*, 11(2): 448–459.

Gregory, D., R. Johnston, G. Pratt, M. Watts and S. Whatmore (2011) *The Dictionary of Human Geography*, Blackwell Publishing, Oxford.

Gadgil, M. and Guha, R. (1992) *This Fissured Land: An Ecological History of India*, Oxford University Press, New Delhi.

Harkness, J. (1998) Recent trends in forestry and conservation of biodiversity in China, *The China Quarterly*, 156: 911–934.

Hatanaka, M., C. Bain and L. Busch (2005) Third-party certification in the global agri-food system, *Food Policy*, 30(3): 354–369.

Igoe, J. and D. Brockington (2007) Neoliberal conservation: a brief introduction, *Conservation and Society*, 5(4): 432–449.

Jha, S., C.M. Bacon, S.M. Philpott, R.A. Rice, V.E. Mendez and P. Lederach (2011) A review of ecosystem services, farmer livelihoods, and value chains in shade coffee agroecosystems, in W.B. Campbell and S. López Ortíz (eds.) *Integrating Agriculture, Conservation and Ecotourism: Examples from the Field*, Springer, Dordrecht, 141–208.

Kleijn, D. and W.J. Sutherland (2003) How effective are European agri-environment schemes in conserving and promoting biodiversity?, *Journal of Applied Ecology*, 40(6): 947–969.

Larson, A.M., P. Cronkleton, D. Barry and P. Pacheco (2008) *Tenure Rights and Beyond: Community Access to Forest Resources in Latin America*, Center for International Forestry Research (CIFOR), Bogor, Indonesia.

Laurance, W.F. (2004) The perils of payoff: corruption as a threat to global biodiversity, *Trends in Ecology and Evolution*, 19(8): 399–401.

Lee, H.L. and C.Y. Lee (2010) *Building Supply Chain Excellence in Emerging Economies*, Springer, Dordrecht.

Leroy, M., C. Garcia, P. Aubert, V. Jeremy, C. Bernard, J. Brams, C. Caron, C. Junker, G. Payet, C. Rigal and S. Thevenet (2011) *Thinking the Future: Coffee, Forests and People: Conservation and Development in Kodagu*, AgroParisTech – ENGREF, Paris.

Linton, A. (2005) Partnering for sustainability: business–NGO alliances in the coffee industry, *Development in Practice*, 15(3–4): 600–614.

Lyon, S. (2009) What good will two more trees do? The political economy of sustainable coffee certification, local livelihoods and identities, *Landscape Research*, 34(2): 223–240.

Martin, A., A. Blowers and J. Boersema (2008) Paying for environmental services: can we afford to lose a cultural basis for conservation?, *Environmental Sciences*, 5(1): 1–5.

Moguel, P. and V.M. Toledo (1999) Biodiversity conservation in traditional coffee systems of Mexico, *Conservation Biology*, 13(1): 11–21.

MSC (2013) Marine Stewardship Council: about us. *Retrieved 23/12/2017*, from www.msc.org/about-us.

Muradian, R. and W. Pelupessy (2005) Governing the coffee chain: the role of voluntary regulatory systems, *World Development*, 33(12): 2029–2044.

Mutersbaugh, T. (2004) To serve and to certify: organic coffee, certification services and village cargo service in Mexico, *Environment and Planning D: Society and Space*, Special Issue: *New Geographies of Work*, 22(4): 533–552.

Nachappa, N.U. (2006) *Social, Political and Constitutional Rights and Entitlements of the Codavas*, Codava National Council. Retrieved 18/12/2013, from www.google.co.uk/url?sa=t&rct=j&q=&esrc=s&source=web&cd=1&ved=0CDEQFjAA&url=http%3A%2F%2Fcodavanationalcouncil.com%2Fdownload.doc&ei=6dGxUobmNqvb7AaX1oF4&usg=AFQjCNE87b2ZMuO8SCVnJTyWufiyqn9g5Q&sig2=gpW40msJPH7NeNJVrRdxDw&bvm=bv.58187178,d.Z G4.

Nath, C.D., R. Pélissier, B. Ramesh and C. Garcia (2011) Promoting native trees in shade coffee plantations of southern India: comparison of growth rates with the exotic Grevillea robusta, *Agroforestry Systems*, 83(2): 107–119.

National Informatics Centre (2011) Official Website of Kodagu District. Retrieved 27/03/2012, from www.kodagu.nic.in/.

Neilson, J. and B. Pritchard (2007) Green coffee? The contradictions of global sustainability initiatives from an Indian perspective, *Development Policy Review*, 25(3): 311–331.

Ninan, K. and J. Sathyapalan (2005) The economics of biodiversity conservation: a study of a coffee growing region in the Western Ghats of India, *Ecological Economics*, 55(1): 61–72.

Peluso, N.L. (1993) Coercing conservation? The politics of state resource control, *Global Environmental Change*, 3(2): 199–217.

Perfecto, I., R.A. Rice, R. Greenberg and M.E. v. d. Voort (1996) Shade coffee: a disappearing refuge for biodiversity, *BioScience*, 46(8): 598–608.

Perfecto, I., J. Vandermeer, A. Mas and L.S. Pinto (2005) Biodiversity, yield, and shade coffee certification, *Ecological Economics*, 54(4): 435–446.

Perfecto, I., I. Armbrecht, S.M. Philpott, L. Soto-Pinto and T.V. Dietsch (2007) Shaded coffee and the stability of rainforest margins in northern Latin America, in T. Tscharntke, C. Leuschner, M. Zeller, E. Guhardja and A. Bidin (eds.) *Stability of Tropical Rainforest Margins*, Springer, Berlin, 225–261.

Philpott, S.M., P. Bichier, R. Rice and R. Greenberg (2007) Field-testing ecological and economic benefits of coffee certification programs, *Conservation Biology*, 21(4): 975–985.

RA (2012) Mission Statement of the Rainforest Alliance. *Retrieved 02/04/2017*, from www.rainforest-alliance.org/about.

Raynolds, L.T., D. Murray and A. Heller (2007) Regulating sustainability in the coffee sector: a comparative analysis of third-party environmental and social certification initiatives, *Agriculture and Human Values*, 24(2): 147–163.

Ribot, J.C. and N.L. Peluso (2003) A theory of access, *Rural Sociology*, 68(2): 153–181.

Rice, R. (2002) Symposium: direct payments as an alternative conservation investment, *16th Annual Meetings of the Society for Conservation Biology*, Canterbury, England.

Scott, J.C. (1985) *Weapons of the Weak: Everyday Forms of Peasant Resistance*, Yale University Press, New Haven, CT.

SMBC (2013) Smithsonian Migratory Bird Center: Bird-friendly Coffee Certification. *Retrieved 11/12/2016*, from http://nationalzoo.si.edu/scbi/migratorybirds/coffee/lover.cfm.

Smith, R.J. and M.J. Walpole (2005) Should conservationists pay more attention to corruption?, *Oryx*, 39(3): 251–256.

Sommerville, M.M., J.P. Jones and E. Milner-Gulland (2009) A revised conceptual framework for payments for environmental services, *Ecology and Society*, 14(2): art. 34.

Soto-Pinto, L., I. Perfecto, J. Castillo-Hernandez and J. Caballero-Nieto (2000) Shade effect on coffee production at the northern Tzeltal zone of the state of Chiapas, Mexico, *Agriculture, Ecosystems and Environment*, 80(1–2): 61–69.

Svadlenak-Gomez, K., T. Clements, C. Foley, N. Kazakov, D. Lewis, D. Miquelle and R. Stenhouse (2007) *Paying for Results: WCS Experience with Direct Incentives for Conservation*, TransLinks, Wildlife Conservation Society, Bronx, New York.

Swinton, S.M., F. Lupi, G.P. Robertson and S.K. Hamilton (2007) Ecosystem services and agriculture: cultivating agricultural ecosystems for diverse benefits, *Ecological Economics*, 64(2): 245–252.

Turner, R. and G. Daily (2008) The ecosystem services framework and natural capital conservation, *Environmental and Resource Economics*, 39(1): 25–35.

Uthappa, K. (2004) *Land Tenure, Land Holding, and Tree Rights of Kodagu*, Kodagu Model Forest Trust, College of Forestry, Mysore, India.

West, P. (2010) Making the market: specialty coffee, generational pitches, and Papua New Guinea, *Antipode*, 42(3): 690–718.

10 Conclusions

Reimagining wilderness

Shonil Bhagwat

Conservation and development for the rich?

Conservation and development both have their own moral agendas (Adams *et al.* 2004; Bhagwat *et al.* 2011a). Conservation is motivated by the desire to save non-human species, primarily because of the perceived responsibility of humans to safeguard life on earth. Similarly, development is motivated by the desire to help other human beings who, for one reason or another, may be in a less privileged position (Bhagwat *et al.* 2011b). However, these well-intentioned moral agendas do not always deliver the goods.

Conservation in India has primarily focused on creating inviolate areas for wilderness where the iconic megafauna of the country can be saved. But who are these iconic species serving? In today's India, they have become the objects of entertainment for the urban elite who flock the national parks and sanctuaries to watch wildlife and expect the wild animals to 'perform' for them. The cover of this book portrays such an interaction – with tiger walking majestically in the foreground and jeep-loads of tourists with their sophisticated digital cameras vying to capture every single move of the tiger. If the moral agenda is to save species, then what about species that are less iconic, inconspicuous, invisible or even invasive? How can their value be paid sufficient attention to in Indian conservation?

Similarly, development in India is all about fast-tracking the clearance of 'development' projects such as mining, construction and other infrastructure. These projects are also mainly serving the urban elite – whether mining of bauxite or iron for the automobile industry or the construction of motorways to connect the cities. The logic is that the benefits of these developments will eventually trickle down to the less well-off. But India still remains a country of extreme contrasts where material wealth and abject poverty coexist, often side-by-side in large metropolises. The nationwide welfare programmes have made promises of food, clothing and shelter for the poorest living in rural India, but they have not always delivered on the promises. Why has development failed to deliver for the poorest? What about the forest-dwelling communities whose generations have depended on natural resources that the elite urban India is increasingly staking its claim on? How does Indian conservation and development play out for their livelihoods?

It is evident that these thorny issues force us to think beyond the confines of what 'conservation' and development' have come to mean in a narrow sense (Newsham and Bhagwat 2015). Even though protected areas have long been seen as the cornerstone of Indian conservation, these issues force us to look beyond them. Similarly, they force us to look beyond what development means in the conventional sense. The chapters in this book have taken that broad view and raised questions that are relevant to addressing the key challenges for conservation and development in India.

Key challenges for conservation and development

This section outlines five key challenges for conservation and development that India will need to grapple with over the course of the twenty-first century. Some of these challenges have been around since Indian Independence, but many have added new dimensions since the wave of neoliberalism in post-1990s India. Five challenges that particularly stand out are: (1) meeting the Sustainable Development Goals; (2) effective use of protected area designations; (3) moderating human–wildlife interactions; (4) recognising community-conserved areas; and (5) using market-based instruments. This section looks at each in turn.

Meeting the Sustainable Development Goals

In 2015, 193 Member States of the United Nations agreed 17 Sustainable Development Goals (SDGs) and 169 targets to be achieved by 2030 (UN 2015). The Government of India is committed to these goals and targets (GoI 2015). In his statement to the UN Summit for the adoption of post-2015 Development Agenda Narendra Modi, the Prime Minister of India, confidently promised to rise to the challenges of meeting these goals and targets:

> There is no cause greater than shaping a world, in which every life that enters it can look to a future of security, opportunity and dignity; and, where we leave our environment in better shape for the next generation. And, no cause that is more challenging.
>
> (GoI 2015: 1)

Meeting the SDGs is indeed a challenge, not least because meeting the 17 goals – let alone 169 targets – at once is very difficult. For example, meeting the seventh SDG, to 'Ensure access to affordable, reliable, sustainable and modern energy for all', or the ninth, to 'Build resilient infrastructure, promote sustainable industrialization and foster innovation' may compromise the fifteenth, to 'Sustainably manage forests, combat desertification, halt and reverse land degradation, halt biodiversity loss'. As Damodaran (this volume) shows, historically mining and forest conservation have been at loggerheads in India and, while the former has helped rapid industrialisation, the obstacles in the latter have compromised the interests of forest-dwelling tribes as Rai and Madegowda (this volume) also show.

In modern-day India, environment–environment conflicts are also evident as Lakhanpal and Chhatre (this volume) demonstrate: in a number of places in India, often adjacent to protected areas, the renewable energy generation has come in direct competition with biodiversity conservation. Meeting one SDG without compromising others is going to be a major challenge for India as the country treads a fine line between conservation and development.

Effective use of protected area designations

It is evident that there is a vast array of protected area designations in India and some geographical spaces have multiple overlapping designations as Saigal *et al.* (this volume) demonstrate. The reasons for this diversity are rooted in three factors: (1) India's colonial legacy; (2) renewed commitment to environmental conservation since the 1970s; and (3) strong local conservation ethic among many communities. The colonial legacy has given India its wildlife sanctuaries, national parks and tiger reserves – many of which were the hunting reserves during the British colonial period. India's renewed commitment to environmental conservation in the 1970s expanded the network of protected areas and added to its repertoire international designations such as biosphere reserves and Ramsar sites, albeit at the cost of displacing people from their homelands. Despite this, many community-conserved areas have a long history of protection as Rai and Madegowda (this volume) demonstrate. Some of these were subsumed within formal protected areas while others remain outside of this network. During the wave of community-based conservation in the 1990s, 'joint forest management' (JFM) was seen as the panacea by the authorities trying to work with the local communities to protect forests. However, as Shahabuddin and Thadani (this volume) show, this form of management has not been successful, particularly where 'top-down' management structures within state forestry departments still persist. The failure of JFM in many places has compromised the ecological integrity of forests. In contrast, culturally sensitive approaches (e.g. the practice of sprinkling saffron water around sites in northwest India to restore them) have proven more successful (Bhagwat and Rutte 2006). Effectively using the vast array of protected area designations to strike a balance between conservation and development is going to be a significant challenge in a country where the outlook on conservation is deeply divided between those who favour strict reserves and those who push for community-conserved areas.

Moderating human–wildlife interactions

In a country that is divided on the model for wildlife protection, human–wildlife interactions is also a topic for much debate. Those who favour strict protection generally also favour the approach of keeping wildlife within bounds of protected areas, creating corridors that connect protected areas and generally keeping the human–wildlife interaction limited to tourists visiting the wildlife parks with a specific purpose of watching wildlife. Those who favour a greater ownership

of conservation by communities point to the nuances in human–wildlife interactions that often go beyond conflict. They also point to the impracticality of
keeping wildlife separate from humans in a country where humans and wild
animals are never far away from each other. As India embraces fast-track development, moderating the interaction between humans and wildlife, such that there
is less hostility and more acceptance, is going to be a significant challenge. This
kind of 'thrown togetherness' (Massey 2005) of humans and wildlife is particularly relevant in a wildlife-rich and highly populous country like India, where the
'capacity to live with difference' (Hall 1993) of multi-ethnic and multi-religious
communities has been lauded as a key secular value. But making secularism work
has proven challenging and by the same measure moderating human–wildlife
interactions will also be a challenge. There have been calls for a uniform 'solution' to mitigating human–wildlife conflict across the country but experience has
made it clear that there will need to be multiple 'solutions' that are context-spe-
cific (Karanth and Surendra, this volume; Thekaekara, this volume). In a country
where much emphasis is put on state ownership of conservation, letting go of
some control and passing on the ownership to communities to find their own
solutions is a challenge with which the wildlife protection machinery in India
will need to grapple.

Recognising community-conserved areas

Community-conserved areas in India have a long history, much longer than
that of the formal protected areas network. These areas, albeit small in their
geographical extent, are far more numerous than formal reserves. Mapping
these areas is seen as a way of helping the custodian communities to stake their
claims on land in a country where the development machine has been ever more
hungry for land – be it for agriculture, construction or mining. Dubbed 'counter-
mapping' (Peluso 1995), it helps to create an instrument with which to protect
ancestral land that has no formal legal protection. The Recognition of Forest
Rights Act (2006) in India has to a great extent provided a legal mechanism
to support such ancestral claims on land as Rai and Madegowda (this volume)
demonstrate. However, there are a number of challenges in making the maps of
community-conserved areas work for the communities: first, the highly distrib-
uted network of these areas makes it challenging to map them, particularly as
some of these areas are known only to the local custodian communities. Second,
conventional mapping strives to represent these areas in the two dimensions of
a paper or digital map and this may not accurately capture traditional knowledge
associated with these areas. Third, as Kitchin and Dodge (2007: 340) point out,
'[conventional] maps [as objects] have no ontological security, they are of-the-
moment; transitory, fleeting, contingent, relational and context-dependent'. This
view encourages us to move from how things are (ontology) to how things come
into being (ontogenesis). In other words, a conventional map can capture the
ontology, but it does not have the flexibility to capture ontogenesis. Therefore,
in conventional mapping of community-conserved areas the layers of cultural

information that have accumulated over the historical, and even archaeological, past can get lost (e.g. Louis *et al.* 2012). At the same time, mapping or counter-mapping forms a useful tool in empowering forest-dwelling communities who have, thus far, remained disadvantaged. Based on a particular forest-dwelling community that has historically been disadvantaged, Rai and Madegowda (this volume) open up wider discussion about indigenous cartography. The key challenge then is to find a balance between safeguarding the traditional knowledge and layers of cultural information over space and time associated with community-conserved areas and finding ways to empower the custodian communities.

Using market-based instruments

As much of India follows the course of modernisation and embraces the free-market economy, markets are moving into every walk of life. Market-based instruments are also making headway into conservation in India, particularly certification for environmental sustainability standards in agricultural commodities. These standards are developed internationally and in coffee production, for example, many such certification schemes exist. The Smithsonian Migratory Bird Center's bird-friendly coffee certification requires coffee farms to be organic and retain native shade tree canopy that covers at least 40 per cent of the plantation, has at least two layers of vegetation, and is made up of at least ten woody species (SMBC 2017). Rainforest Alliance's certification is more 'light-touch' with no requirement for shade and organic methods of production (RA 2017). Fair Trade certification on the other hand puts emphasis on reducing poverty through market-based instruments. Their standards are designed to empower producers in poor countries in the world and encourage traders to follow ethical standards for engaging with these producers (Fair Trade 2017). A common feature of all these standards is that in order to be certified, farmers have to pay annual fees. For some farmers, particularly smallholders, these fees are unaffordable. Furthermore, there is a feeling among some farmers that the certification bodies are imperialistic, as Bose (this volume) suggests. A combination of these factors means that if domestic markets do not apply sustainability standards, then farmers are reluctant to sign-up to the international criteria developed by the certification bodies. Although smallholder coffee growers in India have traditionally followed practices in coffee cultivation that are inherently biodiversity friendly, the market-based instruments have thus far had little benefit for farmers. The future adoption of market-based instruments in India will need to develop locally appropriate standards for certification that are supportive of smallholder farmers.

Towards a reimagined wilderness

So for the Cloud Messenger (from Kalidasa's fifth-century epic Meghaduta) drifting over the Indian subcontinent today, what would a reimagined wilderness look like? What differences will the Cloud Messenger notice? Will today's landscapes be as beautiful as the landscapes it witnessed on its fifth-century journey from south to north?

First, we must acknowledge the widespread presence of people across the subcontinent. If we do, then the considerably transformed ecology of Indian landscapes with fragmented pockets of wilderness becomes palatable. But on closer look we will also notice that there is wilderness in between these fragments. It is a somewhat different type of wilderness, consisting of non-charismatic species, non-native species, novel species assemblages and new kinds of habitats. This is largely the creation of people's own making and something of which people are part. So, the reimagined wilderness will include people, as opposed to separating people from nature.

Second, the reimagined wilderness is more durable and more sustainable in everyday landscapes that we depend on for food, fuel and fodder. Letting a little bit of wilderness in our farming landscapes can support forms of agriculture that, in the long term, are economically more sustainable, environmentally more responsible, and socially more ethical. The desire to modernise agriculture has led to the loss of generations of traditional knowledge, traditional crops and traditional cultivation practices that work with the land. Locally appropriate models of agriculture, farming and food production will be more durable over the long term. This is not about discarding today's technology, but it is about adopting technology in ways that are locally more appropriate. It is also about putting long-term sustainability at the heart of today's landscapes.

Third, the reimagined wilderness is everywhere and it is for everyone. It is not there just to entertain the urban elite, but it is present in everyday landscapes where people live, work and play. If we develop a culture of tolerance, learning from communities in India who already have cherished such a culture, it will be possible to accept wilderness more easily in our everyday lives – whether it means large charismatic megafauna or less charismatic species or even non-native invasive species. The reimagined wilderness will transcend hard boundaries of all kinds: between protected areas and land outside, between urban and rural, and between humans and non-human species. The reimagined wilderness can help conservation and development – for everyone and everywhere.

References

Adams, W.M., Aveling, R., Brockington, D., Dickson, B., Elliott, J., Hutton, J., Roe, D., Vira, B. and Wolmer, W. (2004) Biodiversity conservation and the eradication of poverty. *Science* 306, 1146–1149.

Bhagwat, S.A. and Rutte, C. (2006) Sacred groves: potential for biodiversity management. *Frontiers in Ecology and the Environment* 4(10): 519–524.

Bhagwat, S.A., Dudley, N. and Harrop, S.R. (2011a) Religious following in biodiversity hotspots: challenges and opportunities for conservation and development. *Conservation Letters* 4: 234–240.

Bhagwat, S.A., Ormsby, A.A., Rutte, C. (2011b) The role of religion in linking conservation and development: challenges and opportunities. *Journal for the Study of Religion, Nature and Culture* 5, 39–60.

Fair Trade (2017) Fair Trade International Standards. www.fairtrade.net/standards.html (last seen: 13 July 2017).

GoI (2015) National Institution for Transforming India (NITI Aayog), Government of India: India's Commitment to the SDGs. http://niti.gov.in/india-s-commitment-to-the-sdgs (last seen: 11 July 2017).

Hall, S. (1993) Cultural identity and diaspora. In *Colonial Discourse and Post-colonial Theory: A Reader*. Ed. Patrick Williams and Laura Chrisman. London: Harvester Wheatsheaf, 392–403.

Kitchin, R. and Dodge, M. (2007) Rethinking maps. *Progress in Human Geography* 31: 331–344.

Louis, R.P., Johnson, J.T. and Pramono, A.H. (2012) Introduction: indigenous cartographies and counter-mapping. *Cartographica* 47(2): 77–79.

Massey, D. (2005) *For Space*. London: Sage.

Newsham, A. and Bhagwat, S.A. (2015) *Conservation and Development*. London and New York: Routledge.

Peluso, N.L. (1995) Whose woods are these? Counter-mapping forest territories in Kalimantan, Indonesia. *Antipode* 27(4): 383–406.

RA (2017) Rainforest Alliance: Engage your agricultural business. www.rainforest-alliance.org/business/agriculture (last seen: 13 July 2017).

SMBC (2017) Smithsonian Migratory Bird Center's Bird-friendly coffee: shade management criteria. https://nationalzoo.si.edu/migratory-birds/bird-friendly-coffee-criteria (last seen: 13 July 2017).

UN (2015) Sustainable Development Goals: 17 goals to transform our world. www.un.org/sustainabledevelopment/sustainable-development-goals/ (last seen: 11 July 2017).

Index

Printed and bound by CPI Group (UK) Ltd, Croydon, CR0 4YY
01/05/2025
01858432-0002